Text-Based Intelligent Systems: Current Research and Practice in Information Extraction and Retrieval

Text-Based Intelligent Systems:
Current Research and Practice in Information Extraction and Retrieval

Edited by Paul S. Jacobs
Artificial Intelligence Laboratory
GE Research and Development Center

First published 1992 by Lawrence Erlbaum Associates, Inc.

Published 2014 by Psychology Press
711 Third Avenue, New York, NY 10017

and by Psychology Press
27 Church Road, Hove, East Sussex, BN3 2FA

Psychology Press is an imprint of the Taylor & Francis Group, an informa business

Library of Congress Cataloging-in-Publication Data

Text-based intelligent systems: current research and practice in information extraction and
   retrieval / edited by Paul S. Jacobs.
      p.   cm.
   Includes bibliographical references and index.
   1. Text processing (Computer science) 2. Natural language processing (Computer science) 3.
      Artifical intelligence.
   I. Jacobs, Paul Schafran
   QA76.9. T48T469   1992
   006.3'5-dc20   92-17802
                                                                                   CIP

ISBN 13: 978-0-805-81188-9 (hbk)

Contents

v

Preface

This volume started with a Symposium in 1990, sponsored by AAAI and titled "Text-Based Intelligent Systems". The push for this get-together, which included about 50 scientists with a variety of backgrounds, was a rapidly-emerging set of technologies for exploiting the massive quantity of textual information that has become increasingly available through advances in computing technology.

The challenge for this group was to explore new ways to take advantage of the power of on-line text. We intuit that a billion words of text can be a lot more generally useful than a few hundred logical rules, if we can use advanced computation (1) to extract useful information from streams of text, and (2) to help find (retrieve) what we need in the sea of available material. The extraction task has become a hot topic for the field of Natural Language Processing, while the retrieval task has been solidly in the field of Information Retrieval. These two disciplines came together at our Symposium, and have been cross-breeding more than ever.

This text has gone to press very quickly, in order to provide a "snapshot" of current research and practice and to help others to contribute to this new discipline. In fact, enough has happened since the 1990 Symposium that the papers in this book bear little resemblance to the original versions presented. Since then, there have been some new commercial applications, the government has undertaken a substantial research program called TIPSTER along with a series of formal evaluations (known as MUC and TREC) for testing text-processing technologies, and computer programs have scaled up from handling a few texts in simple domains to getting useful information out of millions of words of naturally occurring text. The contributors here are representative of the individuals, groups, and approaches that are behind this progress.

Not all the contributors here like the word "intelligent" in the title: It is meant not to ascribe any real intelligence to our programs, but rather to connote the innovative nature of the work. The systems are meant to be fast, effective, and helpful—"Text-based Fast, Effective, Helpful Systems" does not roll off the tongue as well, so we have chosen Text-Based Intelligent Systems (TBIS) to represent the nature of the science and the applications.

The book is organized in three parts. The first group of papers describes the current set of natural language (NL) processing techniques that are used for interpreting and extracting information from quantities of text. The second group gives some of the historical perspective, methodology, and current practice of Information Retrieval (IR) work. The third set covers some of the current and emerging application.

The volume is aimed at an audience of computer professionals who have at least some knowledge of natural language and IR, but it has also been prepared with advanced students in mind. While there are now good texts in both NL and IR, the changes in both fields have been substantial enough that the texts do not capture much of current practice with respect to TBIS. This collection of readings should give students and scientists alike a good idea of the current techniques as well as a general concept of how to go about developing and testing systems to handle volumes of text.

This work is the result of the cooperative efforts of the contributors, to whom I am indebted for their timely and appropriate response. Every word has been prepared, submitted, reviewed, and typeset electronically (in "soft copy") to keep the material current and correct. I am also thankful for the support of AAAI for the original Symposium, to Norm Sondheimer and the Artificial Intelligence Laboratory at GE for helping to promote this type of work, and to Lisa Rau for helping me put everything together.

Introduction: Text Power and Intelligent Systems

Paul S. Jacobs
Artificial Intelligence Program
GE Research and Development Center
Schenectady, NY 12301 USA

1.1 A New Opportunity

Huge quantities of readily available on-line text raise new challenges and opportunities for artificial intelligence systems. The ease of acquiring text knowledge suggests replacing, or at least augmenting, knowledge-based systems with "text-based" intelligence wherever possible. Making use of this text knowledge demands more work in robust processing, retrieval, and presentation of information, but raises a host of new applications of AI technologies, where on-line information exists but knowledge bases do not.

Most AI programs have failed to "scale up" because of the difficulty of developing large, robust knowledge bases. At the same time, rapid advances in networks and information storage now provide access to knowledge bases millions of times larger—in text form. No knowledge representation claims the expressive power or the compactness of this raw text. The next generation of AI applications, therefore, may well be "text-based" rather than knowledge based, deriving more power from large quantities of stored text than from hand-crafted rules.

Text-based intelligent systems can combine artificial intelligence techniques with more robust but "shallower" methods. Natural language processing (NLP) research has been hampered, on the one hand, by the limitations of deep systems that work only on a very small number of texts (often only one), and, on the other hand, by the failure of more mature technologies, such as parsing, to apply to practical systems. Information retrieval (IR) systems offer a vehicle where selected NLP methods can produce useful results; hence, there is a natural and potentially important marriage between IR and NLP. This synergy extends beyond the traditional realms of either technology to a variety of emerging applications.

As examples, we must consider what a knowledge-based system can offer in the domain of medical diagnosis, on-line operating systems, fault diagnosis in engines, or financial advising, that cannot be found in a medical textbook, a user's manual, a design specification, or a tax preparation handbook. Computers should help make the right information from these documents accessible and comprehensible to the user. Harnessing the power of volumes of available text—through information retrieval, natural language analysis, knowledge representation, and conceptual information extraction—will pose a major challenge for AI into the next century.

Advocates of the text-based approach to intelligent systems must accept its inherent limitations. Some of the traditional AI problems, such as reasoning, inference, and pragmatics, must necessarily play a limited role. But there is evidence of substantial progress in building robust text processing systems that rely more heavily on shallower methods. The rest of this paper describes the combination of applications, methodologies and techniques that forms the backbone of work on Text-Based Intelligent Systems.

1.2   A New Name

To merit their own label, "text-based intelligent systems" must suggest something distinctly different from prevailing research. As the introduction has implied, a text-based intelligent system (TBIS) is a program that derives its power from large quantities of raw text, in an intelligent manner. Such systems differ from traditional information retrieval systems in that they must be more flexible and responsive, possibly segmenting, combining, or synthesizing a response rather than just retrieving texts. The systems differ from traditional natural language programs in that they must be much more robust.

The category of text-based intelligent systems includes, for example:

- *Text extraction systems*—programs that analyze volumes of unstructured text, selecting certain features from the text and potentially storing such features in a structured form. These systems currently exist in limited domains. Examples of this type of system are news reading programs [Jacobs and Rau, 1990] (see the papers by Hobbs *et al.* and McDonald in this volume), database generation programs that produce fixed-field information from free text, and transaction handling programs, such as those that read banking transfer messages [Lytinen and Gershman, 1986; Young and Hayes, 1985].

- *Automated indexing and hypertext*—knowledge-based programs that determine key terms and topics by which to select texts or portions of text [Jonak, 1984] or automatically link portions of text that relate to one another (see the paper by Salton and Buckley in this volume).

- *Summarization and abstracting*—programs that integrate multiple texts that repeat, correct, or augment one another, as in following the course of a news story over time such as a corporate merger or political event [Rau, 1987].

- *Intelligent information retrieval*—systems with enhanced information retrieval capabilities, through robust query processing, user modeling, or limited inference [IPM, 1987] (see also the paper by Croft and Turtle in this volume).

This volume contains position papers covering all of the topics above, along with discussions of underlying problems in constructing TBIS's, such as the representation and storage of knowledge about texts or about language, and robust text processing techniques. Many of the positions describe research related to substantial systems in one of the above categories, and virtually all address the issue of robust processing of some sort. The next section describes the apparent methodological themes of this sort of research.

1.3   No More "Donkeys"

Much of this research combines the discipline of information retrieval with some of the techniques of natural language processing. Historically, the methodology of information retrieval has been to develop new methods and conduct experiments to compare those methods with other approaches. By contrast, the methodology of natural language processing has been either to develop theories that apply to broad but carefully selected linguistic phenomena, or to develop programs that apply to carefully selected texts. In other words, there has been very little effort within natural language to produce results such as "This program performs the following task with 95% accuracy on the following set of 1000 texts".

As a result of its more theoretical orientation, natural language as a field has devoted much of its attention to paradigmatic but improbable examples. Researchers in natural language were trained to think about contrived sentences—"Every man who owns a donkey beats it" or "The box is in the pen." These are so familiar that one might stand up with a question at the end of a presentation and ask, "But what about the 'donkey' sentences?" Researchers are acquainted enough with the examples that they needn't be repeated, in spite of the fact that they hardly seem representative of examples or problems that we might encounter.

The current methodological shift in the experimental element of natural language processing (by no means the dominant segment of the field) brings text processing, as experimental computer science, closer to information retrieval. Rather than seek out examples that support or challenge theories, the experimental methodology uses sets of naturally occurring examples as test cases, possibly ignoring certain interesting problems that simply do not occur in a particular task. While this approach has some disadvantages, it has the benefit of focussing work on the issues in natural language processing that inhibit robustness.

Another example of the experimental shift is the area of language acquisition. During the 1970's and most of the 1980's, the field of language acquisition concentrated on the *techniques* through which knowledge, especially grammatical knowledge, could be acquired. The result of this effort was a host of theories and techniques, but very little in the way of sizable knowledge bases. Recently, however, the research focus in language acquisition has been on achieving the *goal* of acquisition rather than on the *process*, resulting in extensive lexicons and knowledge bases for use in processing texts [Zernik, 1991].

While the methodology of natural language may be drifting toward information retrieval, information retrieval is slowly changing in focus. The extreme difficulty of producing significant improvements using traditional document retrieval metrics suggests exploring new retrieval strategies as well as devising new measures. As the combined fields of natural language processing and information retrieval continue to make progress, the demand grows for test collections and metrics that evaluate meaningful tasks, including not only the accuracy of document retrieval, but also the accuracy, speed, transportability, and ease of use of systems that perform functions such as those outlined in the previous section. This new direction involves the constant interplay of two goals: (1) produce new measurable results and (2) produce new measures of new results.

The resulting experimental methodology has spawned a host of research projects emphasizing robust processing, large-scale systems, knowledge acquisition, and performance evaluation. As the new research is still taking shape, one shouldn't expect any breakthroughs as yet. The next section considers the limited progress that has already resulted.

1.4 Where We Are Now

While text-based intelligent systems are very much a futuristic concept, the recent emphasis on experiment and performance has brought some noticeable changes during the last several years:

- *Evaluation*:
  In government, academia, and industry, the desire for results has led to new metrics for evaluating system performance. While metrics and benchmarks often spark debate, they also show clear progress. For example, a government-sponsored message processing conference three years ago featured a small set of programs performing different functions in different domains, while a more recent similar conference included nine substantial programs performing a common task on a set of over 100 real messages, and produced meaningful results [Sundheim, 1989] (see Hobbs *et al.*, this volume). New evaluation metrics have appeared also in other tasks, such as text categorization (cf. Hayes, this volume).

- *Scale*:
  Natural language programs typically have operated on a handful of texts; recently, programs have emerged that process streams of hundreds of thousands of words or more, depending on the level of semantic processing. Along with their broader capabilities, the knowledge bases that such programs use have been expanding. While a typical lexicon recently might have included 100 or 200 words, many systems now have real lexicons of 10,000 roots or more.

- *Commercialization*:
  The number of industrial scientists represented in this volume is an indicator of the emerging commercial applications of robust text processing and information retrieval technology, as is the increasing number of commercially available systems. Many commercial applications that formerly used relational databases or other structured knowledge sources are shifting to textual databases because of the availability of on-line text information, and many hardware and software vendors are packaging their products with substantial text databases. These products generally do not employ the sort of technology discussed here, but do provide a vehicle for the ultimate application of the technology.

- *Cooperation and Competition*:
  Until recently, schools of thought in text processing and information retrieval were dogmatic enough to ignore most other related work. In many areas, recent projects have spawned cooperative efforts in collecting data and lexical knowledge, assembling test collections, and cooperating between industry and academia. Competition, on the other hand, was never allowed because of the general lack of evaluation criteria. Now there is a growing interest in holding "showdowns" that objectively compare different methods.

While there has been some visible progress toward text-based intelligent systems, we aren't very close to a desirable state of technology. The next section addresses some of the obstacles we must overcome.

1.5 Why We Aren't There Yet

Many of us have workstations on top of our desks that have access via computer networks to trillions of words of text—encyclopedias, almanacs, dictionaries, literature, news, and electronic bulletin boards. Ironically, we are loath to attempt to use most of this information because a combination of factors—mainly the difficulty of finding any particular bit of knowledge we desire—makes it a gross waste of time.

Much of this problem in crudeness of information access boils down to issues that are relatively mundane, having little to do with text content—the speed of transmission across networks, compatibility of hardware, security, legal and copyright concerns, the lack of standards for storing and transmitting on-line text, etc. As the motivation for using on-line text helps to dissolve some of these issues, we can hope for better opportunities to use the advanced technologies for content analysis that are reported here.

In addition to these mundane communication and standardization issues, there is a more relevant problem of how to market the technology that we are developing. Too often we ignore the strengths of the competition—in this case, simple text search, Boolean query, and keyword retrieval methods. While these simpler methods lack the power and intuitive appeal, say, of natural language analysis or concept-based information retrieval, they have certain features that appeal to users of large text databases: they are fast, portable, relatively inexpensive, and relatively easy to learn. The techniques are compatible with many software packages, run on many hardware platforms, and are easier to implement in hardware. By contrast, natural language processing can be slow, brittle, and expensive. In order to bring the technology to the marketplace in the near future (such as the next dozen or so years), we will either have to minimize these disadvantages or prove dramatic improvements over simpler methods.

Some key technical barriers stand in the way of the all-knowing desktop librarian. These technical barriers will form some of the focal points the research reported in this volume as well as the progress that is likely to be made in the rest of the century. Four such issues are (1) robustness of analysis, (2) retrieval strategy, (3) presentation of information, and (4) cultivation of applications. The next section will outline the technical challenges in each of these areas.

1.6   Challenges for the 1990's

The intelligent access to information from texts is the central theme of this research. The following are some of the key thrusts of this theme, including the topics of many of the papers here:

- *Robustness*:
  The next generation of language analyzers must do much of the same sort of processing that current systems do, but must do it more accurately, faster, and with less domain-dependent knowledge. Robustness applies both to extending techniques that are already robust, such as parsing and morphology, and to increasing the robustness of more knowledge-intensive techniques, such as semantic analysis.

- *Retrieval Strategy*:
  Current retrieval methods are oriented toward the retrieval of documents, not information in general. Text-based systems must address the broader issue of satisfying the information needs of many different

systems and users. Within this broader information processing context, the concept of success but be redefined to be more than reproducing "relevant" texts, and new retrieval strategies must address this new notion of success. For example, if a user wants to know a specific piece of information and the system produces an extremely long text containing relevant information, this is somehow not as good as producing a direct answer to the user's question.

- *Presentation*:
A big problem with on-line text retrieval is that people do not like to read. On-line text is even harder to read than printed material. Current systems depend on users' reading skills rather than presenting information that satisfy's a user's needs. We have only begun to address the many different ways textual information can be effectively displayed. For example, hypertext systems can link together pieces of text from different parts of a document or different documents, making it easier for the user to control the presentation. For all the "hype" that hypertext has received, we have a long way to go in presenting texts intelligently—for example, generating a summary by combining different portions of text, highlighting sections of text that contain information that is asked for, or compressing a text so that only key portions appear. Many of these techniques must be developed to suit the requirements of new applications.

- *Applications*:
One of the limitations of information retrieval research is that it has narrowly defined its territory, possibly overlooking appropriate application areas. Many different types of content-based text applications have already emerged, such as routing (selective dissemination of information), text categorization, database generation, and transaction handling. The range of application areas continues to grow. Some provocative application areas are: skimming news stories about political issues to determine whether a figure is "for" or "against" (cf. Hearst, this volume); selecting and ordering requirements from a large software specification; and generating a help system from on-line documentation (Maarek, this volume). Research in text-based systems must consider these new testbed applications along with the underlying technical issues.

While each of these areas poses some substantive problems, text-based systems are bound to grow steadily in their capabilities. After all, the use of information retrieval systems is expanding in spite of relatively poor accuracy. It's a good bet that many of the developments in text-based intelligent systems will pan out as they apply more robust methods to use the increasing power of on-line text.

1.7   Summary

The emerging field of text-based intelligent systems marries the content-based analysis of natural language processing with the experimental methodology of information retrieval. This combination can overcome many of the limitations of current knowledge-based systems by applying shallow methods of analysis to huge bodies of text. This new focus has already produced an expansion in robust text processing capabilities, and is likely to produce a wave of maturing applications in the next decade.

Bibliography

[IPM, 1987] *Information Processing and Management, Special Issue on Artificial Intelligence for Information Retrieval, 23*(4), 1987.

[Jacobs and Rau, 1990] Paul Jacobs and Lisa Rau. SCISOR: Extracting information from on-line news. *Communications of the Association for Computing Machinery, 33*(11):88–97, November 1990.

[Jonak, 1984] Zdenek Jonak. Automatic indexing of full texts. *Information Processing and Management, 20*(5-6):619–627, 1984.

[Lytinen and Gershman, 1986] Steven Lytinen and Anatole Gershman. ATRANS: Automatic processing of money transfer messages. In *Proceedings of the Fifth National Conference on Artificial Intelligence*, pages 1089–1093, Philadelphia, 1986.

[Rau, 1987] Lisa F. Rau. Information retrieval in never-ending stories. In *Proceedings of the Sixth National Conference on Artificial Intelligence*, pages 317–321, Seattle, Washington, July 1987. Morgan Kaufmann Inc.

[Sundheim, 1989] Beth Sundheim. Second message understanding (MUCK-II) report. Technical Report 1328, Naval Ocean Systems Center, San Diego, CA, 1989.

[Young and Hayes, 1985] S. Young and P. Hayes. Automatic classification and summarization of banking telexes. In *The Second Conference on Artificial Intelligence Applications*, pages 402–208, IEEE Press, 1985.

[Zernik, 1991] U. Zernik, editor. *Lexical Acquisition: Using On-Line Resources to Build a Lexicon.* Lawrence Erlbaum Associates, Hillsdale, NJ, 1991.

Part I

Broad-Scale NLP

Part I: Broad-Scale NLP

Two forces drive the emergence of text-based systems: the power of on-line text and the increased ability of computers to process text. This section covers the techniques that have changed the way computers interpret texts in recent years, from increased coverage and completeness of traditional linguistic processing to the integration of statistical or "weak" methods with deeper interpretation.

The paper by Hobbs *et al.* argues that augmenting the detailed models of parsing and inference that have been explored in the past can provide much of what's needed to extract information from quantities of real text. Wilks *et al.* and Hirst and Ryan lean more heavily on weak methods, while McDonald presents an alternative model of parsing. The Zernik paper gives one view of how weak methods can aid, rather than replace, linguistic processing.

Robust Processing of Real-World Natural-Language Texts

Jerry R. Hobbs, Douglas E. Appelt, John Bear,
Mabry Tyson, and David Magerman

Artificial Intelligence Center
SRI International
Menlo Park, California

Abstract

It is often assumed that when natural language processing meets the real world, the ideal of aiming for complete and correct interpretations has to be abandoned. However, our experience with TACITUS, especially in the MUC-3 evaluation, has shown that principled techniques for syntactic and pragmatic analysis can be bolstered with methods for achieving robustness. We describe and evaluate a method for dealing with unknown words and a method for filtering out sentences irrelevant to the task. We describe three techniques for making syntactic analysis more robust—an agenda-based scheduling parser, a recovery technique for failed parses, and a new technique called terminal substring parsing. For pragmatics processing, we describe how the method of abductive inference is inherently robust, in that an interpretation is always possible, so that in the absence of the required world knowledge, performance degrades gracefully. Each of these techniques has been evaluated, and the results of the evaluations are presented.

2.1 Introduction

If automatic text processing is to be a useful enterprise, it must be demonstrated that the completeness and accuracy of the information extracted is adequate for the application one has in mind. While it is clear that certain applications require only a minimal level of competence from a system, it is also true that many applications require a very high degree of completeness and accuracy, and an increase in capability in either area is a clear advantage. Therefore, we adopt an extremely high standard against which the performance of a text processing system should be measured: it should recover all information that is implicitly or explicitly present in the text, and it should do so without making mistakes.

This standard is far beyond the state of the art. It is an impossibly high standard for human beings, let alone machines. However, progress toward adequate text processing is best served by setting ambitious goals. For this reason we believe that, while it may be necessary in the intermediate term to settle for results that are far short of this ultimate goal, any linguistic theory or system architecture that is adopted should not be demonstrably inconsistent with attaining this objective. However, if one is interested, as we are, in the potentially successful application of these intermediate-term systems to real problems, it is impossible to ignore the question of whether they can be made efficient enough and robust enough for actual applications.

2.1.1   The TACITUS System

The TACITUS text processing system has been under development at SRI International for the last six years. This system has been designed as a first step toward the realization of a system with very high completeness and accuracy in its ability to extract information from text. The general philosophy underlying the design of this system is that the system, to the maximum extent possible, should not discard any information that might be semantically or pragmatically relevant to a full, correct interpretation. The effect of this design philosophy on the system architecture is manifested in the following characteristics:

- TACITUS relies on a large, comprehensive lexicon containing detailed syntactic subcategorization information for each lexical item.

- TACITUS produces a parse and semantic interpretation of each sentence using a comprehensive grammar of English in which different possible predicate-argument relations are associated with different syntactic structures.

- TACITUS relies on a general abductive reasoning mechanism to uncover the implicit assumptions necessary to explain the coherence of the explicit text.

These basic design decisions do not by themselves distinguish TACITUS from a number of other natural-language processing systems. However, they are somewhat controversial given the intermediate goal of producing systems that are useful for existing applications. Criticism of the overall design with respect to this goal centers on the following observations:

- The syntactic structure of English is very complex, and no grammar of English has been constructed that has complete coverage of the syntax one encounters in real-world texts. Much of the text that needs to be processed will lie outside the scope of the best grammars available, and therefore cannot be understood by a system that relies on a complete syntactic analysis of each sentence as a prerequisite to other processing.

- Typical sentences in newspaper articles are about 25-30 words in length. Many sentences are much longer. Processing strategies that rely on producing a complete syntactic analysis of such sentences will be faced with a combinatorially intractable task, assuming in the first place that the sentences lie within the language described by the grammar.

- Any grammar that successfully accounts for the range of syntactic structures encountered in real-world texts will necessarily produce many ambiguous analyses of most sentences. Assuming that the system can find the possible analyses of a sentence in a reasonable period of time, it is still faced with the problem of choosing the correct one from the many competing ones.

Designers of application-oriented text processing systems have adopted a number of strategies for dealing with these problems. Such strategies involve de-emphasizing the role of syntactic analysis [Jacobs et al., 1991], producing partial parses with stochastic or heuristic parsers [deMarcken, 1990; Weischedel et al., 1991] or resorting to weaker syntactic processing methods such as conceptual or case-frame based parsing (e.g., [Schank and Riesbeck, 1981]) or template matching techniques [Jackson et al., 1991]. A common feature shared by these weaker methods is that they ignore certain information that is present in the text, which could be extracted by a more comprehensive analysis. The information that is ignored may be irrelevant to a particular application, or relevant in only an insignificant handful of cases, and thus we cannot argue that approaches to text processing based on weak or even nonexistent syntactic and semantic analysis are doomed to failure in all cases and are not worthy of further investigation. However, it is not obvious how such methods can scale up to handle fine distinctions in attachment, scoping, and inference, although some recent attempts have been made in this direction [Cardie and Lehnert, 1991].

In the development of TACITUS, we have chosen a design philosophy that assumes that a complete and accurate analysis of the text is being undertaken. In this paper we discuss how issues of robustness are approached from this general design perspective. In particular, we demonstrate that:

- A statistical keyword filter can select the sentences to be processed, with a great savings in time and little loss of relevant information.

- Useful partial analyses of the text can be obtained in cases in which the text is not grammatical English, or lies outside the scope of the grammar's coverage.

- Substantially correct parses of sentences can be found without exploring the entire search space for each sentence.

- Useful pragmatic interpretations can be obtained using general reasoning methods, even in cases in which the system lacks the necessary

world knowledge to resolve all of the pragmatic problems posed in a
sentence.

- All of this processing can be done within acceptable bounds on computational resources.

Our experience with TACITUS suggests that extension of the system's
capabilities to higher levels of completeness and accuracy can be achieved
through incremental modifications of the system's knowledge, lexicon, and
grammar, while the robust processing techniques discussed in the following
sections make the system usable for intermediate term applications. We have
evaluated the success of the various techniques discussed here, and conclude
from this evaluation that TACITUS offers substantiation of our claim that a
text processing system based on principles of complete syntactic, semantic,
and pragmatic analysis need not be too brittle or computationally expensive
for practical applications.

2.1.2   Evaluating the System

SRI International participated in the recent MUC-3 evaluation of text-understand
systems [Sundheim, 1991]. The methodology chosen for this evaluation was
to score a system's ability to fill in slots in templates summarizing the content
of newspaper articles, approximately one page in length, on Latin American
terrorism. The template-filling task required identifying, among other things,
the perpetrators and victims of each terrorist act described in the articles, the
occupation of the victims, the type of physical entity attacked or destroyed,
the date, the location, and the effect on the targets. Frequently, articles
described multiple incidents, while other texts were completely irrelevant.

An example of a relatively short terrorist report is the following from a
news report dated March 30, 1989:

> A cargo train running from Lima to Lorohia was derailed before
> dawn today after hitting a dynamite charge.
> Inspector Eulogio Flores died in the explosion.
> The police reported that the incident took place past midnight in
> the Carahuaichi-Jaurin area.

Some of the corresponding database entries are as follows:

Incident: Date	30 Mar 89
Incident: Location	Peru: Carahuaichi-Jaurin (area)
Incident: Type	Bombing
Physical Target: Description	"cargo train"
Physical Target: Effect	Some Damage: "cargo train"
Human Target: Name	"Eulogio Flores"
Human Target: Description	"inspector": "Eulogio Flores"
Human Target: Effect	Death: "Eulogio Flores"

The fifteen participating sites were given a development corpus of 1300 such texts in October 1990. In early February 1991, the systems were tested on 100 new messages (the TST1 corpus), and a workshop was held to debug the testing procedure. In May 1991 the systems were tested on a new corpus of 100 messages (TST2); this constituted the final evaluation. The results were reported at a workshop at NOSC in May 1991.

The principal measures in the MUC-3 evaluation were recall and precision. *Recall* is the number of answers the system got right divided by the number of possible right answers. It measures how comprehensive the system is in its extraction of relevant information. *Precision* is the number of answers the system got right divided by the number of answers the system gave. It measures the system's accuracy. For example, if there are 100 possible answers and the system gives 80 answers and gets 60 of them right, its recall is 60% and its precision is 75%.

The database entries are organized into templates, one for each relevant event. In an attempt to factor out some of the conditionality among the database entries, recall and precision scores were given, for each system, for three different sets of templates:

- Templates for events the system correctly identified (Matched Templates).

- Matched templates, plus templates for events the system failed to identify (Matched/Missing).

- All templates, including spurious templates the system generated.

The results for TACITUS on the TST2 corpus were as follows.

	Recall	Precision
Matched Templates	44%	65%
Matched/Missing	25%	65%
All Templates	25%	48%

Our precision was the highest of any of the sites participating in the evaluation. Our recall was somewhere in the middle.

We also ran our system, configured identically to the TST2 run, on the first 100 messages of the development set. The results were as follows:

	Recall	Precision
Matched Templates	46%	64%
Matched/Missing	37%	64%
All Templates	37%	53%

Here, recall was considerably better, as would be expected since the messages were used for development.

Although we are pleased with these overall results, a subsequent detailed analysis of our performance on the first 20 messages of the 100-message test set is much more illuminating for evaluating the success of the particular robust processing strategies we have chosen. In the remainder of this paper, we discuss the impact of the robust processing methods in the light of this detailed analysis.

We will divide our discussion into four parts: handling unknown words, our statistical relevance filter, syntactic analysis, and pragmatic interpretation. The performance of each of these processes will be described for Message 99 of TST1 (given in the Appendix) or on Message 100 of the development set (given in Section 2.5). Then their performance on the first 20 messages of TST2 will be summarized.

2.2   Handling Unknown Words

When an unknown word is encountered, three processes are applied sequentially.

1. Spelling Correction. A standard algorithm for spelling correction is applied, but only to words longer than four letters.

2. Hispanic Name Recognition. A statistical trigram model for distinguishing between Hispanic surnames and English words was developed and is used to assign the category Last-Name to some of the words that are not spell-corrected.

3. Morphological Category Assignment. Words that are not spell-corrected or classified as last names, are assigned a category on the basis of morphology. Words ending in "-ing" or "-ed" are classified as verbs. Words ending in "-ly" are classified as adverbs. All other unknown words are taken to be nouns. This misses adjectives entirely, but this is generally harmless, because the adjectives incorrectly classified as nouns will still parse as prenominal nouns in compound nominals. The grammar will recognize an unknown noun as a name in the proper environment.

There were no unknown words in Message 99, since all the words used in the TST1 set had been entered into the lexicon.

In the first 20 messages of TST2, there were 92 unknown words. Each of the heuristics either did or did not apply to the word. If one did, the results could have been correct, harmless, or wrong. An example of a harmless spelling correction is the change of "twin-engined" to the adjective "twin-engine". A wrong spelling correction is the change of the verb "nears" to the preposition "near". An example of a harmless assignment of Hispanic surname to a word is the Japanese name "Akihito". A wrong assignment is the word "panorama". A harmless morphological assignment of a category to a word is the assignment of **Verb** to "undispute" and "originat". A wrong assignment is the assignment of **Noun** to "upriver".

The results were as follows:

	Unknown	Applied	Correct	Harmless	Wrong
Spelling	92	25	8	12	5
Surname	67	20	8	10	2
Morphological	47	47	29	11	7

If we look just at the Correct column, only the morphological assignment heuristic is at all effective, giving us 62%, as opposed to 32% for spelling correction and 40% for Hispanic surname assignment. However, harmless assignments are often much better than merely harmless; they often allow a sentence to parse that otherwise would not, thereby making other information in the sentence available to pragmatic interpretation. If we count both the Correct and Harmless columns, then spelling correction is effective 80% of the time, Hispanic surname assignment 90% of the time, and morphological assignment 86%.

Using the three heuristics in sequence meant that 85% of the unknown words were handled either correctly or harmlessly.

2.3   Statistical Relevance Filter

The relevance filter works on a sentence-by-sentence basis and decides whether the sentence should be submitted to further processing. It consists of two subcomponents—a statistical relevance filter and a keyword antifilter.

The statistical relevance filter was developed from our analysis of the training data. We went through the 1300-text development set and identified the relevant sentences. For each unigram, bigram, and trigram, we determined an n-gram-score by dividing the number of occurrences in the relevant sentences by the total number of occurrences. A subset of these n-grams was selected as being particularly diagnostic of relevant sentences. A sentence score was then computed as follows. It was initialized to the n-gram score for the first diagnostic n-gram in the sentence. For subsequent nonoverlapping, diagnostic n-grams it was updated by the formula:

$$\text{sentence score} \leftarrow \text{sentence score} + (1 - \text{sentence score})$$
$$* \text{next n-gram score}$$

This formula normalizes the sentence score to between 0 and 1. Because of the second term of this formula, each successive n-gram score "uses up" some portion of the distance remaining between the current sentence score and 1.

Initially, a fixed threshold for relevance was used, but this gave poor results. The threshold for relevance is now therefore contextually determined for each text, based on the average sentence score for the sentences in the text, by the formula

.3 + .65 * (1 − average sentence score)

Thus, the threshold is lower for texts with many relevant sentences, as seems appropriate. This cutoff formula was chosen so that we would identify 85% of the relevant sentences and overgenerate by no more than 300%. The component is now apparently much better than this.

The keyword antifilter was developed in an effort to capture those sentences that slip through the statistical relevance filter. The antifilter is based on certain keywords. If a sentence in the text proves to contain relevant information, the next few sentences will be declared relevant as well if they contain those keywords.

In Message 99, the statistical filter determined nine sentences to be relevant. All of these were actually relevant except for one, Sentence 13. No relevant sentences were missed. The keyword antifilter decided incorrectly that two other sentences were relevant, Sentences 8 and 9. This behavior is typical.

In the first 20 messages of the TST2 set, the results were as follows: There were 370 sentences. The statistical relevance filter produced the following results:

	Actually Relevant	Actually Irrelevant
Judged Relevant	42	33
Judged Irrelevant	9	286

Thus, recall was 82% and precision was 56%. These results are excellent. They mean that by using this filter alone we would have processed only 20% of the sentences in the corpus, processing less than twice as many as were actually relevant, and missing only 18% of the relevant sentences.

The results of the keyword antifilter were as follows:

	Actually Relevant	Actually Irrelevant
Judged Relevant	5	57
Judged Irrelevant	4	229

Clearly, the results here are not nearly as good. Recall was 55% and precision was 8%. This means that to capture half the remaining relevant sentences, we had to nearly triple the number of irrelevant sentences we processed. Using the filter and antifilter in sequence, we had to process 37% of the sentences. Our conclusion is that if the keyword antifilter is to be retained, it must be refined considerably.

Incidentally, of the four relevant sentences that escaped both the filter and the antifilter, two contained only redundant information that could have been picked up elsewhere in the text. The other two contained information essential to 11 slots in templates, lowering overall recall by about 1%.

2.4   Syntactic Analysis

Robust syntactic analysis requires a very broad coverage grammar and means for dealing with sentences that do not parse, whether because they fall outside the coverage of the grammar or because they are too long for the parser. The grammar used in TACITUS is that of the DIALOGIC system, developed in 1980-81 essentially by constructing the union of the Linguistic String Project Grammar [Sager, 1981] and the DIAGRAM grammar [Robinson, 1982], which grew out of SRI's Speech Understanding System research in the 1970s. Since that time it has been considerably enhanced. It consists of about 160 phrase structure rules. Associated with each rule is a "constructor" expressing the constraints on the applicability of that rule, and a "translator" for producing the logical form.

The grammar is comprehensive and includes subcategorization, sentential complements, adverbials, relative clauses, complex determiners, the most common varieties of conjunction and comparison, selectional constraints, some coreference resolution, and the most common sentence fragments. The parses are ordered according to heuristics encoded in the grammar.

The parse tree is translated into a logical representation of the meaning of the sentence, encoding predicate-argument relations and grammatical subordination relations. In addition, it regularizes to some extent the role assignments in the predicate-argument structure, and handles arguments inherited from control verbs.

Our lexicon contains about 20,000 entries, including about 2000 personal names and about 2000 location, organization, or other names. This number does not include morphological variants, which are handled in a separate morphological analyzer.

The syntactic analysis component was remarkably successful in the MUC-3 evaluation. This was due primarily to three innovations:

- An agenda-based scheduling chart parser.

- A recovery heuristic for unparsable sentences that found the best sequence of grammatical fragments.

- The use of "terminal substring parsing" for very long sentences.

Each of these techniques will be described in turn, with statistics on their performance in the MUC-3 evaluation.

2.4.1   Performance of the Scheduling Parser and the Grammar

The fastest parsing algorithms for context-free grammars make use of prediction based on left context to limit the number of nodes and edges the parser must insert into the chart. However, if robustness in the face of possibly ungrammatical input or inadequate grammatical coverage is desired, such algorithms are inappropriate. Although the heuristic of choosing the longest possible substring beginning at the left that can be parsed as a sentence could be tried (e.g. [Grishman and Sterling, 1989]) sometimes, the best fragmentary analysis of a sentence can only be found by parsing an intermediate or terminal substring that excludes the leftmost words. For this reason, we feel that bottom-up parsing without strong constraints based on left context is required for robust syntactic analysis.

Bottom-up parsing is favored for its robustness, and this robustness derives from the fact that a bottom-up parser will construct nodes and edges in the chart that a parser with top-down prediction would not. The obvious problem is that these additional nodes do not come without an associated cost. Moore and Dowding (1991) observed a ninefold increase in time required to parse sentences with a straightforward CKY parser as opposed to a shift-reduce parser. Prior to November 1990, TACITUS employed a simple, exhaustive, bottom-up parser with the result that sentences of more than 15 to 20 words were impossible to parse in reasonable time. Since the average length of a sentence in the MUC-3 texts is approximately 27 words, such techniques were clearly inappropriate for the application.

We addressed this problem by adding an agenda mechanism to the bottom-up parser, based on Kaplan [1973], as described in Winograd [1983]. The purpose of the agenda is to allow us to order nodes (complete constituents) and edges (incomplete constituents) in the chart for further processing. As nodes and edges are built, they are rated according to various criteria for how likely they are to figure in a correct parse. This allows us to schedule which constituents to work with first so that we can pursue only the most likely paths in the search space and find a parse without exhaustively trying all possibilities. The scheduling algorithm is simple: Explore the ramifications of the highest scoring constituents first.

In addition, there is a facility for pruning the search space. The user can set limits on the number of nodes and edges that are allowed to be stored in the chart. Nodes are indexed on their atomic grammatical category (i.e., excluding features) and the string position at which they begin. Edges are indexed on their atomic grammatical category and the string position where they end. The algorithm for pruning is simple: Throw away all but the n highest scoring constituents for each category/string-position pair.

It has often been pointed out that various standard parsing strategies correspond to various scheduling strategies in an agenda-based parser. However, in practical parsing, what is needed is a scheduling strategy that enables us to pursue only the most likely paths in the search space and to find the correct parse without exhaustively trying all possibilities. The literature has not been as illuminating on this issue.

We designed our parser to score each node and edge on the basis of three criteria:

- The length of the substring spanned by the constituent.

- Whether the constituent is a node or an edge, that is, whether the constituent is complete or not.

- The scores derived from the preference heuristics that have been encoded in DIALOGIC over the years, described and systematized in [Hobbs and Bear, 1990].

However, after considerable experimentation with various weightings, we concluded that the length and completeness factors failed to improve the performance at all over a broad range of sentences. Evidence suggested that a score based on preference factor alone produces the best results. The reason a correct or nearly correct parse is found so often by this method is that these preference heuristics are so effective.

In Message 99, of the 11 sentences determined to be relevant, only Sentence 14 did not parse. This was due to a mistake in the sentence itself, the use of "least" instead of "at least". Of the 10 sentences that parsed, 5 were completely correct, including the longest, Sentence 7 (27 words in 77 seconds). There were three mistakes (Sentences 3, 4, and 9) in which the preferred multiword senses of the phrases "in front of" and "Shining Path" lost out to their decompositions. There were two attachment mistakes. In Sentence 3 the relative clause was incorrectly attached to "front" instead of "embassy", and in Sentence 8, "in Peru" was attached to "attacked" instead of "interests". All of these errors were harmless. In addition, in Sentence 5, "and destroyed the two vehicles" was grouped with "Police said ..." instead of "the bomb broke windows"; this error is not harmless. In every case the grammar prefers the correct reading. We believe the mistakes were due to a problem in the scheduling parser that we discovered the week of the evaluation but felt was too deep and far-reaching to attempt to fix at that point.

In the first 20 messages of the test set, 131 sentences were given to the scheduling parser, after statistically based relevance filtering. A parse was produced for 81 of the 131 sentences, or 62%. Of these, 43 (or 33%) were completely correct, and 30 more had three or fewer errors. Thus, 56% of the sentences were parsed correctly or nearly correctly.

These results naturally vary depending on the length of the sentences. There were 64 sentences of under 30 morphemes (where by "morpheme" we mean a word stem or an inflectional affix). Of these, 37 (58%) had completely correct parses and 48 (75%) had three or fewer errors. By contrast, the scheduling parser attempted only 8 sentences of more than 50 morphemes, and only two of these parsed, neither of them even nearly correctly.

Of the 44 sentences that would not parse, nine were due to problems in lexical entries. Eighteen were due to shortcomings in the grammar, primarily involving adverbial placement and less than fully general treatment of conjunction and comparatives. Six were due to garbled text. The causes of eleven failures to parse have not been determined. These errors are spread out evenly across sentence lengths. In addition, seven sentences of over 30 morphemes hit the time limit we had set, and terminal substring parsing, as described below, was invoked.

A majority of the errors in parsing can be attributed to five or six causes. Two prominent causes are the tendency of the scheduling parser to lose favored close attachments of conjuncts and adjuncts near the end of long sentences, and the tendency to misanalyze the string

$$[[\text{Noun Noun}]_{NP} \text{ Verb}_{trans} \text{ NP}]_S$$

as

$$[\text{Noun}]_{NP} [\text{Noun Verb}_{ditrans} () \text{ NP}]_{S/NP},$$

again contrary to the grammar's preference heuristics. We believe that most of these problems are due to the fact that the work of the scheduling parser is not distributed evenly enough across the different parts of the sentence, and we expect that this difficulty could be solved with relatively little effort.

Our results in syntactic analysis are quite encouraging since they show that a high proportion of a corpus of long and very complex sentences can be parsed nearly correctly. However, the situation is even better when one considers the results for the best-fragment-sequence heuristic and for terminal substring parsing.

2.4.2   Recovery from Failed Parses

When a sentence does not parse, we attempt to span it with the longest, best sequence of interpretable fragments. The fragments we look for are main clauses, verb phrases, adverbial phrases, and noun phrases. They are chosen on the basis of length and their preference scores, favoring length over preference score. We do not attempt to find fragments for strings of less than five morphemes. The effect of this heuristic is that even for sentences that do not parse, we are able to extract nearly all of the propositional content.

For example, Sentence (14) of Message 99 in the TST1 corpus,

> The attacks today come after Shining Path attacks during which
> least 10 buses were burned throughout Lima on 24 Oct.

did not parse because of the use of "least" instead of "at least". Hence, the best fragment sequence was sought. This consisted of the two fragments "The attacks today come after Shining Path attacks" and "10 buses were burned throughout Lima on 24 Oct." The parses for both these fragments were completely correct. Thus, the only information lost was from the three words "during which least". Frequently such information can be recaptured by the pragmatics component. In this case, the burning would be recognized as a consequence of an attack, and inconsistent dates would rule out "the attacks today."

In the first 20 messages of the TST2 corpus, a best sequence of fragments was sought for the 44 sentences that did not parse for reasons other than timing. A sequence was found for 41 of these; the other three were too short, with problems in the middle. The average number of fragments in a sequence was two. This means that an average of only one structural relationship was lost. Moreover, the fragments covered 88% of the morphemes. That is, even in the case of failed parses, 88% of the propositional content of the sentences was made available to pragmatics. Frequently the lost propositional content is from a preposed or postposed, temporal or causal adverbial, and the actual temporal or causal relationship is replaced by simple logical conjunction of the fragments. In such cases, much useful information is still obtained from the partial results.

For 37% of the 41 sentences, correct syntactic analyses of the fragments were produced. For 74%, the analyses contained three or fewer errors. Correctness did not correlate with length of sentence.

These numbers could probably be improved. We favored the longest fragment regardless of preference scores. Thus, frequently a high-scoring main clause was rejected because by tacking a noun onto the front of that fragment and reinterpreting the main clause bizarrely as a relative clause, we could form a low-scoring noun phrase that was one word longer. We therefore plan to experiment with combining length and preference score in a more intelligent manner.

2.4.3   Terminal Substring Parsing

For sentences of longer than 60 words and for faster, though less accurate, parsing of shorter sentences, we developed a technique we are calling *terminal substring parsing*. The sentence is segmented into substrings, by breaking it at commas, conjunctions, relative pronouns, and certain instances of the word "that". The substrings are then parsed, starting with the last one and working back. For each substring, we try either to parse the substring itself as one of several categories or to parse the entire set of substrings parsed so far as one of those categories. The best such structure is selected, and for subsequent processing, that is the only analysis of that portion of the sentence allowed. The categories that we look for include main, subordinate, and relative clauses, infinitives, verb phrases, prepositional phrases, and noun phrases.

A simple example is the following, although we do not apply the technique to sentences or to fragments this short.

George Bush, the president, held a press conference yesterday.

This sentence would be segmented at the commas. First "held a press conference yesterday" would be recognized as a VP. We next try to parse both "the president" and "the president, VP". The string "the president, VP" would not be recognized as anything, but "the president" would be recognized as an NP. Finally, we try to parse both "George Bush" and "George Bush, NP,

VP". "George Bush, NP, VP" is recognized as a sentence with an appositive on the subject.

This algorithm is superior to a more obvious algorithm we had been considering earlier, namely, to parse each fragment individually in a left-to-right fashion and then to attempt to piece the fragments together. The latter algorithm would have required looking inside all but the last of the fragments for possible attachment points. This problem of recombining parts is in general a difficulty that is faced by parsers that produce phrasal rather than sentential parses (e.g., [Weischedel et al., 1991]). However, in terminal substring parsing, this recombining is not necessary, since the favored analyses of subsequent segments are already available when a given segment is being parsed.

The effect of this terminal substring parsing technique is to give only short inputs to the parser, without losing the possibility of getting a single parse for the entire long sentence. Suppose, for example, we are parsing a 60-word sentence that can be broken into six 10-word segments. At each stage, we will only be parsing a string of ten to fifteen "words", the ten words in the segment, plus the nonterminal symbols dominating the favored analyses of the subsequent segments. When parsing the sentence-initial 10-word substring, we are in effect parsing at most a "15-word" string covering the entire sentence, consisting of the 10 words plus the nonterminal symbols covering the best analyses of the other five substrings. In a sense, rather than parsing one very long sentence, we are parsing six fairly short sentences, thus avoiding the combinatorial explosion.

Although this algorithm has given us satisfactory results in our developmental work, its numbers from the MUC-3 evaluation do not look good. This is not surprising, given that the technique is called on only when all else has already failed. In the first 20 messages of the test set, terminal substring parsing was applied to 14 sentences, ranging from 34 to 81 morphemes in length. Only 1 of these parsed, and that parse was not good. However, sequences of fragments were found for the other 13 sentences. The average number of fragments was 2.6, and the sequences covered 80% of the morphemes. None of the fragment sequences was without errors. However, 8 of the 13 had three or fewer mistakes. The technique therefore allowed us to make use of much of the information in sentences that have hitherto been beyond the capability of virtually all parsers.

2.5   Robust Pragmatic Interpretation

When a sentence is parsed and given a semantic interpretation, the relationship between this interpretation and the information previously expressed in the text, as well as the interpreter's general knowledge, must be established. Establishing this relationship comes under the general heading of pragmatic interpretation. The particular problems that are solved during this step include:

- Making explicit information that is only implicit in the text. This includes, for example, explicating the relationship underlying a compound nominal, or explicating causal consequences of events or states mentioned explicitly in the text.

- Determining the implicit entities and relationships referred to metonymically in the text.

- Resolving anaphoric references and implicit arguments.

- Viewing the text as an instance of a schema that makes its various parts coherent.

TACITUS interprets a sentence pragmatically by proving that its logical form follows from general knowledge and the preceding text, allowing a minimal set of assumptions to be made. In addition, it is assumed that the set of events, abstract entities, and physical objects mentioned in the text is to be consistently minimized. The best set of assumptions necessary to find such a proof can be regarded as an explanation of its truth, and constitutes the implicit information required to produce the interpretation [Hobbs *et al.*, 1990]. The minimization of objects and events leads to anaphora resolution by assuming that objects that share properties are identical, when such an assumption is consistent.

In the MUC-3 domain, explaining a text involves viewing it as an instance of one of a number of explanatory schemas representing terrorist incidents of various types (e.g., bombing, arson, assassination) or one of several event types that are similar to terrorist incidents, but explicitly excluded by the task requirements (e.g., an exchange of fire between military groups of opposing factions). This means that assumptions that fit into incident schemas are preferred to assumptions that do not, and the schema that ties together the most assumptions is the best explanation.

In this text interpretation task, the domain knowledge performs two primary functions:

1. It relates the propositions expressed in the text to the elements of the underlying explanatory schemas.

2. It enables and restricts possible coreferences for anaphora resolution.

It is clear that much domain knowledge may be required to perform these functions successfully, but it is not necessarily the case that more knowledge is always better. If axioms are incrementally added to the system to cover cases not accounted for in the existing domain theory, it is possible that they can interact with the existing knowledge in such a way that the reasoning process becomes computationally intractable, and the unhappy result would be failure to find an interpretation in cases in which the correct interpretation is entailed by the system's knowledge. In a domain as broad and diffuse as the terrorist domain, it is often impossible to guarantee by inspection that a domain theory is not subject to such combinatorial problems.

The goal of robustness in interpretation therefore requires one to address two problems: A system must permit a graceful degradation of performance in those cases in which knowledge is incomplete, and it must extract as much information as it can in the face of a possible combinatorial explosion.

The general approach of abductive text interpretation addresses the first problem through the notion of a "best interpretation." The best explanation, given incomplete domain knowledge, can succeed at relating some propositions contained in the text to the explanatory schemas, but may not succeed for all propositions. The combinatorial problems are addressed through a particular search strategy for abductive reasoning described as *incremental refinement of minimal information proofs.*

The abductive proof procedure as employed by TACITUS [Stickel, 1988] will always be able to find *some* interpretation of the text. In the worst case—the absence of any commonsense knowledge that would be relevant to the interpretation of a sentence—the explanation offered would be found by assuming each of the literals to be proved. Such a proof is called a "minimal information proof" because no schema recognition or explication of implicit relationships takes place. However, the more knowledge the system has, the more implicit information can be recovered.

Because a minimal information proof is always available for any sentence of the text that is internally consistent, it provides a starting point for incremental refinement of explanations that can be obtained at next to no cost. TACITUS explores the space of abductive proofs by finding incrementally better explanations for each of the constituent literals. A search strategy is adopted that finds successive explanations, each of which is better than the minimal information proof. This process can be halted at any time in a state that will provide at least *some* intermediate results that are useful for subsequent interpretation and template filling.

Consider again Message 100 from the MUC-3 development corpus:

A cargo train running from Lima to Lorohia was derailed before dawn today after hitting a dynamite charge.
Inspector Eulogio Flores died in the explosion.
The police reported that the incident took place past midnight in the Carahuaichi-Jaurin area.

The correct interpretation of this text requires recovering certain implicit information that relies on commonsense knowledge. The compound nominal phrase "dynamite charge" must be interpreted as "charge composed of dynamite." The interpretation requires knowing that dynamite is a substance, that substances can be related via compound nominal relations to objects composed of those substances, that things composed of dynamite are bombs, that hitting bombs causes them to explode, that exploding causes damage, that derailing is a type of damage, and that planting a bomb is a terrorist act. The system's commonsense knowledge base must be rich enough to derive each of these conclusions if it is to recognize the event described as a terrorist act, since all derailings are not the result of bombings. This example underscores the need for fairly extensive world knowledge in the comprehension of text. If the knowledge is missing, the correct interpretation cannot be found. (A few simple heuristics can capture some of the information, but at the expense of accuracy.)

However, if there is missing knowledge, all is not necessarily lost. If, for example, the knowledge was missing that hitting a bomb causes it to explode, the system could still hypothesize the relationship between the charge and the dynamite to reason that a bomb was placed. When processing the next sentence, the system may have trouble figuring out the time and place of Flores' death if it can't associate the explosion with hitting the bomb. However, if the second sentence were "The Shining Path claimed that their guerrillas had planted the bomb," the partial information would be sufficient to allow "bomb" to be resolved to dynamite charge, thereby connecting the event described in the first sentence with the event described in the second.

It is difficult to evaluate the pragmatic interpretation component individually, since to a great extent its success depends on the adequacy of the syntactic analysis it operates on. However, in examining the first 20 messages of the MUC-3 test set in detail, we attempted to pinpoint the reason for each missing or incorrect entry in the required templates.

There were 269 such mistakes, due to problems in 41 sentences. Of these, 124 are attributable to pragmatic interpretation. We have classified their causes into a number of categories, and the results are as follows:

Reason	Mistakes
Simple Axiom Missing	49
Combinatorics	28
Unconstrained Identity Assumptions	25
Complex Axioms or Theory Missing	14
Underconstrained Axiom	8

An example of a missing simple axiom is that "bishop" is a profession. An example of a missing complex theory is one that assigns a default causality relationship to events that are simultaneous at the granularity reported in the text. An underconstrained axiom is one that allows, for example, "damage to the economy" to be taken as a terrorist incident. Unconstrained identity assumptions result from the knowledge base's inability to rule out identity of two different objects with similar properties, thus leading to incorrect anaphora resolution. "Combinatorics" simply means that the theorem-prover timed out, and the minimal-information proof strategy was invoked to obtain a partial interpretation.

It is difficult to evaluate the precise impact of the robustness strategies outlined here. The robustness is an inherent feature of the overall approach, and we did not have a non-robust control to test it against. However, the implementation of the minimal information proof search strategy virtually eliminated all of our complete failures due to lack of computational resources, and cut the error rate attributable to this cause roughly in half.

2.6   Conclusion

We felt that the treatment of unknown words was for the most part adequate. The statistical relevance filter was extremely successful. The keyword antifilter, on the other hand, is apparently far too coarse and needs to be refined or eliminated.

We felt syntactic analysis was a stunning success. At the beginning of this effort, we despaired of being able to handle sentences of the length and complexity of those in the MUC-3 corpus, and indeed, many sites abandoned syntactic analysis altogether. Now, however, we feel that the syntactic analysis of material such as this is very nearly a solved problem. The coverage of our grammar, our scheduling parser, and our heuristic of using the best sequence of fragments for failed parses combined to enable us to get a very high proportion of the propositional content out of every sentence. The mistakes that we found in the first 20 messages of TST2 can, for the most part, be attributed to about five or six causes, which could be remedied with a moderate amount of work.

On the other hand, the results for terminal substring parsing, our method for dealing with sentences of more than 60 morphemes, are inconclusive, and we believe this technique could be improved.

In pragmatics, much work remains to be done. A large number of fairly simple axioms need to be written, as well as some more complex axioms. In the course of our preparation for MUC-3, we made sacrifices in robustness for the sake of efficiency, and we would like to re-examine the tradeoffs. We would like to push more of the problems of syntactic and lexical ambiguity into the pragmatics component, rather than relying on syntactic heuristics. We would also like to further constrain factoring, which now sometimes results in the incorrect identification of distinct events.

It is often assumed that when natural language processing meets the real world, the ideal of aiming for complete and correct interpretations has to be abandoned. However, our experience with TACITUS, especially in the MUC-3 evaluation, has shown that principled techniques for syntactic and pragmatic analysis can be bolstered with methods for achieving robustness, yielding a system with some utility in the short term and showing promise of more in the long term.

Acknowledgments

This research has been funded by the Defense Advanced Research Projects Agency under Office of Naval Research contracts N00014-85-C-0013 and N00014-90-C-0220.

Bibliography

[Cardie and Lehnert, 1991] Claire Cardie and Wendy Lehnert. A cognitively plausible approach to understanding complex syntax. In *Proceedings of the Ninth National Conference on Artificial Intelligence*, pages 117–124, Anaheim, CA, July 1991.

[Grishman and Sterling, 1989] Ralph Grishman and John Sterling. Preference semantics for message understanding. In *Proceedings of the DARPA Speech and Natural-Language Workshop*, pages 71–74, 1989.

[Hobbs, 1978] Jerry R. Hobbs. Resolving pronoun references. *Lingua* 44:311–338. Also in *Readings in Natural Language Processing*, Barbara Grosz, Karen Sparck Jones, and Bonnie Webber, editors, pages 339–352, Morgan Kaufmann Publishers, Los Altos, CA, 1978.

[Hobbs and Bear, 1990] Jerry R. Hobbs and John Bear. Two principles of parse preference. In H. Karlgren, editor, *Proceedings of the Thirteenth International Conference on Computational Linguistics*, Vol. 3, pages 162–167, Helsinki, Finland, August 1990.

[Hobbs et al., 1990] Jerry R. Hobbs, Mark Stickel, Douglas Appelt, and Paul Martin. Interpretation as abduction. SRI International Artificial Intelligence Center Technical Note 499, December 1990.

[Jackson et al., 1991] Eric Jackson, Douglas Appelt, John Bear, Robert Moore, and Ann Podlozny. A template matcher for robust NL interpretation. In *Proceedings of the DARPA Speech and Natural Language Workshop*, pages 190–194, Asilomar, CA, February 1991.

[Jacobs et al., 1991] Paul S. Jacobs, George R. Krupka, and Lisa F. Rau. Lexico-semantic pattern matching as a companion to parsing in text understanding. In *Proceedings of the DARPA Speech and Natural Language Workshop*, pages 337–341, Asilomar, CA, February 1991.

[Kaplan, 1973] Ronald Kaplan. A general syntactic processor. In Randall Rustin, editor, *Natural Language Processing*, pages 193–241, Algorithmics Press, New York, 1973.

[deMarcken, 1990] Carl G. de Marcken Parsing the LOB corpus. In *Proceedings of the 28th Annual Meeting of the Association for Computational Linguistics*, pages 243–251, Helsinki, Finland, August 1990.

[Moore and Dowding, 1991] Robert C. Moore and John Dowding. Efficient bottom-up parsing. In *Proceedings of the DARPA Speech and Natural Language Workshop*, pages 200–203, Asilomar, CA, February 1991.

[Robinson, 1982] Jane Robinson. DIAGRAM: A grammar for dialogues. *Communications of the Association for Computing Machinery*, 25(1):27–47, January 1982.

[Sager, 1981] Naomi Sager. *Natural Language Information Processing: A Computer Grammar of English and Its Applications*. Addison-Wesley, Reading, MA, 1981.

[Schank and Riesbeck, 1981] Roger Schank and C. Riesbeck. *Inside Computer Understanding: Five Programs Plus Miniatures*. Lawrence Erlbaum Associates, Hillsdale, NJ, 1981.

[Stickel, 1988] Mark E. Stickel. A Prolog-like inference system for computing minimum-cost abductive explanations in natural-language interpretation. In *Proceedings of the International Computer Science Conference-88*, pages 343–350, Hong Kong, December 1988. Also published as Technical Note 451, Artificial Intelligence Center, SRI International, Menlo Park, CA, September 1988.

[Sundheim, 1991] Beth Sundheim, editor. *Proceedings of the Third Message Understanding Conference (MUC-3)*. San Diego, CA, May 1991.

[Weischedel et al., 1991] Ralph Weischedel, Damaris Ayuso, Sean Boisen, Robert Ingria, and J. Palmucci. Partial parsing: A report on work in progress. In *Proceedings of the DARPA Speech and Natural Language Workshop*, pages 204–209, Asilomar, CA, February 1991.

[Winograd, 1983] Terry Winograd. *Language as a Cognitive Process*. Addison-Wesley, Reading, MA, 1983.

Appendix

Message 99 of the TST1 corpus:

(1)   Police have reported that terrorists tonight bombed the embassies of the PRC and the Soviet Union.

(2)   The bombs caused damage but no injuries.

(3)   A car-bomb exploded in front of the PRC embassy, which is in the Lima residential district of San Isidro.

(4)   Meanwhile, two bombs were thrown at a USSR embassy vehicle that was parked in front of the embassy located in Orrantia district, near San Isidro.

(5)   Police said the attacks were carried out almost simultaneously and that the bombs broke windows and destroyed the two vehicles.

(6)   No one has claimed responsibility for the attacks so far.

(7)   Police sources, however, have said the attacks could have been carried out by the Maoist "Shining Path" group or the Guevarist "Tupac Amaru Revolutionary Movement" (MRTA) group.

(8)   The sources also said that the Shining Path has attacked Soviet interests in Peru in the past.

(9)   In July 1989 the Shining Path bombed a bus carrying nearly 50 Soviet marines into the port of El Callao.

(10) Fifteen Soviet marines were wounded.

(11) Some 3 years ago two marines died following a Shining Path bombing of a market used by Soviet marines.

(12) In another incident 3 years ago, a Shining Path militant was killed by Soviet embassy guards inside the embassy compound.

(13) The terrorist was carrying dynamite.

(14) The attacks today come after Shining Path attacks during which least 10 buses were burned throughout Lima on 24 Oct.

Combining Weak Methods in Large-Scale Text Processing

Yorick Wilks
Louise Guthrie
Joe Guthrie
Jim Cowie
Computing Research Laboratory
New Mexico State University
Las Cruces, New Mexico

Pat Suppes used to say 20 years ago that he would pay attention to AI and natural language processing (NLP) only when it could "do something of book length". That day is now pretty close, though old-fashioned machine translation systems like SYSTRAN [Toma, 1977] met his criterion at a low level many years ago. The present could seem like a rerun (in NLP) of the struggles within machine vision in the late 1970's: the high-level, top-down paradigm of scene analysis (Guzman, Brady, Waltz, etc.) was crumbling in the face of low-level, bottom-up, arguments posed by Marr. NLP has been told for some time that it should be more scientific "like machine vision," so perhaps the current emergence of connectionist, statistical and associationist techniques in NLP is a form of progress by virtue of that fact alone.

The first major program of the first author ran on texts, using a coherence-based approach later called Preference Semantics [Wilks, 1975]. The program processed philosophical argument texts with newspaper editorials as controls. None of that was on a very large scale, although it was probably pretty big for Lisp programs in the mid-sixties. The aim was to locate coherent text structures that were more revealing and information-providing than those coming from the information retrieval (IR) and associationist methods of the period. It seemed to many at the time that IR techniques had been totally discredited, at least as far as the extraction of text content was concerned. The goal of Preference Semantics, like other techniques of that period, was to find an appropriate level of structure, lying above those of IR, yet without going impossibly deeply into what later came to be called *knowledge-based text understanding*. But, as Augustine used to point out, truth may not be in the middle at all, but in both extremes.

The last paragraph was to make the point, if it still needs making, that the current statistical/connectionist etc. approaches are not essentially novel or revolutionary, as their proponents tend to claim: Their techniques are, by and large, well-known and long-rejected. The interesting question now is: Can those techniques be optimised in some way by software or hardware methods, so as to produce more plausible results than before? Another possibility, and one at the center of this book's concerns, is whether the benefits of "higher" and "lower" level methods can be combined to scale up NLP in the way we all now accept as necessary.

Let us attempt a brief and cursory taxonomy of large-scale text processing efforts, to see if the range is larger or smaller than one first thought. We could distinguish at least the following components or phases:

1. The SYSTRAN machine translation system [Toma, 1977]: its core is 25 years old but it still does whole books in a few minutes every day at the Federal Translation Division at Dayton. It is certainly massive text processing by any standard, and gets a rate of something like 75% of Russian sentences acceptably translated into English. SYSTRAN is very efficiently programmed, but the core consists of routines no one fully understands anymore and which cannot be edited: it certainly has little or no high-level semantics and no knowledge-based capacity, but works by means of a very large lexicon of linguistic cases.

2. The FRUMP system by DeJong at Yale [DeJong, 1979] analyzed the AP newswires with "sketchy scripts." Its final hit rate was about 38% of the stories it should have gotten. It had a system of structured key words although it claimed derivation from a higher-level representational system (conceptual dependency). A key fact was that its performance was never compared with standard IR techniques over similar materials. Here one should also mention Lebowitz's IPP parser [Lebowitz, 1983], which made many of the same assumptions.

3. Leech's [Atwell et al., 1984] automatic tagging system for parts of speech in the Brown text corpus used low-level probabilistic procedures. AI workers mocked it for years, but it turned out to have a success rate of the order of 95% and is now being reimplemented by Marcus with the addition of intonational tagging as the Pennsylvania Tree Bank Project.

4. Waltz's [Mott et al., 1986] (see also Waltz and Stallfill, this volume) implementation of key-word IR for texts on a connection machine also embodied a range of interesting string-matching techniques. This is certainly not connectionism (albeit Waltz's simultaneous interest in connectionist methods) but is large-scale text analysis; it is certainly not impeded by the scale-up problems of connectionism (including connectionist IR, see Belew 1988 [Belew and Rose, 1988]). Waltz's proposals are much more like a combination of weak methods such as we advocate below.

5. Church's [Church and Hanks, 1989] recent work uses the mutual information statistic to compute word associations in large corpora. One application is to give probable successor information for English words. Related work is reported over dictionaries and texts by Boguraev *et al.* [Boguraev *et al.*, 1989]. This is undoubtedly large-scale computation but the relationship to "meaning" that Church and Hanks claim is totally unclear, since no individual (who presumably knows the "meanings of words") has such statistical information, which is also, almost by definition, subject to none of the conventional hierarchical relationships such as transitivity of inference. That fact may make it hard to use in any practical application.

6. Jelinek [Brown *et al.*, 1988] and his colleagues at IBM are attempting machine translation based on models of redundancy in text, applied to parallel text in two languages. So, they have a model of collocational forms within the two languages as well as between them, based on one-to-one sentence alignments. This technique seems to rely on similar orders of "related" words in the source and target languages, a condition not normally met between, say, English and German, because of their very different sentence order for words. Even between two languages that have some such relationship (e.g., English and French) the hit rate claimed (65%) is very low, even when compared with SYSTRAN over much less constrained text.

What can one say by way of generalization about this sample of massive text processing methods? They are a very mixed bag: (1), for example, relies on hand-coding like almost all machine translation, whereas the IBM approach (6) is wholly automatic, all its information being derived from the text with no hand-coding or foreign language expertise. One could rate the systems on whether or not they do achieve their (even if limited) goals: (3) clearly does. Or one could ask whether one can be fairly certain that no amount of optimization could allow the chosen method to reach the chosen goal (as in 1 and 6), whereas other systems do not have goals clear enough to be sure (e.g., 5).

In spite of differences in the goals of these systems, they are all key efforts in text processing which have been driving forces for new interests and continued research. SYSTRAN holds a unique place due to its continued development over a long period and it's ongoing use for real work. New research projects in Machine Translation such as the DARPA funded IBM statistical project and the Carnegie Mellon, New Mexico State, University of Southern California joint project will surely be evaluated on the basis of whether the new methods can potentially be improved to a level beyond that of SYSTRAN.

The FRUMP system inspired two major research initiatives in text understanding. MUC (Message Understanding Conferences) were conferences designed to discuss the results of a competition on extracting information from news articles reporting terrorist incidents in South America [Lehnert and Sundheim, 1991]. An innovation of this effort was the development of a standard scheme for evaluation of the various competing text extraction methods. The success of this project has led to the recent initiation of the ambitious TIPSTER project to extract more complex information from text.

The statistical work of the IBM group and of Church and Hanks has renewed interest in statistical methods for processing texts. The availability of large corpora and the low cost of large memories and large file stores has made these approaches realistic to pursue at this time. On the other hand, massively parallel machines, such as the connection machine, are not widely available and the adoption of the work of Mott *et al.* has been slower. Nevertheless, the ideas here have been influential both in information retrieval and in the research on massively parallel architectures.

The Leech, Atwell and Garside work illustrates a major success in natural language processing. This work has surely satisfied the "reproducibility" goal of scientific experiments. Today, many part-of-speech taggers exist that automatically tag texts with accuracy that cannot be attained in many other important natural language tasks. Part-of-speech tagging is now viewed as an important initial processing stage for text analysis and all indications are that this work will improve the overall quality of language processing systems.

What is the future of large-scale text processing? Which of the trends that are apparent now will be dominant in the systems of tomorrow? We believe that rather than any one method triumphing, the future lies in the combination of methods, that the better way ahead is one we are following at CRL: one where different types of methods are combined, "higher" and "lower", hopefully to give a strong combination of what Newell [Newell, 1973] called inherently weak methods.

3.1   A "Weak Method" Hybrid Approach at CRL

The New Mexico State Computing Research Laboratory has been working on large-scale analysis of dictionaries, which are special texts but texts nonetheless. The machine readable dictionary text (MRD) we used initially is *The Longman Dictionary of Contemporary English* (LDOCE, [Procter and others, 1978]), and we have applied a range of different methods to it, each of which may be considered weak in itself, but which we hope later to combine to make a strong approach for text analysis. The methods differ in the amount of knowledge they start with and the kinds of knowledge they provide, and are almost wholly automatic.

The goal of our work on large scale analysis of dictionaries is to provide a representation of each dictionary sense entry which can then be used for automatic creation of lexical entries for natural language processing systems. We are using a simple, but we believe adequate, frame-based representation for storing the dictionary senses. Our interest lies not in the format of this representation, but rather in the extraction of syntactic and semantic information about word senses that can be found either explicitly or implicitly in a dictionary sense entry.

Thus it could be said we intend to bring out the "unconscious" of the lexicographers, as well as their "conscious", i.e., what they actually intended to express. Our aim is to produce a *Machine Tractable Dictionary* (MTD) for general NLP use in the form of a Lexical Data Base, containing both symbolic and statistically-derived information. One aspect of that task will be the use of both types of information to produce a dictionary whose defining terms (or primitives) have themselves been tagged, on each occurrence, with the right sense.

At this point we have transformed each entry from LDOCE into a frame-based representation from which we have semi-automatically generated lexical entries for the open class words[1] of one of the lexicons of the ULTRA machine translation system [Farwell *et al.*, 1991]. We mean by semi-automatically that completed lexical entries were generated when possible (for example, in the case of lexical items corresponding to nouns), and when this was not possible, incomplete entries were created and then completed interactively.

To make lexicon creation fully automatic, we need to provide a better representation of the information in each entry. To do this, we define a hybrid SPIRAL procedure that combines and refines much of the previous work of the laboratory in a way that allows each procedure to enrich the information contained in the frame corresponding to a dictionary entry.

The first stages of the SPIRAL procedure are shown in Figure 3.1.

We have used the Lexicon Provider of Slator [Slator and Wilks, 1987; Wilks *et al.*, 1989]) to enrich each frame by providing a parse of the definition string. The Genus Processor [Guthrie *et al.*, 1990; Bruce and Guthrie, 1991]) identifies and disambiguates the genus terms of definitions and this links the frames into a semantic network of word senses. This project has been completed for noun senses and will eventually include similar procedures for verbs.

There are strong empirical assumptions behind these approaches: one can be called Extricability. **Extricability** is concerned with whether it is possible to specify a set of computational procedures that operate on an MRD and extract, through their operation alone and without any human intervention, general and reliable semantic information on a large scale, and in a general format suitable for, though independent of, a range of subsequent NLP tasks. A second assumption is **Sufficiency**: that there is enough world knowledge present, explicitly or implicitly, to enable parsing of general text to be carried out with the aid of the information extracted from the MRD. Finally, there is the assumption of **Bootstrapping**: the viability, for subsequent text parsing,

---

[1]Open class words are the types of words which are frequently added to the language. In English the open class words include nouns, verbs, adjectives, and adverbs.

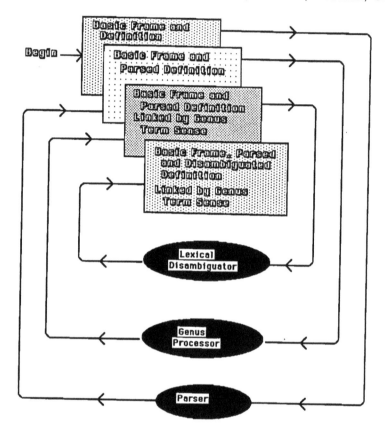

Figure 3.1: The Spiral Procedure

of the process of collecting initial information from the in an MRD.

There are differences of opinion in computational lexicography regarding these assumptions. Slocum and Morgan [1986] are pessimistic about the use of machine readable dictionaries in machine translation, and Kay [1989] has argued all work on MRDs for NLP is misguided. Others (e.g., Amsler [1980]; Boguraev [1989]; Kegl [1987]) appear to believe that the semantic information in dictionaries can be extricated but only with some external bootstrapping, that is, only if at least some prior knowledge is hand-coded into an analysis program. Our assumptions in this work are empirically based and our evaluation criteria practical. Our plan is large-scale testing of techniques based on these assumptions.

Our current research plan aims to produce the lexical data base by integrating further structures derived from parsing the dictionary itself with more computationally-tractable associationist methods. Here, however, since the main topic is text processing, we move on to describe two techniques developed in the course of this work that will be incorporated into this hybrid technology, but which can be applied to the task of sense-tagging beyond the dictionary text to general text itself.

3.2   The Lexical Disambiguator

Our most recent work has been on the next cycle of the SPIRAL: the lexical disambiguator, which will allow the parsed word sense definitions to be sense-tagged relative to the senses provided in LDOCE. Although we have developed several techniques that are specific to LDOCE for disambiguating SOME words in some definitions [Guthrie et al., 1990; Bruce and Guthrie, 1991; Wilks et al., 1989; Guthrie et al., 1991], we believe that we will need to develop tools for the lexical disambiguation of general text before we can make significant progress in disambiguating the remaining words in the dictionary definitions.

This is an ambitious task, but we believe that significant progress in this area is necessary before we can actually extract the other meaningful relationships which are present in dictionary definitions and are commonly considered necessary for language processing.

We are exploring two major techniques for lexical disambiguation on which we only have preliminary experimental results. The first method involves constraining the statistical disambiguation techniques of McDonald and Plate [Wilks et al., 1989; Guthrie et al., 1991] by prior application of the LDOCE subject area codes. This hybrid technique enormously enhances the sense-tagging percentage in text, both dictionary and general text. The second approach is an extension to sense-disambiguation (in lexicons and general text) of the technique of simulated annealing (Sampson [Sampson, 1986]) for solving large-scale problems of combinatorial maximization. This has been applied experimentally to the LDOCE word sense codings for the words of general text (*Grolier's Encyclopedia*) to optimize the technique of Lesk [1986]. These hybrid procedures are in the process of refinement, both for general text disambiguation and for the production of an unambiguous Lexical Data Base.

3.3   Word Sense Disambiguation by Subject-Dependent Co-occurrence

Word associations have been studied in the fields of psycholinguistics (by testing human subjects on words), linguistics (where meaning is based on how words co-occur with each other in areas like lexical field theory) and, more recently, they have been revived after a long interval by researchers in natural language processing (Church and Hanks [1989]; Dagan and Itai

[1990]; McDonald *et al.* [1990]; Wilks *et al.* [Wilks *et al.*, 1989; Guthrie *et al.*, 1991]) using statistical measures to identify sets of associated words for use in natural language processing tasks. One of the tasks where the statistical data on associated words has been used with some success is lexical disambiguation. However, associated word sets gathered from a general corpus may contain words that are associated with many different senses. For example, vocabulary associated with the word *bank* includes *money*, *rob*, *river* and *sand*. In this section, we describe an additional method for obtaining subject-dependent associated word sets, or "neighborhoods" of a given word, relative to a particular (subject) domain. Using the subject classifications of Longman's *Dictionary of Contemporary English* (LDOCE), we have established subject-dependent co-occurrence links between words of the defining vocabulary to construct these neighborhoods. We will describe a method of word sense disambiguation based on these co-occurrences. This work was first reported on in Guthrie *et al.* [1991].

3.3.1   Co-occurrence Neighborhoods

Words that occur frequently with a given word may be thought of as forming a "neighborhood" of that word. If we can determine which words (i.e., spelling forms) co-occur frequently with each word sense, we can use these neighborhoods to disambiguate the word in a given text. Assume that we know of only the two classic senses of the word *bank*:

1. A repository for money

2. A pile of earth on the edge of a river

We can expect the "money" sense of *bank* to co-occur frequently with such words as *money*, *loan*, and *robber*, while the "river" sense would be more frequently associated with *river*, *bridge*, and *earth*. In order to disambiguate *bank* in a text, we would produce neighborhoods for each sense, and intersect them with the text, our assumption being that the neighborhood which shared more words with the text would determine the correct sense. Variations of this idea appear in [Lesk, 1986; McDonald *et al.*, 1990; Veronis and Ide, 1990].

As we noted above, McDonald and Plate [McDonald *et al.*, 1990; Schvaneveldt, 1990] used the collection of all LDOCE definitions as their text, in order to generate co-occurrence data for the 2,187 words in the LDOCE control (defining) vocabulary. They used various methods to apply this data to the problem of disambiguating control vocabulary words as they appear in the LDOCE example sentences. In every case, however, the set of associated words for a given word was a co-occurrence neighborhood for its spelling form over all the definitions in the dictionary.

3.3.2 Subject-Dependent Neighborhoods

The study of word co-occurrence in a text is based on the cliche (attributed to Firth) that "a word is known by the company it keeps". We hold that it also makes a difference *where* that company is kept: Since a word may occur with different sets of words in different contexts, we construct word neighborhoods which depend on the subject of the text in question. We call these, naturally enough, "subject-dependent neighborhoods". A unique feature of the electronic version of LDOCE is that many of the word sense definitions are marked with a subject field code which tells us which subject area the sense pertains to.

For example, the "money"-related senses of *bank* are marked *EC* (Economics), and for each such main subject heading, we consider the subset of LDOCE definitions that consists of those sense definitions which share that subject code. These definitions are then collected into one file, and co-occurrence data for their defining vocabulary is generated. Word x is said to co-occur with word y if x and y appear in the same sense definition; the total number of times they co-occur is denoted as f_{xy}. We construct a matrix (2,187 × 2,187) where each row and column corresponds to one word of the defining vocabulary, and the entry in the xth row and yth column is the number of times the xth word co-occurred with the yth word. (This is a symmetric matrix, and therefore it is only necessary to maintain half of it.) We denote by f_x the total number of times word x appeared. While many statistics may be used to measure the relatedness of words x and y, we used the following function:

$$r(x,y) = \frac{f_{xy}}{f_x + f_y - f_{xy}}$$

We choose a co-occurrence neighborhood of a word x from a set of closely related words. We may choose the ten words with the highest relatedness statistic, for instance. Neighborhoods of the word *metal* in the categories "Economics" and "Business" are presented below:

Table 3.1: Economics neighborhood of *metal*

Subject Code EC = Economics				
metal	idea	coin	them	silver
	real	should	pocket	gold
	well	him		

In this example, the neighborhoods reflect a fundamental difference between the two subject areas. Economics is a more theoretical subject, and therefore its neighborhood contains words like *idea*, *gold*, *silver*, and *real*,

Table 3.2: Business neighborhood of *metal*

Subject Code BU = Business				
metal	bear	apparatus	mouth	inside
	spring	entrance	plate	brass
	tight	sheet		

while in the more practical domain of Business, we find the words *brass*, *apparatus*, *spring*, and *plate*. We can expect the contrast between subject neighborhoods to be especially great for words with senses that fall into different subject areas. Consider the actual neighborhoods of our original example, *bank*.

Table 3.3: Economics neighborhood of *bank*

Subject Code EC = Economics				
bank	account	cheque	money	by
	into	have	keep	order
	out	pay	at	put
	from	draw	an	busy
	more	supply	it	safe

Table 3.4: Engineering neighborhood of *bank*

Subject Code EG = Engineering				
bank	river	wall	flood	thick
	earth	prevent	opposite	chair
	hurry	paste	spread	overflow
	walk	help	we	throw
	clay	then	wide	level

Notice that even though we included the 20 most closely related words in each neighborhood, they are still unrelated or disjoint, although many of the words that appear in the lists are indeed suggestive of the sense or senses which fall under that subject category. In LDOCE, 3 of the 11 senses of *bank* are marked with the code *EC* for Economics, and these represent the "money" senses of the word. It is a quirk of the classification in LDOCE that the "river" senses of bank are not marked with a subject code. This lack of a subject code for a word sense in LDOCE is not uncommon, however, and as was the case with *bank*, some word senses may have subject codes, while others do not.

We label this lack of a subject code the "null code", and form a neighborhood of this type of sense by using all sense definitions without code as text. This "null code neighborhood" can reveal the common, or "generic", sense of the word. The table below gives the 20 most frequently occurring words with *bank* in definitions with the null subject code.

Table 3.5: Null Code neighborhood of *bank*

Subject Code NULL = no code assigned			
bank	rob	river	account	lend
	overflow	flood	money	criminal
	lake	flow	snow	cliff
	police	shore	heap	thief
	borrow	along	steep	earth

It is obvious that approximately half of these words are associated with our two main senses of *bank*— but a new element has crept in: the appearance of four out of eight words that refer to the "money" sense (*rob, criminal, police,* and *thief*) reveal a sense of *bank* that did not appear in the EC neighborhood. In the null code definitions, there are quite a few references to the potential for a bank to be robbed. Finally, for comparison, consider the neighborhood in the next table for *bank*, which uses *all* the LDOCE definitions (see McDonald *et al.* [McDonald *et al.*, 1990]; Schvaneveldt [Schvaneveldt, 1990]; Wilks *et al.* [Wilks *et al.*, 1989; Guthrie *et al.*, 1991]).

Only four of these words (*bank, earn, sand,* and *thief*) are not found in the other three neighborhoods, and the number of words in the intersection of this neighborhood with the Economics, Engineering, and Null neighborhoods are: 6, 4, and 11, respectively. Recalling that the Economics and Engineering neighborhoods are disjoint, this data supports our hypothesis that the subject-dependent neighborhoods help us to distinguish senses more easily than neighborhoods that are extracted from the whole dictionary. There are over 100 main subject field codes in LDOCE, and over 300 sub-divisions within these. For example, "Medicine-and-Biology" is a main subject field (coded "MD"), and has 22 sub-divisions such as "Anatomy" and "Biochemistry". These main codes and their sub-divisions constitute the only two

Table 3.6: Unrestricted neighborhood of *bank*

Subject Code All			
bank	account	bank	busy	cheque
	criminal	earn	flood	flow
	interest	lake	lend	money
	overflow	pay	river	rob
	safes	and	thief	wall

levels in the LDOCE subject code hierarchy, and main codes such as "Golf" and "Sports" are not related to each other.

There are certain drawbacks in using LDOCE to construct the subject-dependent neighborhoods: the amount of text in LDOCE about any one subject area is rather limited. It is comprised of a control vocabulary for dictionary definitions only, and uses sample sentences which were concocted with non-native English speakers in mind. In the next phase of our research, large corpora consisting of actual documents from a given subject area will be used, in order to obtain neighborhoods which more accurately reflect the sorts of texts which will be used in applications. In the future, these neighborhoods may replace those constructed from LDOCE, while leaving the subject code hierarchy and various applications intact.

3.3.3   Word-Sense Disambiguation

The resolution of lexical ambiguity is central to text processing. In machine translation, for example, it is necessary to decide which sense of a word in the source langauge is being used before it can be correctly translated it into the target language. Lexical disambiguation is also important in other text-processing applications such as information retrieval. The ability to resolve lexical ambiguities in a query and in documents would allow a more precise selection of relevant documents.

In this section, we describe an application of subject-dependent co-occurrence neighborhoods to the problem of word-sense disambiguation. The subject-dependent co-occurrence neighborhoods are used as building blocks for the neighborhoods used in disambiguation. For each of the subject codes (including the null code) which appear with a word sense to be disambiguated, we intersect the corresponding subject-dependent co-occurrence neighborhood with the text being considered (the size of text can vary from a sentence to a paragraph). The intersection must contain a preselected minimum number of words to be considered. But if none of the neighborhoods intersect at greater than this threshold level, we replace the neighborhood N by the neighborhood *N(1)*, which consists of *N* together with the first word from each neighborhood of words in *N*, using the same subject code. If necessary, we add the second most strongly associated word for each of the words in the original neighborhood *N*, forming the neighborhood *N(2)*.

We continue this process until a subject-dependent co-occurrence neighborhood has intersection above the threshold level. Then, the sense or senses with this subject code is selected. If more than one sense has the selected code, we use their definitions as cores to build distinguishing neighborhoods for them. These are again intersected with the text to determine the correct sense. The following two examples illustrate this method. Note that some of the neighborhoods differ from those given earlier since the text used to construct these neighborhoods includes any example sentences that may occur in the sense definitions. Those neighborhoods presented earlier ignored the example sentences. In each example, we attempt to disambiguate the word *bank* in a sentence that appears as an example sentence in the Collins COBUILD English Language Dictionary. The disambiguation consists of choosing the correct sense of *bank* from among the 13 senses given in LDOCE. These senses are summarized below.

bank(1) : [ ] : land along the side of a river, lake, etc.

bank(2) : [ ] : earth which is heaped up in a field or garden.

bank(3) : [ ] : a mass of snow, clouds, mud, etc.

bank(4) : [AU] : a slope made at bends in a road or race-track.

bank(5) : [ ] : a sandbank in a river, etc.

bank(6) : [AU] : to move a car or aircraft with one side higher than the other.

bank(7) : [ ] : a row, especially of oars in an ancient boat or keys on a typewriter.

bank(8) : [EC] : a place in which money is kept and paid out on demand.

bank(9) : [MD] : a place where something is held ready for use, such as blood.

bank(10) : [GB] : (a person who keeps) a supply of money or pieces for payment in a gambling game.

bank(11) : [ ] : break the bank is to win all the money in bank(10).

bank(12) : [EC] : to put or keep (money) in a bank.

bank(13) : [EC] : to keep one's money in a bank.

Table 3.7: Automotive neighborhood of *bank*

Subject Code AU = Automotive			
bank make	go	up	move
so	they	high	also
round	car	side	turn
road	aircraft	slope	bend
safe			

Table 3.8: Economics neighborhood of *bank*

Subject Code EC = Economics			
bank have	it	person	out
into	take	money	put
write	keep	pay	order
another	paper	draw	supply
account	safe	sum	cheque

Example 1. The sentence is "The aircraft turned, banking slightly."

The neighborhoods of *bank* for the five relevant subject codes are given below.

The AU neighborhood contains two words, *aircraft* and *turn*, which also appear in the sentence. Note that we consider all forms of *turn* (*turned*, *turning*, etc.) to match *turn*. Since none of the other neighborhoods have any words in common with the sentence, and since our threshold value for this short sentence is 2, AU is selected as the subject code. We must now decide between the two senses that have this code. At this point we remove the function words from the sense definitions and replace each remaining word by its root form. We obtain the following neighborhoods.

Since bank(4) has no words in common with the sentence, and bank(6) has two (*turn* and *aircraft*), bank(6) is selected. This is indeed the sense of *bank* used in the sentence.

Example 2. The sentence is "We got a bank loan to buy a car."

The original neighborhoods of *bank* are, of course, the same as in Example 1. The threshold is again 2. None of the neighborhoods has more than one word in common with the sentence, so the iterative process of enlarging the neighborhoods is used. The AU neighborhood is expanded to include

Table 3.9: Gambling neighborhood of *bank*

Subject Code GB = Gambling				
bank	person	use	money	piece
	play	keep	pay	game
	various	supply	chance	

Table 3.10: Medical neighborhood of *bank*

Subject Code MD = Medicine and Biology				
bank	something	use	place	hold
	medicine	ready	blood	human
	origin	organ	store	hospital
	treatment	product	comb	

engine since it is the first word in the AU neighborhood of *make*. The first word in the AU neighborhood of *up* is *increase*, so *increase* is added to the neighborhood. If the word to be added already appears in the neighborhood of *bank*, no word is added. On the fifteenth iteration, the EC neighborhood contains *get* and *buy*. None of the other neighborhoods have more than one word in common with the sentence, so EC is selected as the subject code. Definitions 8, 12, and 13 of *bank* all have the EC subject code, so their definitions are used as cores to build neighborhoods to allow us to choose one of them. After 23 iterations, bank(8) is selected. Experiments are underway

Table 3.11: Null Code neighborhood of *bank*

Subject Code NULL = No code assigned				
bank	game	earth	stone	boat
	river	bar	snow	lake
	sand	shore	mud	framework
	flood	cliff	heap	harbor
	ocean	parallel	overflow	clerk

Table 3.12: Words in sense 4 of *bank*

Definition bank(4)				
slope	make	bend	road	so
they	safe	car	go	round

Table 3.13: Words in sense 6 of *bank*

Definition bank(6)			
car	aircraft	move	side
high	make	turn	

to test this method and variations of it on large numbers of sentences so that its effectiveness may be compared with other disambiguation techniques.

Although the words in the LDOCE definitions constitute a small text (almost 1,000,000 words, compared with the mega-texts used in other co-occurrence studies), the unique feature of subject codes which can be used to distinguish many definitions, and LDOCE's small control vocabulary (2,187 words) make it a useful corpus for obtaining co-occurrence data. The development of techniques for information retrieval and word-sense disambiguation based on these subject-dependent co-occurrence neighborhoods is very promising indeed.

3.4   Further Use of Statistical Methods: Lexical Disambiguation Using Simulated Annealing

It was pointed out in the last section that the problem of lexical disambiguation is very important in text processing, and we examined a method which appears to be powerful for single word disambiguation. Ideally, we would like to disambiguate every word in a sentence or text (or maybe more realistically, every content word). This must be done in such a way that the choices of the word senses are interdependent. Thus the sense chosen for each word influences the choice of sense for each other word. Below we describe a method which makes this task computationally tractable. Our eventual goal is to incorporate the subject dependent co-occurrence method described above into the technique we give in this section. For the moment, we are developing the technique for large-scale lexical disambiguation using a variation of a simple word counting method pioneered by Lesk.

Lesk [1986] originally described a symbolic technique which measured the amount of overlap between a dictionary sense definition and the local context of the word to be disambiguated to successfully disambiguate the word *cone* in the phrases "pine cone" and "ice cream cone". Later researchers have extended this basic idea in various ways. In earlier sections above, we described Wilks *et al.* [Wilks *et al.*, 1989; Guthrie *et al.*, 1991] who identified neighborhoods of the 2,187 control vocabulary words in LDOCE based on the co-occurrence of words in the dictionary definitions. These neighborhoods were then used to expand the word sense definitions of the word to be disambiguated, and the overlap between the expanded definitions and the local context was used to select the correct sense of a word.

The method described in the last section above extended this basic technique by defining subject specific neighborhoods of words, using the subject area markings in the machine readable version of LDOCE. Hearst [1991] has suggested using syntactic information and part-of-speech tagging to aid in the disambiguation. She gathered co-occurrence information from manually sense-tagged text. Zernik and Jacobs [1990] also derived their neighborhoods from a training text that had been sense-tagged by hand. Their method incorporated other clues as to the sense of the word in question found in the morphology or by first tagging the text as to part of speech.

These techniques, including our own described above, have only been applied to several words, and the results have been based on experiments which repeatedly disambiguate a single word (or in Zernik and Jacobs [1990], one of three words) in a large number of sentences. In the cases where a success rate for the technique is reported, the results vary from 35% to 80%, depending on whether the correct sense is desired, or some coarser grained distinction is considered acceptable. For even the most successful of these techniques, the success of the application to the processing of text is limited because of the work needed to construct the neighborhoods of the words and the amount of computation necessary to disambiguate each word in a sentence. If only one sense is computed at a time, as is the case in all of the numerically based work on disambiguation, the question arises as to whether and how to incorporate the fact that a sense has been chosen for a word when attempting to disambiguate the next. Should this first choice be changed in light of how other word senses are selected? A sentence that has 10 words, several of which have multiple senses, can easily generate a million possible combinations of senses.

In this section we report on the application of a computational method called *simulated annealing* to this general class of methods (including some of the numerical methods referenced above) to allow all senses to be determined at once in a computationally effective way. We describe the application of simulated annealing to a basic method similar to that of Lesk [1986] The simplicity of the technique makes it fully automatic, and it requires no hand-tagging of text or hand-crafting of neighborhoods. When this basic method operates under the guidance of the simulated annealing algorithm, sense selections are made concurrently for all ambiguous words in the sentence in a way designed to optimize their choice. The system's performance on a set of test sentences was encouraging and can be expected to improve when such features as part-of-speech tagging or subject area codes are incorporated. This can be done in a way that is still fully automatic.

3.4.1   Simulated Annealing

The method of simulated annealing ([Metropolis *et al.*, 1953; Kirkpatrick *et al.*, 1983]) is a technique for solving large-scale problems of combinatorial minimization. It has been successfully applied to the famous traveling salesman problem of finding the shortest route for a salesman who must visit a number of cities in turn, and is now a standard method for optimizing the placement of circuit elements on large-scale integrated circuits. Simulated annealing was applied to parsing by Sampson[1986], but since the method has not yet been widely applied to Computational Linguistics or Natural Language Processing, we describe it briefly. The name of the algorithm is an analogy to the process by which metals cool and anneal. A feature of this phenomenon is that slow cooling usually allows the metal to reach a uniform composition and a minimum energy state, while fast cooling leads to an amorphous state with higher energy. In simulated annealing, a parameter T which corresponds to temperature is decreased slowly enough to allow the system to find its minimum. The process requires a function E of configurations of the system which corresponds to the energy. It is E that we seek to minimize. From a starting point, a new configuration is randomly chosen, and a new value of E is computed. If the new E is less than the old one, the new configuration is chosen to replace the older.

An essential feature of simulated annealing is that even if the new E is larger than the old (indicating that this configuration is farther away from the desired minimum than the last choice), the new configuration may be chosen. The decision of whether or not to replace the old configuration with the new inferior one is made probabilistically. This feature of allowing the algorithm to "go up hill" helps it to avoid settling on a local minimum which is not the actual minimum. In succeeding trials, it becomes more difficult for configurations which increase E to be chosen, and finally, when the method has retained the same configuration for long enough, that configuration is chosen as the solution. In the traveling salesman example, the configurations are the different paths through the cities, and E is the total length of the trip. The final configuration is an approximation to the shortest path through the cities. The next section describes how the algorithm may be applied to word-sense disambiguation.

3.4.2   Word-Sense Disambiguation

Given a sentence with N words, we may represent the senses of the ith word as $s_{i1}, s_{i2}, \ldots s_{ik_i}$, where k_i is the number of senses of the ith word which appear in LDOCE. A configuration of the system is obtained by choosing a sense for each word in the sentence. Our goal is to choose that configuration which a human disambiguator would choose. To that end, we must define a function E whose minimum we may reasonably expect to correspond to the correct choice of the word senses. The value of E for a given configuration is calculated in terms of the definitions of the N senses which make it up. All words in these definitions are stemmed, and the results stored in a list. The redundancy R is computed by giving a stemmed word form which appears n times a score of n-1 and adding up the scores. Finally, E is defined to be $\frac{1}{1+R}$. The rationale behind this choice of E is that word senses which belong together in a sentence will have more words in common in their definitions (larger values of R) than senses which do not belong together. Minimizing E will maximize R and determine our choice of word senses. The starting configuration C is chosen to be that in which sense number 1 of each word is chosen.

Since the senses in LDOCE are generally listed with the most frequently used sense first, this is a likely starting point. The value of E is computed for this configuration. The next step is to choose at random a word number i and a sense S_{ij} of that ith word. The configuration C' is constructed by replacing the old sense of the ith word by the sense S_{ij}. Let δE be the change from E to the value computed for C'. If $\delta E < 0$, then C' replaces C, and we make a new random change in C'. If $\delta E >= 0$, we change to C' with probability $P = \frac{e^{-\delta E}}{T}$. In this expression, T is a constant whose initial value is 1, and the decision of whether or not to adopt C' is made by calling a random number generator. If the number generated is less than P, C is replaced by C'. Otherwise, C is retained. This process of generating new configurations and checking to see whether or not to choose them is repeated on the order of 1000 times, T is replaced by $0.9\,T$, and the loop entered again. Once the loop is executed with no change in the configuration, the routine ends, and this final configuration tells which word senses are to be selected.

3.4.3   An Experiment

The algorithm described above was used to disambiguate 50 example sentences from LDOCE. The sentences were among those used in the experiment described in Section 3.3. A stop list of very common words such as *the*, *as*, and *of* was removed from each sentence. The sentences then contained from 2 to 15 words, with an average of 5.5 ambiguous words per sentence. Definitions in LDOCE are broken down first into broad senses which we call *homographs*, and then into individual senses which distinguish among the various meanings. For example, one homograph of *bank* means roughly "something piled up." There are five senses in this homograph which distinguish whether the thing piled up is snow, clouds, earth by a river, etc. Results of the algorithm were evaluated by having a literate human disambiguate the sentences and comparing these choices of word senses with the output of the program. Using the human choices as the standard, the algorithm correctly disambiguated 47% of the words to the sense level, and 72% to the homograph level. In the case of several of the simpler sentences, it was verified by hand that the simulated annealing algorithm had indeed selected a configuration which minimized the value of E.

Direct comparisons of these success rates with those of other methods is difficult. None of the other methods was used to disambiguate the same text, and while we have attempted to tag every ambiguous word in a sentence, other methods were applied to one, or at most a few, highly ambiguous words. It appears that in some cases the fact that our success rates include not only highly ambiguous words, but some words with only a few senses is offset by the fact that other researchers have used a broader definition of word sense. For example, the four senses of *interest* used by Zernik and Jacobs [1990] may correspond more closely to our two homographs and not our ten senses of *interest*. Their success rate in tagging the three words *interest*, *stock*, and *bond* was 70%. Thus it appears that the method we propose is comparable in effectiveness to the other computational methods of word-sense disambiguation, and has the advantages of being automatically applicable to all the 28,000 words in LDOCE and of being computationally practical.

We have described a method for word-sense disambiguation based on the simple technique of choosing senses of the words in a sentence so that their definitions in a machine readable dictionary have the most words in common. The amount of computation necessary to find this optimal choice exactly quickly becomes prohibitive as the number of ambiguous words and the number of senses increase. The computational technique of simulated annealing allows a good approximation to be computed quickly. Advantages of this technique over previous work are that all the words in a sentence are disambiguated simultaneously, in a reasonable time, and automatically (with no hand disambiguation of training text). Results using this technique are comparable to other computational techniques and enhancements incorporating co-occurrence, part-of-speech, and subject code information, which have been exploited in one-word-at-a-time techniques, may be expected to improve the performance.

3.5   Conclusion

Given the present development of NLP systems, the debate on the usefulness of machine readable dictionaries is a valid one. In many ways, to use the full power of these resources we need NLP techniques which are beyond the current state of the art. However, much of the information in MRD's can be made available using current techniques, and the developer of large scale NLP systems would be foolish to ignore the potential of MRD's. We at CRL have undertaken a research program to develop methods for constructing a MTD automatically (or semiautomatically) from a machine readable dictionary. Several of these methods are described here. Although each method is itself "weak" in the sense that it cannot handle the task of providing a rich representaion of each dictionary sense by itself, or do its portion of the task with great accuracy, we hope that the combination of the weak methods in a manner such as outlined here will prove to be effective and result in the efficient construction of a useful, reliable and flexible MTD.

Bibliography

[Amsler, 1980] R. Amsler. The structure of the Merriam-Webster pocket dictionary. Technical Report TR-164, University of Texas at Austin, 1980.

[Atwell et al., 1984] E. Atwell, G. Leech, and R. Garside. Analysis of the LOB corpus: progress and prospects. In J. Aarts and W. Meijs, editors, Corpus Linguistics. Rodopi, 1984.

[Belew and Rose, 1988] R. K. Belew and R. E. Rose. Learning Semantics from Word Use. University of California at San Diego, La Jolla, CA, 1988.

[Boguraev et al., 1989] B. Boguraev, R. J. Byrd, J. Klavans, and M. Neff. From structural analysis of lexical resources to semantics in a lexical knowledge base. In IJCAI Workshop on Lexical Acquisition, Detroit, MI, 1989.

[Brown et al., 1988] P. Brown, J. Cocke, S. Della Pietra, V. Della Pietra, F. Jelinek, R. Mercer, and P Roosin. A statistical approach to language translation. In Proceedings of the International Congress on Computational Linguistics, pages 71–75, Budapest, Hungary, 1988.

[Bruce and Guthrie, 1991] Rebecca Bruce and Louise Guthrie. Genus disambiguation: A study in weighted preference. Submitted, 1991.

[Church and Hanks, 1989] K. Church and P. Hanks. Word association norms, mutual information and lexicography. In Proceedings of the 27th Annual Meeting of the Assn. for Comput. Linguistics, pages 76–83, Vancouver, BC, 1989.

[Dagan and Itai, 1990] Ido Dagan and Alon Itai. Processing large corpora for reference resolution. In Proceedings of the 13th International Conference on Computational Linguistics (COLING-90), volume 3, pages 330–332, Helsinki, Finland, 1990.

[DeJong, 1979] G. DeJong. Skimming stories in real time: An experiment in integrated understanding. Technical Report 158, Computer Science Dept, Yale University, 1979.

[Farwell et al., 1991] David Farwell, Louise Guthrie, and Yorick Wilks. Automatic creation of lexical entries for a multilingual MT system. Submitted, 1991.

[Guthrie et al., 1990] L. Guthrie, B. Slator, Y. Wilks, and R. Bruce. Is there content in empty heads? In *Proceedings of the 13th International Conference on Computational Linguistics (COLING-90)*, volume 3, pages 138–143, Helsinki, Finland, 1990.

[Guthrie et al., 1991] Joe A. Guthrie, Louise Guthrie, Yorick Wilks, and Homa Aidinejad. Subject-dependent co-occurrence and word sense disambiguation. In *Proceedings of the 29th Annual Meeting of the Association for Computational Linguistics*, pages 146–152, Berkeley, CA, 1991.

[Hearst, 1991] M. Hearst. Toward noun homonym disambiguation - using local context in large text corpora. In *Proceedings of the Seventh Annual Conference of the UW Centre for the New OED and Text Research, Using Corpora*, pages 1–22, Oxford, 1991.

[Kay, 1989] M. Kay. The concrete lexicon and the abstract dictionary. In *Proceedings of the Fifth Annual Conference of the UW Center for the New Oxford English Dictionary*, pages 35–41, Oxford, England, 1989.

[Kegl, 1987] J. Kegl. The boundary between word knowledge and world knowledge. In *Proceedings of the Third Workshop on Theoretical Issues in Natural Language Processing (TINLAP-3)*, pages 26–31, Las Cruces, NM, 1987.

[Kirkpatrick et al., 1983] S. Kirkpatrick, C. D. Gelatt, and M. P. Vecchi. *Science*, 220:671–680, 1983.

[Lebowitz, 1983] Michael Lebowitz. Memory-based parsing. *Artificial Intelligence*, 21:363–404, 1983.

[Lehnert and Sundheim, 1991] W.G. Lehnert and B. Sundheim. A performance evaluation of text analysis technologies. *AI Magazine*, 12:81–94, 1991.

[Lesk, 1986] M. E. Lesk. Automatic sense disambiguation using machine readable dictionaries: How to tell a pine cone from an ice cream cone. In *Proceedings of the ACM SIGDOC Conference*, Toronto, Ontario, 1986.

[McDonald et al., 1990] J.E. McDonald, A.T. Plate, and R.W. Schvaneveldt. Using pathfinder to extract semantic information from text. In R. W. Schvaneveldt, ed., *Pathfinder Associative Networks: Studies in Knowledge Organization*. Ablex, Norwood, NJ, 1990.

[Metropolis *et al.*, 1953] N. Metropolis, A. Rosenbluth, M. Rosenbluth, and
A. Teller. *Journal of Chemical Physics*, *21*:1087, 1953.

[Mott *et al.*, 1986] P. Mott, D. Waltz, H. Resnikoff, and G. Robertson. Automatic indexing of text. Technical Report 86-1, Thinking Machines Corp.,
Cambridge, MA, 1986.

[Newell, 1973] A. Newell. Artificial intelligence and the concept of mind. In
R. Schank and K. Colby, eds., *Computer Models of Thought and Language*,
pages 1–60. W.H. Freeman, San Francisco, 1973.

[Procter and others, 1978] P. Procter et al. *Longman's Dictionary of Contemporary English*. Longman, Harlow, Essex, England, 1978.

[Sampson, 1986] G. Sampson. A stochastic approach to parsing. In *Proceedings of the 11th International Conference on Computational Linguistics
(COLING-86)*, pages 151–155, Bonn, BRD, 1986.

[Schvaneveldt, 1990] R. W. Schvaneveldt, ed., *Pathfinder Associative Networks: Studies in Knowledge Organization*, Ablex, Norwood, NJ, 1990.

[Slator and Wilks, 1987] B. M. Slator and Y. A. Wilks. Toward semantic
structures from dictionary entries. In *Proceedings of the Second Annual
Rocky Mountain Conference on Artificial Intelligence*, pages 85–96, Boulder, CO, 1987.

[Slocum and Morgan, 1986] J. Slocum and M. Morgan. The role of dictionaries and machine readable lexicons in translation. Presented at the Workshop on Automating the Lexicon, Grosseto, Italy, 1986.

[Toma, 1977] P. Toma. Systran as a multi-lingual machine translation system. In *Commission of European Communities: Overcoming the Language
Barrier*, pages 129–160. Dokumentation Verlag, Munich, 1977.

[Veronis and Ide, 1990] J. Veronis and N. M. Ide. Word sense disambiguation
with very large neural networks extracted from machine readable dictionaries. In *Proceedings of the 13th International Conference on Computational
Linguistics (COLING-90)*, Helsinki, Finland, 1990.

[Wilks, 1975] Y. Wilks. An intelligent analyser and understander for English.
Communications of the ACM, *18*:264–274, 1975.

[Wilks *et al.*, 1989] Y. Wilks, D. Fass, C. Guo, J. McDonald, and T. Plate. A
tractable machine dictionary as a resource for computational semantics. In
B. Boguraev and T. Briscoe, eds., *Computational Lexicography for Natural
Language Processing*. Longman, Harlow, Essex, England, 1989.

[Zernik and Jacobs, 1990] Uri Zernik and Paul Jacobs. Tagging for learning:
  Collecting thematic relations from corpus. In *Proceedings of the 13th International Conference on Computational Linguistics (COLING-90)*, volume 1, pages 34–39, Helsinki, Finland, 1990.

Mixed-Depth Representations for Natural Language Text

Graeme Hirst and Mark Ryan*
Department of Computer Science
University of Toronto
Toronto, Canada M5S 1A4

4.1 The Limitations of Surface Representations

Text understanding is usually hard for computers and easy for people, so we tend to forget about the times when it's hard for people, too. But even smart, knowledge-based people, and not just dumb computers, can find text understanding extremely difficult. We all know this from our experiences with writing that presents complex ideas—advanced technical papers, for example—and writing that's just plain bad—incomprehensible instructions for assembling a Christmas toy, textbooks that present ideas sloppily, government tax-return guides that try hard to be clear but never quite succeed.[1] So it's no shame if a natural language understanding program, like a human, has to occasionally capitulate and say, in effect, that it cannot fully understand some difficult piece of text.

Now, intelligent text-based systems will vary as to the degree of difficulty of the texts they deal with. Some may have a relatively easy time with texts for which fairly superficial processes will get useful results, such as, say, *The New York Times* or *Julia Child's Favorite Recipes*. But many systems will have to work on more difficult texts. Often, it is the complexity of the text that makes the system desirable in the first place. It is for such systems that we need to think about making the deeper methods that are already studied in AI and computational linguistics more robust and suitable for processing long texts without interactive human help.

A domain that demonstrates some of the most difficult problems is that of searching legal cases for relevant precedents. What makes a legal case a

---

*Mark Ryan's present address: IBM Canada Ltd, (Station 21, Dept 870), 844 Don Mills Road, North York, Ontario, Canada M3C 1V7.

[1] "You write with ease to show your breeding, / But easy writing's curst hard reading." — Sheridan.

precedent does not necessarily have anything much to do with the domain of the case, but rather the structure of the argument.[2]

Our colleague Judith Dick [1987; 1991] has developed methods for the representation of the texts of judicial decisions in order to permit conceptual searches. Dick's representations are based on Toulmin's [1958] model of argument structures, Sowa's [1984] Conceptual Graph formalism, and Somers's [1987] system of thematic relations, which she has revised and extended. One important sub-goal of the work is just to find what problems arise in representation that cannot be addressed by conventional techniques. For example, present-day formalisms have great difficulty representing entities whose existence is not definite; but many legal texts are, in fact, discussions of whether some entity (usually an abstract entity such as intent or liability) does or doesn't exist. We have addressed this topic in detail elsewhere [Hirst, 1989; Hirst, 1991].

4.2   Mixed and Partial Representations

The dilemma is that on one hand, we have the limitations of raw text databases and superficial processing methods; on the other we have the difficulty of deeper methods and conceptual representations. Our proposal here is to have the best of both, and accordingly we develop the notion of a heterogeneous, or mixed, type of representation.

In our model, a text base permits two parallel representations of meaning: the text itself, for presentation to human users, and a *conceptual encoding*[3] of the text, for use by intelligent components of the system. The two representations are stored in parallel; that is, there are links between each unit of text (a sentence or paragraph in most cases) and the corresponding conceptual encoding. This encoding could be created en masse when the text was entered into the system.[4] But if it is expected that only a small fraction of

---

[2] "There is a story of a Vermont justice of the peace before whom a suit was brought by one farmer against another for breaking a churn. The justice took time to consider, and then said that he had looked through the statutes and could find nothing about churns, and gave judgment for the defendant. The same state of mind is shown in all our common digests and textbooks. Applications of rudimentary rules of contract or tort are tucked away under the head of Railroads or Telegraphs or go to swell treatises on historical subdivisions, such as Shipping or Equity, or are gathered under an arbitrary title which is thought likely to appeal to the practical mind, such as Mercantile law." (Oliver Wendell Holmes, "The path of the law" (1897). In: MacGuigan, Mark R. *Jurisprudence: Readings and cases.* University of Toronto Press, 1966, 48–62.)

[3] What we have in mind at present is close to a conventional first-order AI knowledge representation, modified as we describe below; but we use this deliberately 'neutral' term because we don't want to prejudice consideration of other possibilities.

[4] The development of interlingual methods of machine translation also offers interesting possibilities here. Many text bases—laws and regulations in multilingual jurisdictions such as Canada and the European Community, for example—have to be translated anyway. The interlingual representation generated as a by-product of machine translation could be retained and stored in the text base along with the surface text and its translations. Although probably shallower than a regular AI representation, and possibly even erroneous

the text base will ever be looked at by processes that need the conceptual representations, then the encoding could be performed on each part of the text as necessary for inference and understanding to answer some particular request. The results could then be stored so that they don't have to be redone if the same area of the text is searched again. Thus, a text would gradually *grow* its encoding as it continues to be used. (And the work will never be done for texts or parts of texts that are never used.)

So far, this is straightforward. But we can go one step further. The encoding itself may be deep or shallow at different places, depending on what happened to be necessary at the time it was generated—or on what was possible. Or, to put it a different way, we can view natural-language text and AI-style knowledge representations as two ends of a spectrum.

Our goal is the development of a conceptual representation of text that encompasses this entire spectrum—that is, the representation includes natural language, a first-order (at present, anyway) formalism, and mixtures of both of them at various levels of concentration. Such an encoding could tolerate vagueness, but permit precision. For example, the representation of a sentence might have a piece of natural language embedded in a logical form, or vice versa. Thus, anything that needs (or permits) only partial interpretation or disambiguation may stay in its partially encoded form until dealt with later (if ever).

Some of the aspects of language understanding that would be optional in this representation are: lexical disambiguation; marking case relations; attachment of modifiers of uncertain placement; reference resolution; quantifier scoping; and distinguishing extensional, intensional, generic, and descriptive noun phrases. If all optional parts are omitted, then one just has the surface string. If all are included, one has a full-blown AI-style knowledge representation. Anything in the middle would also be perfectly legal, and be acceptable to the inference and search processes that use the representation. In practice, one would expect to at least include some syntactic markings or bracketings.

For example, if such a system were given a sentence such as *John bought a vrzfl* (where *vrzfl* represents some word or phrase that the system simply can't understand), it should be able to answer the question *Did he pay for it? (Yes)*, and pass gracefully on *Could he eat it? (I don't know)*.

In summary, there are three separate proposals included in this model:

- The usefulness of partial or incomplete encodings.

- Surface natural-language forms as a special case of an incomplete encoding.

- Mixing together encodings of different levels of completeness.

---

in places, this representation might well serve as a conceptual encoding for many purposes, or as a first step to a deeper encoding.

Aspects of the first two of these have already been suggested in various forms in the literature; the third, we believe, is novel. The following sections will discuss each in turn.

4.3   Incomplete Encodings

The first proposal is that if it is not possible to create the conceptual encoding of a piece of text (a sentence or other fragment), because there is insufficient information, because the text is somehow ill-formed, or simply because it looks like it would require too much work, one may usefully create a *partial* or *incomplete* encoding.

Recognizing word senses and thematic relations.   At the lexical level, incomplete encoding means incomplete lexical disambiguation.   In earlier work [Hirst, 1987; Hirst, 1988a; Hirst, 1988b], we described the *Polaroid Words* system for lexical and thematic disambiguation.   In this system, a variety of information sources, including semantic associations and selectional restrictions, were used to eliminate potential readings of an ambiguous word or case marker until just one was left. If a unique meaning could not be determined, the system was unhappy. Our present suggestion is that it need not be unhappy, but simply report a list of the remaining possible meanings (i.e., a disjunction of possibilities). And if a word that the system encounters is not even in its lexicon, the surface form, marked as such, may be retained.

Syntactic analysis.   At the syntactic level, incomplete encodings can be used when it is not possible to determine a unique parse for part of a sentence.   Such a situation occurs, for example, when a modifier such as a prepositional phrase or relative clause has two (or more) seemingly permissible points of attachment, and when lexical ambiguity permits more than one distinct structure for a clause (as in *Time flies like an arrow*).

A number of writers have suggested methods for the representation of the set of choices in such multiple parses. For example, Church's YAP parser [1980] was able to 'pseudo-attach' nodes; that is, if a unique parent couldn't be determined, the node kept a list of the possibilities. Seo and Simmons [1989] propose the more general method of 'packed parse forests', graphs that compactly represent a number of trees. An algorithm for finding each tree in the forest is given.

Metzler *et al.* [1989] suggest a slightly different kind of partial representation for a parse tree. Rather than even trying to decide where a prepositional phrase or the like might be attached, their 'Constituent Object Parser' simply assumes attachment to the right-most available node. For Metzler *et al.*'s application, which is information retrieval by matching the dependency trees created by the parser, the consequent imprecision is easily tolerated (the same simplifying assumption being made for both the target text and the query).

Except for Metzler *et al.*'s, the expectation is usually that such representations are just a stage on the way to choosing one of the options. But if the choice must be (indefinitely) postponed, a system could continue to use the incomplete representation as is—provided subsequent processes so permit. We will discuss this point in section 4.5.

Semantic interpretation. Most of the time, any incompleteness at the lexical or syntactic levels will give rise to a corresponding incompleteness in semantic interpretation.[5] And of course even a representation that is complete at the lower levels can give rise to an incomplete semantic interpretation.

Perhaps the most important ambiguity at this level is in the scope of quantification. Alshawi and van Eijck [1989] have described a representation in which quantifier scoping and certain modifiers are unresolved. (As with some of the incomplete syntactic representations, this is intended just as an intermediary step, not a possibly-final form; that is, it is a *logical form* in the sense made precise by Allen [1991].) And Hobbs [1983] has proposed a 'scope-neutral' representation of quantification that would be amenable to subsequent inference processes.

Ambiguities of intension and description also occur at this level. As far as we are aware, the only notation that even describes all the possible readings is that of Fawcett and Hirst [1986], but there is no attempt to permit incompleteness.

Discourse structure and pragmatics. Full text comprehension includes resolving anaphors, understanding the role of each sentence in the discourse, and deriving pragmatic inferences such as presuppositions and conventional implicatures. In practice, an intelligent text retrieval system will probably not need to figure out every last ounce of the writer's intent. But certainly anaphor resolution will be necessary, and perhaps also the recognition of some simple indirect speech acts such as asserting by asking a question.

An unresolvable anaphor or definite reference can be treated much as an unresolvable lexical ambiguity—that is, regarded as a disjunction of possible referents. Unresolved discourse connections are somewhat harder, as the possibilities are open-ended, and it seems likely that if a unique connection is not found, then almost anything is possible. The connection then must just be recorded as 'I don't know', rather than as a small disjunction.

---

[5] The exceptions are cases where two distinct possibilities end up 'saying the same thing'. For example, if the PP in *Nadia kissed the boy in the park* is attached to the VP, then the kissing took place in the park, and we may infer that the participants were in the park, too. If it is attached to the object NP, then the boy was in the park, and we may infer that Nadia and the kissing were, too. So either way, everything is in the park, and it's not actually necessary to worry about which PP attachment is correct; they both are. Such cases are not as rare as one might expect, but it's certainly not worth a system's time to check for them especially.

Interaction between levels. Information available at one level of an NLU program will often permit the resolution of uncertainties at another. Hirst [1987; 1988a] describes an architecture for a system in which the flow of information supports this to the greatest extent possible. We assume such a mechanism here, so that incompletenesses may indeed be only temporary. The difference here is that nothing *requires* an incompleteness to be patched up.

4.4 Natural Language as its Own Representation

If for some reason, the system could create only very incomplete representations at all levels of analysis for a particular sentence, then the representation of the sentence would be effectively little more than its unaltered surface form. In fact, a system might sometimes decide that a hard-to-process fragment is better left wholly in its surface form. Despite our earlier remarks concerning the limitations of surface representations (section 4.1), such forms would not necessarily be useless. After all, information retrieval systems have for many years operated on surface forms, with some fair success (but see Dick [1991] for discussion of the limitations).[6] Moreover, some recent research in AI has used natural language as a form for inference [Kayser *et al.* , 1987; Jayez, 1988] and as an interlingua in machine translation [Schubert, 1988; Guzmán, 1988]. We don't have space here to discuss the advantages and disadvantages of these approaches (but see Hirst [1993]), but we just need to point out that, contrary to the impression one gets from some AI research, natural language can be used, at least in some ways, as a knowledge representation. Indeed, it is the only knowledge representation we have so far that meets the fundamental requirement of having the expressive power of natural language.

4.5 Mixed-depth Encodings

If the representation of a sentence or text is incomplete in different ways in different places, the result is a *mixed-depth encoding*. For example, one might obtain a vaguely scoped logical form with a piece of surface text and a disjunction of attachments embedded in it. In fact, a mixed-depth encoding could be quite a mess, as we will see in the examples below.

If such representations are to be useful, it will be necessary to devise inference and search methods that can operate upon them. For example, given

---

[6] "We actually made a map of the country, on the scale of *a mile to the mile!*" "Have you used it much?" I enquired. "It has never been spread out, yet," said Mein Herr: "the farmers objected; they said it would cover the whole country, and shut out the sunlight! So now we use the country itself, as its own map, and I assure you it does nearly as well."—Lewis Carroll, *Sylvie and Bruno Concluded* (1893), chapter 11.

our earlier example, *John bought a vxzfl*, it should be possible to infer that if the *vxzfl* was bought, it was paid for, even if the description of it is missing or incomplete. (One approach to this is exemplified by Granger's FOUL-UP program [Granger, 1977], which used expectations in context, including a library of scripts for stereotypical situations, to perform such inferences.) As well as the usual kinds of matching and inference, these processes should be able to continue refining the encodings—that is, removing some of the uncertainties—if they find themselves able to do so.

One possible weakness of incomplete encodings is a vulnerability to a sort of 'snowballing' of incompleteness. Since understanding a sentence generally requires understanding the preceding text, one might find each sentence understood a little less than the one before it, until the system eventually becomes completely confused. This is not uncommon in undergraduates, and there's nothing to prevent it happening to any NLU system that is given a text that far exceeds its abilities. So the proposal here crucially depends on incompleteness not being resorted to too often. Mixed-depth representations are intended to add flexibility, not to act as a substitute for intelligence.

This proposal is to be distinguished from others that involve multiple kinds of representation. For example, Sparck Jones [1983] has proposed the simultaneous use of several different representations of text, each optimized for different aspects of the tasks of the system that uses them. While such representations may be 'partial', in the sense that they won't all contain full information about the text (*cf.* Sloman [1985]), they are not incomplete in our sense; that is, each is as fully refined as intended. In addition, the representations are not fragments mixed together; each individually covers the full text.

4.6   An Example

In order to demonstrate what mixed-depth representations might look like, we now present an extended example. A relatively complex paragraph is presented, along with a parse of each sentence and a semantic interpretation. We will assume that neither the parser nor the interpreter can cope with the full complexity of the text, and they therefore resort to incomplete encodings where necessary.

It should be understood that our example representation is constructed by hand, and is not the output of any actual system. Our point is the general nature of the representation, rather than the strengths and weaknesses of any particular system of parsing or semantic interpretation. Consequently, we have constructed our example by making reasonable assumptions about the abilities and limitations typical of state-of-the-art parsers and interpreters operating under time pressure.

We have chosen Dick's [1991] interpretation of Sowa's conceptual graphs (CGs) [Sowa, 1984] as a typical first-order knowledge representation scheme

Table 4.1: Abbreviations for case roles used in our conceptual graphs.

AGNT   Agent: Relates an action to the entity performing it.
ATTR   Attribute: Relates an entity to one of its properties.
BENF   Beneficiary: Relates an action to the entity for whom it
        was performed.
CAUS   Cause: Relates a state to its cause.
CHRC   Characteristic: Relates an entity to an inalienable or
        characterizing property.
DUR   Duration: Relates an action to the time period over which
        it occurs.
LOC   Location: Relates an action to the place at which it occurs.
MANR   Manner: Relates an action to the manner in which it is
        carried out.
POSS   Possession: Relates an entity to another entity it possesses.
PTNT   Patient or theme: Relates an action to the entity upon
        which it is performed.
TEMPL   Temporal location: Relates an action to the point in time
        over which it occurs.

upon which to base our extensions for representations that are incomplete or
varying in depth. Readers unfamiliar with the notation should still find its
meaning fairly obvious; the abbreviations for case roles that we use (following
Sowa and Dick) are shown in Table 4.1. We chose CGs merely for generality
and readability, and have no particular commitment to this notation.

For reasons of space, we do not show any attempt at processing the discourse relations in the text; rather, we simply show the CG output for each
sentence or clause. In practice, of course, an interpreter would have to tie
these graphs together with discourse-level relations such as ELABORATION or
EXAMPLE; this process is vulnerable to the same kinds of uncertainties, and
leading to the same kinds of representational gaps, as sentence interpretation.

4.6.1   Incompleteness

There are two ways that both the parse and the semantic interpretation can
be incomplete:

1. A structure in the original sentence may be left *uncoded* if there is
   no appropriate representation for it.

2. A structure in the original sentence may have more than one encoding
   because the system cannot choose a single encoding. We call such a
   structure *multicoded*.

Even if the parse produces a complete encoding, it is still possible that the
semantic interpretation be incomplete.

In order to control the number of uncoded elements, we assume that default assumptions can be made in certain situations. For example, if one sense of an ambiguous word is much more common than the others, that sense is chosen in the absence of any positive evidence for the alternatives (cf Hirst [1987]).

When the parser or semantic interpreter is faced with a structure that it cannot uniquely encode, it goes through a list of possible encodings for the structure and discards those that are not possible given what it has already been able to interpret. If there are no possibilities left, the structure is left uncoded. If there is more than one possibility left, and no unique default applies, the structure is multicoded with the remaining allowable defaults. This method of eliminating the impossible and taking what is left as the only possible encoding is used in such systems as Polaroid Words [Hirst, 1987; Hirst, 1988a] and constraint grammars [Karlsson, 1990; Karlsson et al. , 1991].

4.6.2 The Example in Detail

In this section, we present the parse trees and multiple-depth semantic interpretations for each sentence of the example paragraph.

The parse trees are drawn in a simple, linear fashion. Syntactic elements are underlined and labelled. If an element cannot be identified, it is labelled with a question mark. If the parser has to make a guess about the role of an element, that element is underlined with a dotted line, and its name is followed by a question mark. Once the parser makes a guess about the role of an element, all of the higher-level constituents that the element is taken to be part of are also treated as guesses. Key relationships between parts of a sentence are identified with arrows. If the relationship is ambiguous or the result of a guess, the arrow is dotted. The top-level structure of each sentence is S; in order to keep the parse trees as simple as possible, we have omitted this level from the graphs of longer sentences (sentences (4), (5), and (7) below).

In the conceptual graphs, uncoded elements are denoted by a question mark followed by the problematic surface string in quotation marks. Unspecified conceptual relations are represented as question marks. We add to Sowa's notation the disjunction operator "or", which is used to indicate alternatives that the interpreter cannot decide between. For example, "(AGNT or PTNT)" is an *uncertain representation* of a relation that might be (AGNT) or might be (PTNT); the interpreter can't decide which. This is distinguished from the standard CG operators "(OR)" and "|" [Sowa, 1984, p. 118–119], which are *certain representations*, and can be used to represent sentences that explicitly talk about disjunctive possibilities.

We have followed the style of Sowa's linear notation rather than network diagrams for CGs. This means that when an instance of a concept or structure participates in more than one relation, it might have to be written more than once. We do this by assigning it a name to the instance (using the notation *concept=#name*), and then, when necessary, using the name. For example, [SAILOR: {*}=#ss] denotes a set, named #ss, of sailors. A subsequent occurrence of [SAILOR: {*} #ss] would refer to the same set. It should be understood, however, that in an implementation there would be only one copy of the structure, with pointers deployed as necessary. Similarly, when literal strings of the original text are incorporated into the conceptual structures, these could, in an implementation, be pointers to the text rather than copies of it.

Our names for relations are mostly taken from Sowa's catalogue of conceptual relations [Sowa, 1984, p. 415ff]. Our names for concepts are, for ease of reading, mostly suggestive English words.

Our example text is taken from a review[7] of *Dreadnought*, a book by Robert K. Massie that describes British naval history in the period leading up to the First World War. The following paragraph describes the state of the Royal Navy prior to its Edwardian revival:

> Without warships, Britain was perilously vulnerable to blockade or invasion. But Britannia's capacity to rule the waves, as Massie also points out, was somewhat illusory; the Royal Navy during much of Victoria's reign was largely unfit for combat. Weighed down by moribund traditions that Winston Churchill acidly defined as "rum, sodomy, and the lash," British tars were ill fed and worse led. While their social-climbing officers fopped and preened, sailors spent long days at sea scrubbing decks and polishing brightwork, or wielding cutlasses in boarding drills as if they were still in the age of sail. Meanwhile, gunnery practice was cursory even though naval bombardments were ludicrously inaccurate. In 1881, for example, eight British battleships fired 3,000 rounds at forts guarding the Egyptian city of Alexandria and scored precisely 10 hits.

We will show the parse tree and semantic interpretation for each sentence in turn, illustrating various aspects of incomplete and mixed-depth representation.

Sentence (1)

(1) Without warships, Britain was perilously vulnerable to blockade or invasion.

Figure 4.1(a) contains the parse tree for sentence (1). There are no ambiguities or guesses in this parse. The conceptual graph for sentence (1), shown in Figure 4.1(b), is not complete, because the semantic interpreter

---

[7]Elson, John. "When Britannia Ruled", *Time*, **138**(19), 11 November 1991.

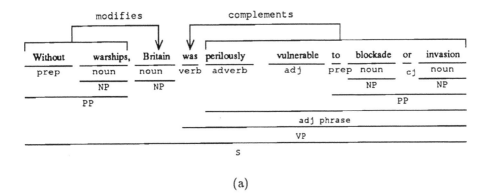

(a)

[STATE: [COUNTRY:Britain] -> (ATTR) -> [VULNERABLE] <- (ATTR) <- [PERILOUS]] -
      (CAUS) -> [[COUNTRY:Britain] -> (⁻POSS) -> [WARSBIP:{*}]]].

[[BLOCKADE] <- (OR) -> [INVASION]].

(b)

Figure 4.1: Parse and interpretation of sentence (1)

cannot find a way to connect the phrase *to blockade or invasion* to the graph
for the rest of the sentence. Thus, the interpretation of this phrase forms
its own separate graph. Notice also that the (OR) relation in this graph expresses a disjunction in the semantic content of the original sentence, not in
its interpretation.

Sentence (2)

(2)   But Britannia's capacity to rule the waves, as Massie also points out,
      was somewhat illusory;

Figure 4.2(a) contains the parse tree for sentence (2). This shows that
the parser cannot determine whether the dependent clause *as Massie also
points out* modifies *Britannia's capacity* or the sentence as a whole.

The conceptual graph for sentence (2), shown in Figure 4.2(b), is almost complete. But the ambiguous attachment of the dependent clause *as
Massie also points out* is reflected in the CG by the disjunction in the PTNT
("patient") relationship for POINT_OUT. The patient of POINT_OUT is either
[COUNTRY:Britain] or [CAPACITY: #cap] depending on whether the dependent clause modifies the whole sentence or the NP *Britannia's capacity*.

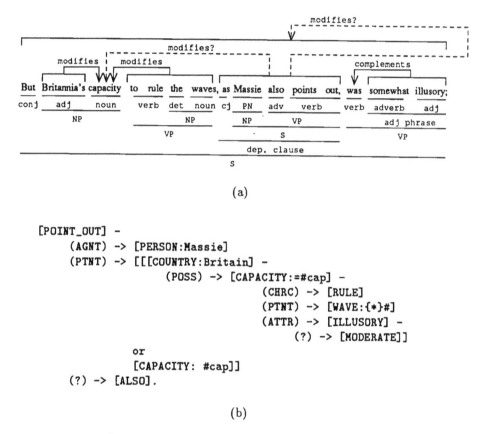

(a)

```
[POINT_OUT] -
    (AGNT) -> [PERSON:Massie]
    (PTNT) -> [[[COUNTRY:Britain] -
                    (POSS) -> [CAPACITY:=#cap] -
                                    (CHRC) -> [RULE]
                                    (PTNT) -> [WAVE:{*}#]
                                    (ATTR) -> [ILLUSORY] -
                                            (?) -> [MODERATE]]]
            or
            [CAPACITY: #cap]]
    (?) -> [ALSO].
```

(b)

Figure 4.2: Parse and interpretation of sentence (2)

And while the parser identifies *also* as a modifier of *points out*, the semantic interpreter cannot identify the exact relationship, so the relationship is
left unspecified in the graph. The same happens for *somewhat* as a modifier
of *illusory*. And the idiom *to rule the waves* has not been recognized, the
interpreter representing it quite literally.

Sentence (3)

(3)   the Royal Navy during much of Victoria's reign was largely unfit for
      combat.

Figure 4.3(a) contains the parse tree for sentence (3). There are no ambiguities or guesses in this tree. But we shall assume that the interpreter cannot
determine if the *Royal Navy* is the agent or the patient of the action implicit

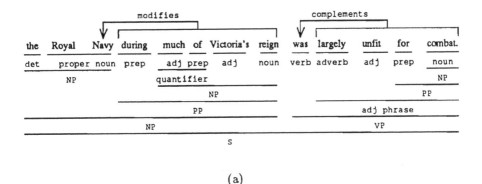

(a)

```
[[COMBAT] -
    (AGNT or PTNT) -> [NAVY:Royal Navy] -
    (ATTR) -> [UNFIT]
    (DUR) -> [[[PERSON:Victoria] -> (POSS) -> REIGN]]:@much]].
```

(b)

Figure 4.3: Parse and interpretation of sentence (3)

in the phrase *unfit for combat* (*cf. The food was unfit for consumption*). The CG therefore shows the disjunction of the alternatives. In addition, the interpreter has not taken the time to consider the subtleties of the possessive in the phrase *Victoria's reign*, and has simply encoded it as the reign that Victoria possesses, just as if it were a physical possession like *Victoria's carriage* or *Victoria's nose*. The resulting conceptual graph is shown in Figure 3(b).

Sentence (4)

> (4) Weighed down by moribund traditions that Winston Churchill acidly defined as "rum, sodomy, and the lash," British tars were ill fed and worse led.

Figure 4.4(a) contains the parse tree for sentence (4). We assume that the lexicon does not recognize *sodomy* or *lash*, but the parser can guess that both words are nouns, and that the entire phrase *rum, sodomy, and the lash* is a conjunctive NP. The structures in the sentence that include this NP are also recorded as guesses in the parse tree. In addition, we assume that the lexicon does not recognize *tars*, knowing *tar* only as a mass noun meaning black, sticky stuff; it guesses that *British tars* is an NP. Finally, it guesses that the introductory phrase *Weighed ... lash* modifies *tars*.

Because of these uncertainties, the conceptual graph for sentence (4), in Figure 4.4(b), has some significant holes in it. To begin with, the focus of the sentence, *tars*, has to be left uncoded. The interpreter makes the default choice that this element represents the patient of the verb *weighed down* and is what is modified by the phrase *ill fed and worse led*. In the phrase *rum, sodomy, and the lash*, only the noun *rum* is encoded. The knowledge representation scheme makes the default choice that this phrase has a conceptual relationship with the verb *defined*, but it cannot specify which relationship.

Sentence (5)

(5) While their social-climbing officers fopped and preened, sailors spent long days at sea scrubbing decks and polishing brightwork, or wielding cutlasses in boarding drills as if they were still in the age of sail.

Figure 4.5(a) contains the parse tree for sentence (5). The lexicon does not recognize the neologism *fopped*, nor does it have an entry for *preened* as an intransitive verb (a usage that is not included in the *Oxford Advanced Learner's Dictionary*). The parser guesses that both words are being used as intransitive verbs. The lexicon also does not have an entry for *brightwork*, but the parser guesses that it is a noun. The parser cannot determine the attachment of the dependent clause *as if they were still in the age of sail*. It guesses that this clause modifies the verb phrase *wielding cutlasses in boarding drills*.

The conceptual graph for sentence (5), shown in Figure 4.5(b), also has many holes and uncertainties in it. To begin with, the interpreter guesses that the agent of the unknown words *fopped* and *preened* is *their social-climbing officers*. We shall assume also that it falls short in its representation of the clause *as if they were still in the age of sail*. The phrase *the age of sail* is not recognized as an idiom, nor can the system determine the relationship between [AGE] and [SAIL]. Thus, it leaves the relationship unspecified. This uncertainty, plus the great polysemy of the word *in*, means that, in turn, the relationship between this phrase and the pronoun *they* has to be represented as the disjunction of a TEMPL relationship and a LOC relationship; the interpreter can't determine whether the preposition *in* in the phrase *in the age of sail* flags a physical location or a period in time, so it records both. And lastly, it cannot determine whether *they* refers to the officers or the sailors. (The representation of *as if* as a manner relationship between an action and a state labeled as counterfactual is clearly inadequate, but that is a separate issue in semantics.)

Sentence (6)

(6) Meanwhile, gunnery practice was cursory even though naval bombardments were ludicrously inaccurate.

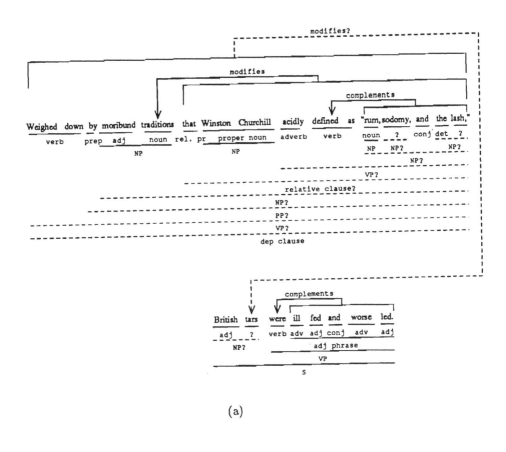

(a)

```
[WEIGH_DOWN] -
    (PTNT) -> [ ? 'tars' ] -
        (CHRC) -> [BRITISH]
        (ATTR) -
                [[[FED] -> (ATTR) -> [BADLY]] and [[LED] -> (ATTR) -> [BADLY]]]
    (AGNT) -> [TRADITION:{*}=#trad] -> (ATTR) -> [MORIBUND]]
[DEFINE] -
    (PTNT) -> [TRADITION:{*} #trad]
    (AGNT) -> [PERSON:Winston_Churchill]
    (?) -> [[RUM] and [? 'sodomy'] and [? 'the lash']].
```

(b)

Figure 4.4: Parse and semantic interpretation of sentence (4)

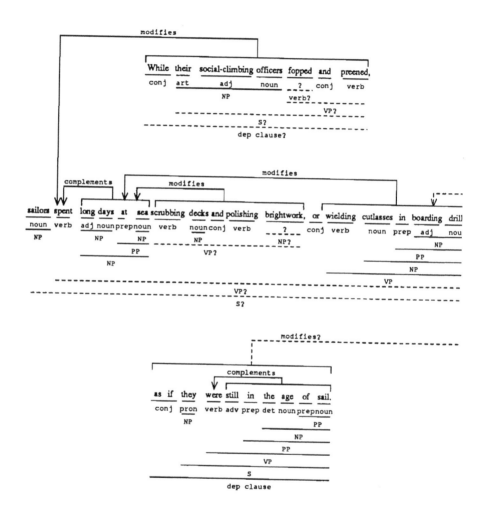

(a)

```
[ ? 'fopped']
[ ? 'preened'] -
    (AGNT) -> [OFFICER:{*}=#offs] -
          (ATTR) -> [SOCIAL_CLIMBING]
          (POSS) -> [SAILOR:{*}=#ss]
[SPEND_TIME] -
    (AGNT) -> [SAILOR:{*} #ss]
    (LOC) -> [SEA]
    (PTNT) -> [DAY:{*}] -> (ATTR) -> [LONG]
[SCRUB] -
    (AGNT) -> [SAILOR:{*} #ss]
    (PTNT) -> [DECK:{*}]
[POLISH] -
    (AGNT) -> [SAILOR:{*} #ss]
    (PTNT) -> [ ? 'brightwork']
[WIELD] -
    (AGNT) -> [SAILOR:{*} #ss]
    (PTNT) -> [CUTLASS:{*}]
    (LOC) -> [DRILL:{*}] -> (CHRC) -> [BOARDING]
    (MANR) -> [COUNTERFACTUAL:
                    [[SAILOR:{*} #ss] or [OFFICER:{*} #offs]] -
                        (TEMPL or LOC) -> [AGE] -> (?) -> [SAIL]].
```

(b)

Figure 4.5: Parse and interpretation of sentence (5)

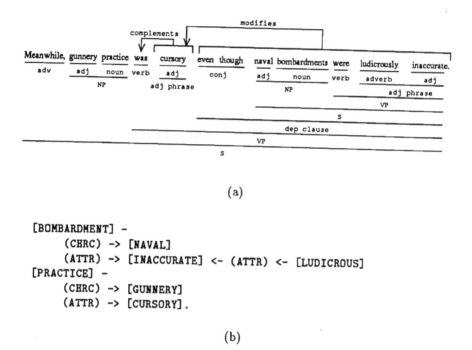

(a)

```
[BOMBARDMENT] -
    (CHRC) -> [NAVAL]
    (ATTR) -> [INACCURATE] <- (ATTR) <- [LUDICROUS]
[PRACTICE] -
    (CHRC) -> [GUNNERY]
    (ATTR) -> [CURSORY].
```

(b)

Figure 4.6: Parse and interpretation of sentence (6)

Figure 4.6(a) contains the parse tree for sentence (6). There are no ambiguities or guesses in this parse tree. The conceptual graph for the sentence, in Figure 4.6(b) is relatively complete, but the causal relationship between the two clauses has been lost. The sentence is represented as two unrelated conceptual graphs, one with the head BOMBARDMENT and the other with the head PRACTICE.

Sentence (7)

(7) In 1881, for example, eight British battleships fired 3,000 rounds at forts guarding the Egyptian city of Alexandria and scored precisely 10 hits.

Figure 4.7(a) contains the parse tree for sentence (7). There are no ambiguities or guesses in this parse tree. But the sentence is quantificationally ambiguous: Did the eight battleships fire 3,000 rounds each or 3,000 in total; and did they score 10 hits each or 10 in total? In standard conceptual graphs [Sowa, 1984, p. 118], the notation [BATTLESHIP: dist{*}@8] means each element of the set of battleships acts independently, giving the first reading of each pair, while [BATTLESHIP: {*}@8] means all the battleships act together as a single agent, giving the second reading of each pair.

We represent the uncertainty by the disjunction [BATTLESHIP: (dist or set){*}@8] (adding the word "set", implicit in Sowa's notation, to explicitly disjoin with "dist"). The CG is shown in Figure 4.7(b).

4.6.3 Using This Representation

The purpose of a representation such as we have shown is, of course, to permit conceptual retrieval by matching queries that are similarly represented (*cf.* Dick [1991]). The matching process might take into account inheritance of properties and even inference of arbitrary complexity. While the development of such processes is a topic of continuing research, it should be clear that the general principles of matching processes that operate on complete representations will carry over to our mixed-depth partial representations.

4.6.4 What We Have Shown

Our example demonstrates a number of points about incomplete and multiple-depth representations.

Many inaccuracies are benign: for example, the representation of the NP *Victoria's reign* as a possession of the person *Victoria* in sentence (3), rather than as a time period. Thus, if this representation were used to retrieve entities belonging to Victoria, her reign would be one of the entities retrieved, which is incorrect but probably harmless. On the other hand, because of inaccuracy, the conceptual graph for sentence (3) would probably *not* match queries about the nineteenth century, a more serious error. Such errors are the price paid for being unwilling or unable to analyze the text as deeply as an ideal language understander could. Nevertheless, a partial representation is better than none at all. (And often, redundancy in the text will come to the rescue. In this example, other sentences in the text, including sentence (7) of the same paragraph, would presumably match such a query.)

Metaphors can be taken literally. The CG for sentence (2) has *rule the waves* represented as a literal ruling over waves rather than the intended meaning: military (and perhaps economic) domination of the seas. The representation is not correct, but it does provide some relevant information, the notion of British rule.

Even completely uncoded text can still be useful in certain situations. In the fourth sentence of the example, the lexical units *sodomy* and *the lash* are unknown, but the entire unit *rum, sodomy, and the lash* can still be identified as text that the person *Winston Churchill* used to define the *traditions* that are mentioned earlier in the sentence. An information retrieval system can still present such a text as a whole in answer to a query about naval traditions (or about quotations by Winston Churchill).

The incomplete representations preserve ambiguities that are present in the text itself. In sentence (7), for example, the phrase *eight British battleships fired 3,000 rounds ... and scored precisely 10 hits* is quantificationally

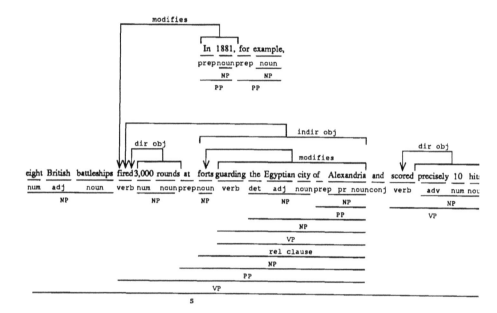

(a)

```
[FIRED] -
     (AGNT) -> [BATTLESHIP:(dist or set){*}@8 =#ships] <- (CHRC) <- [BRITISH]
     (PTNT) -> [ROUND:{*}@3000]
     (BENF) -> [FORT:{*} =#ff]
     (TEMPL) -> [DATE:1881]
[GUARD] -
     (AGNT) -> [FORT:{*} #ff]
     (PTNT) -> [CITY:Alexandria]
[SCORE] -
     (AGNT) -> [BATTLESHIP:(dist or set){*}@8 #ships]
     (PTNT) -> [HIT:{*}@10].
```

(b)

Figure 4.7: Parse and interpretation of sentence (7)

ambiguous. The representation retains this ambiguity.

4.6.5 What We Haven't Shown

By choosing judiciously our "reasonable assumptions about the abilities and limitations typical of state-of-the-art parsers and interpreters operating under time pressure", we have tried to show, in one short example, many of the things that might occur in a mixed-depth representation. But we cannot show all that might arise. While many uncertainties in parsing are only a question of where to attach a modifying constituent, as in sentences (2) and (5), it can sometimes be the case that the parser cannot decide between two completely different structures for much or all of a sentence or clause: the declarative and imperative parses of *Time flies*, for example. The resulting interpretation might be the disjunction of two completely separate CGs; we have not shown such a case here. Nor have we shown disjunctive intepretations of ambiguities of intension and description, where CGs cannot always even represent all the possibilities (*cf.* Fawcett and Hirst [1986]). And we have not even attempted to show any kind of discourse processing.

4.7 Conclusion

The ultimate criterion for adequacy of a mixed representation would be its usefulness, and, in particular, the degree to which inference and understanding processes can be developed or modified to accept such forms. At present, research in the area is very preliminary; a number of representations that are incomplete in one way or another have been proposed, but there has been no previous attempt at integration. However, we believe the basic idea to be a promising one worthy of further development, and have showed, by means of an example, how this might proceed.

Acknowledgments

We are grateful to Judy Dick for many discussions on the role of representations of text in information retrieval, and to Stephen Regoczei, Karen Sparck Jones, Paul Jacobs, and Yorick Wilks for comments on earlier versions of this paper. Our work is supported by grants from the Natural Sciences and Engineering Research Council of Canada and the Information Technology Research Centre.

Bibliography

[Allen, 1991] James Allen. Natural language, knowledge representation, and logical form. Technical report 367, Department of Computer Science, University of Rochester, 1991.

[Alshawi and van Eijck, 1989] Hiyan Alshawi and Jan van Eijck. Logical forms in the Core Language Engine. In *Proceedings of the 27th Annual Meeting, of the Association for Computational Linguistics*, pages 25–32, Vancouver, June 1989.

[Church, 1980] Kenneth Ward Church. *On memory limitations in natural language processing.* MSc thesis / TR 245, Laboratory for Computer Science, MIT, June 1980. Distributed by the Indiana University Linguistics Club, Bloomington, IN.

[Dick, 1987] Judith Dick. Conceptual retrieval and case law. In *Proceedings of the First International Conference on Artificial Intelligence and Law*, pages 106–115, Boston, May 1987.

[Dick, 1991] Judith Dick. *A conceptual, case-relation representation of text for information retrieval.* Doctoral dissertation, Faculty of Library and Information Science, University of Toronto. Published as technical report CSRI-265, Computer Systems Research Institute, University of Toronto.

[Fawcett and Hirst, 1986] Brenda Fawcett and Graeme Hirst. The detection and representation of ambiguities of intension and description. In *Proceedings of the 24th Annual Meeting of the Association for Computational Linguistics*, pages 192–199, New York, June 1986.

[Granger, 1977] Richard H. Granger, Jr. FOUL-UP: A program that figures out meanings of words from context. In *Proceedings of the 5th International Joint Conference on Artificial Intelligence*, pages 172–178, Cambridge, Mass., August 1977.

[Guzmán, 1988] Iván Guzmán de Rojas. "ATAMIRI—Interlingual MT using the Aymara language." In Maxwell *et al.* [1988], pages 123–129.

[Hirst, 1987] Graeme Hirst. *Semantic Interpretation and the Resolution of Ambiguity.* Cambridge University Press (Studies in natural language processing), 1987.

[Hirst, 1988a] Graeme Hirst. Semantic interpretation and ambiguity. *Artificial Intelligence*, 34(2):131–177, March 1988.

[Hirst, 1988b] Graeme Hirst. Resolving lexical ambiguity computationally with spreading activation and Polaroid Words. In Steven Small, Garrison Cottrell and Michael Tanenhaus, editors, *Lexical ambiguity resolution*, 73–107, Morgan Kaufmann, Los Altos, CA, 1988.

[Hirst, 1989] Graeme Hirst. Ontological assumptions in knowledge representation. In *Proceedings of the First International Conference on Principles of Knowledge Representation and Reasoning*, pages 157–169, Toronto, May 1989. Morgan Kaufmann, Los Altos, CA.

[Hirst, 1991] Graeme Hirst. Existence assumptions in knowledge representation. *Artificial Intelligence, 49*:199–242, May 1991.

[Hirst, 1993] Graeme Hirst. Natural language as its own representation. In preparation.

[Hobbs, 1983] Jerry R. Hobbs. An improper treatment of quantification in ordinary English. In *Proceedings of the 21st annual meeting of the Association for Computational Linguistics*, pages 57–63, Cambridge, MA, June 1983.

[Jayez, 1988] Jacques Jayez. *L'inference en langue naturel: Le problème des connecteurs; représentation et calcul.* Hermès (Langue, raisonnement, calcul), Paris, 1988.

[Karlsson, 1990] Fred Karlsson. Constraint grammar as a framework for parsing running text. In *Proceedings of the 13th International Conference on Computational Linguistics (COLING-90)*, vol. III, pages 168–173, Helsinki, August 1990.

[Karlsson et al. , 1991] Fred Karlsson, Atro Voutilainen, Arto Anttila, and Juha Heikkilä. Constraint grammar: A language-independent system for parsing unrestricted text, with an application to English. In *Workshop Notes from the 9th National Conference on Artificial Intelligence (AAAI-90): Natural Language Text Retrieval*, Anaheim, July 1991.

[Kayser et al. , 1987] D. Kayser, P. Fosse, M. Karoubi, B. Levrat, and L. Nicaud. A strategy for reasoning in natural language. *Applied Artificial Intelligence, 1*(3):205–231, 1987.

[Maxwell et al , 1988] Dan Maxwell, Klaus Schubert, and Toon Witkam, editors, *New Directions in Machine Translation*. Foris (Distributed Language Translation 4), Dordrecht, 1988.

[Metzler et al , 1989] Douglas P. Metzler, Stephanie W. Haas, Cynthia L. Cosic, and Leslie H. Wheeler. Constituent object parsing for information retrieval and similar text processing problems. *Journal of the American Society for Information Science, 40*(6):398–423, 1989.

[Schubert, 1988] Klaus Schubert. The architecture of DLT—Interlingual or double direct? In Maxwell et al. [1988], pages 131–144.

[Seo and Simmons, 1989] Jungyun Seo and Robert F. Simmons. Syntactic graphs: A representation for the union of all ambiguous parse trees. *Computational Linguistics, 15*(1):19–32, March 1989.

[Sloman, 1985] Aaron Sloman. Why we need many knowledge representation formalisms. In Max A. Bramer, editor, *Research and Development in Expert Systems*, pages 163–183, Cambridge University Press (British Computer Society workshop series), 1985.

[Somers, 1987] Harold Somers. *Valency and Case in Computational Linguistics*. Edinburgh University Press (Edinburgh Information Technology Series), 1987.

[Sowa, 1984] John Sowa. *Conceptual Structures: Information Processing in Mind and Machine*. Addison-Wesley, Reading, MA, 1984.

[Sparck Jones, 1983] Karen Sparck Jones. Shifting meaning representations. In *Proceedings of the Eighth International Joint Conference on Artificial Intelligence*, pages 621–623, Karlsruhe, August 1983,

[Toulmin, 1958] Stephen Toulmin. *The Uses of Argument*. Cambridge University Press, 1958.

Robust Partial-Parsing Through Incremental, Multi-Algorithm Processing*

David D. McDonald
Brandeis University and Content Technologies, Inc.
14 Brantwood Road, Arlington, MA 02174

5.1   Introduction

The problem that inspired this volume is how to develop intelligent computer systems that are *text-based*—systems that acquire their knowledge by assimilating massive amounts of ordinary natural language text, rather than having to be spoon-fed rules handcrafted by knowledge engineers. [1] A mature text-based system would keep up with current events by simply reading the newspaper as we do. Conceivably, it might even learn new fields by reading the textbooks.

The sheer number of things to be learned, and the pace with which they change, requires us to try to develop systems that can assimilate the information in a text with only a minimum of human oversight. The ready availability of candidate texts in electronic form: encyclopedias, newswires, daily papers, magazines, printer's tapes, etc. gives us every incentive to try.

An example may help to make clear just what this enterprise is. Below is an article from the *Wall Street Journal*, shown exactly as it appears when downloaded electronically from the Dow Jones News Retrieval service.

```
AN    910214-0090
HL    Who's News: Goodyear Tire & Rubber Co.
DD    02/14/91
SO    WALL STREET JOURNAL (J), PAGE B8
```

---

*This paper is an expanded and revised version of a paper originally presented at the AAAI Spring Symposium on *Text-Based Intelligent Systems*, March 1990 at Stanford University.

[1] An excellent example of the "handcrafted" approach is Lenat's CYC project at MCC [Lenat and Guha, 1990], an out-growth of the Atari Encyclopedia project initiated by Allan Kay [Borning *et al.*, 1983]. This kind of careful deliberate work will surely be needed to bootstrap systems to a minimal competence. Large-scale intelligence and currency, however, will only come through the systems' reading what is written for people.

```
CO    *  GT WNEWS
IN       PIPELINE OPERATORS (PIP) PETROLEUM
     (PET) AUTO PARTS AND EQUIPMENT INCLUDING
     TIRES (AUP)
TX       GOODYEAR TIRE & RUBBER Co. (Akron, Ohio) -- George
```
R. Hargreaves, vice president and treasurer of Goodyear, will
become president and chief executive officer of the Celeron Corp.
unit, a holding company for Goodyear's All American Pipeline.
Mr. Hargreaves, 61, will assume the post effective March 1 and
will retain his current posts. Robert W. Milk, Celeron's current
president and chief executive, as well as an executive vice presid
for Goodyear, will be on special assignment until he retires April
30.

The availability of such *Who's News* articles prompted me to consider the task
of automatically extracting information about people's change in position.
(The results of this experiment are given in Section 5.4.) This means that
the article is analyzed by a computer program to recover a set of four tuples
consisting of the action, person or persons affected, their position (title), and
the company or subsidiary. The tuples are then entered into a database.
Below is an example of the first such tuple in this article.

```
#<edge75  80 Job-event 105
event: #<event-type become-title>
title: (#<title ''president''
        #<title ''chief executive officer''>)
person: #<person Hargreaves, George R.>
company: #<subsidiary
        of: #<company Goodyear Tire &
                  Rubber Company>
        name:    #<co-name
               . ''Celeron Corporation''>>>
```

This paper examines the challenges that the effort to develop such a system
will pose for research on natural language understanding. We begin by identifying the two central problems that this research must solve, and then move
to describing the approach taken by the SPARSER system, a mature program
for extracting information in specific domains from unrestricted news articles.

5.2   Two Central Problems

Obviously, if a computer program is to learn anything from an English
text, it must have some procedure for determining the information the text
contains—some kind of natural language understanding system. But while
many understanding systems have been developed over the last 40 years (see
[Grosz *et al.*, 1985] for a definitive set of early reference papers), none can yet

meet the needs of the kind of text-based intelligent system we all envision. I believe that before this can happen, two large problems must be solved.

The first problem is that the information literally present in any naturally occurring text is only a fraction of the information that is conveyed to the person who reads it. These *omissions* must be recognized and the gaps filled before a program will understand from a text what a person would. This is a problem requiring both general inference and very specific textual inferences. Instances of these problems are ubiquitous since almost nothing in a text can be taken at face value: Simple numbers (43) may actually denote amounts in millions of dollars; unknown proper names (April Wednesday) must be categorized from context; the amount a value has plunged will be orders of magnitude different depending on whether it is the value of a stock or of a currency in the international markets. (The first two inferences can be guided by linguistic clues from the rest of the text; the third requires general knowledge.)

This kind of ability to make inferences from what is given literally in a text—*to read in between the lines*—is not a problem for people since we unconsciously recover the missing information from the context provided by the rest of the article, from what we know about the conventions of the author or the publication, and from the general stock of information we already have. In fact, most of the information people see in a text will be facts that they already know. These will be matters of common sense (e.g., all the information needed to make the passage sensible to, say, a three-year-old—or better, a martian), as well as facts and descriptions they have heard before. All that reading the passage does is bring the older information to mind and add or modify particulars.

In short, as they read the literal information a text contains, people bring a wealth of general and situational knowledge to bear, dramatically expanding the total amount of information the text conveys. Computer programs must do the same if they are to take away from what they read all that a human author intends.

The second problem, and the focus of this paper, is the problem of parsing. For present purposes I will define *parsing* as what a program does to determine the literal information a text contains, i.e., the information against which it can then bring its wealth of general knowledge to bear. This is a simpler problem than what some natural language understanding systems have taken as their task. Dyer's BORIS system [Dyer, 1983], for example, both recovered the literal information in the text and drew on background information that enabled it to infer much of what people reading the same passages are able to conclude by *reading between the lines*. There is, however, no principled limit on the scope of the inferences that can be drawn from reading a text. [2]

---

[2]This was demonstrated in the thesis of Chuck Rieger [Rieger, 1975]. The problem is that some inferences seem obvious and lexically driven, for instance that upon reading that *John Doe was appointed CEO, succeeding Mary Roe, who retired*, we all know what

This can greatly complicate the design of a system, because the kinds of knowledge involved in general inferences are very different from those needed to analyze linguistic structure, since they are dependent on just what background information is available and on how many assumptions one is willing to make in coming to conclusions. If we want to distinguish between *parsing*, which can apply generally to any text, and *inference*, which will vary according to the knowledge of the reader, then we must draw a line at some point. A logical place is just at the limit of extracting the information that is literally present, given knowledge of the meaning of the words and grammatical relationships.

As mentioned above, there has already been a vast amount of research on the parsing problem. But I will argue here that, with exceptions, the parsers that this research has produced are inadequate for the task, and that new parsers must be developed along very different lines.

All parsers, from Earley to Riesbeck to Marcus[3], draw on roughly the same "surface linguistic" knowledge to do their analyses, i.e., knowledge of how words combine into phrases because of their positions, their morphology, identities, categories, etc. This much is not controversial; the issue is what the output of the parser should be. Most parsers stop just with a structural description: a tree of nodes that dominate words that have been identified just by their part of speech. These nodes are labeled with syntactic categories (e.g., noun phrase, sentence), and information will be available in the tree about the grammatical relations among the nodes (e.g., subject, prepositional phrase adjunct, theme). A few parsers, however, go further and recover information about "who did what to whom" and identify the intended sense of each word. Only this second kind of parser (one that recovers the semantic content of a text) will be of use to a text-based intelligent system.

To a certain extent, of course, this distinction in parsers is simply termi-

---

position Ms. Roe used to hold. However, what principle would allow us to distinguish that kind of inference, on the basis of structural properties alone, from inferences such as that she no longer receives a salary from her old company, assumptions about her probable age, her possible interest in trust funds, etc. ?

[3]These three people have each had a strong influence on the design of parsers. Jay Earley [Earley, 1970] invented a standard algorithm for parsing with general context-free grammars, establishing the basic efficiency parameters of the process and introducing a set of techniques that widely influenced the design of later parsers, even though it was oriented more toward computer languages than human, *natural* languages. Chris Riesbeck [Riesbeck, 1975] invented the first *conceptual analyzer*, specifically for reading simple English stories. A conceptual analyzer uses heuristics to try to recover the concepts and relations expressed in a text, without particular concern for its syntactic form. Dyer's system is a quite sophisticated conceptual analyzer in terms of the kinds of conceptual knowledge it could employ, but its underlying parsing mechanisms are essentially the same as Riesbeck's and reflect progress within a unified school of thought. Mitch Marcus [Marcus, 1980] invented the so-called *wait and see* parser. His parser was *deterministic*, in the special sense that it constructed only one analysis and never retracted any of its decisions (this is the notion of *indelibility*, see [McDonald, 1980]). It achieved this by waiting on its judgments until it had accumulated enough evidence to be certain. He recovered a description of the syntactic form of a text, designing his parser so that it could account for some of the psychological observations about the human parsing process.

nological. A parser that stops with a structural description can obviously be coupled with a semantic interpretation component that analyzes the structural description and the words to arrive at the same information as the second kind of parser produces directly (i.e., some set of concepts and the relations among them). However, if one looks at the research goals of people working on the first kind of parser, for example, Berwick and Weinberg [1984], they tend to be studying the consequences of using different theories of grammar or how to constrain structural syntactic ambiguities, not how information can be extracted from unrestricted, naturally occurring text to support a text-based intelligent system. Since different goals lead people to be interested in different problems and to adopt different approaches, it seems only realistic to expect that only research aimed directly at how to understand unrestricted texts, and not simply on how to describe them linguistically, is likely to yield an efficient design for a text-based intelligent system.

5.3   Parsing Unrestricted Text

To be useful, our text-based intelligent system of the hopefully not too distant future will have to deal with the actual texts that people read. A business program should read the *Wall Street Journal* every day; it should not have to depend on a person to transcribe the *Journal* into some acceptable computerpidgin. A concomitant requirement is that there can be no restrictions on what texts the system is prepared to process; it cannot depend on a person going through the *Journal* and passing it only those articles that it is likely to know how to handle, but must be able to process any text whatsoever, even if it understands nothing in it. (This capacity simply to get through a text without stopping because of a bug or a request to the user is sometimes known as *robustness*.) Unrestricted text imposes two key goals for the design of a parser.

5.3.1   Goal 1: It Must Be a "Partial" Parser

While there are a number of parsers today that can produce syntactic descriptions of unrestricted texts, [4] no parser even comes close to understanding everything in a real text, such as a news article. While part of the problem is the lack of grammatical analyses for the breadth of constructions found

---

[4] While these parsers have, indeed, robustly analyzed tens of thousands of words of texts (e.g. [Hindle, 1983; de Marcken, 1990]), the analyses they produce are not complete. They produce a forest of phrases rather than complete sentences or larger units, e.g., NPs, verb groups, PPs, minimal clauses, etc. Given that they are making a conventional syntactic analysis, these fragment-sequence analyses are their only way to get a single, definitive analysis. If one insists on full-sentence analyses of unrestricted texts, then one must be prepared to accept potentially enormous ambiguity, sometimes many hundreds of analyses for a single 25-word sentence [Clippinger *et al.*, 1982].

in unrestricted texts, the real, fundamental problems are semantic and conceptual, as today's computer programs simply are not able to make sense out of the bulk of the information in texts they are given to read because they lack the needed concepts and referents. Instead of trying to understand everything, much of the research on parsing today is directed at the problem of extracting very specific information. [5] This has led to the concept of a *partial* parser, one that is specifically designed to recover a particular class of information while ignoring stretches of text on other subjects. A partial parser makes a careful and thorough analysis of the portions of text it is designed for, while skipping over the irrelevant portions. In addition, a partial parser is exceptionally careful that what it does analyze is accurate, i.e., that the analysis would not change if it had been able to make sense of additional parts of the text.

To be concrete, imagine that we have a text-based system that knows something about currency trading and that it sees in the second column of the front page of the *Journal* the lead text, *The dollar plunged, partly on the Treasury's report of an unexpectedly large deficit...*, (n.b.: this is from a real text). It is entirely possible that the system could have the concepts needed to understand the main clause (*the dollar plunged*), while not having those needed for the adjunct (*, partly on ...*). On the basis of those concepts and referents the parser would be able to link the phrase "the dollar" to the object that represents U.S. currency in its domain model, rather than linking it to its unit for the quantity of money worth 100 cents or to some individual dollar bill, etc. Similarly it would be able to determine that the appropriate sense of *plunge* is *fall in value against other nations' currency*, rather than *dive into water* or simply *fall in value*.

Within the adjunct, if we assume that the parser does not know the idiom *..<event>.. on the report of...*, it will not be able to completely analyze the whole phrase (though it may well have a partial analysis). Nevertheless, to be effective the parser must still be reasonably sure that the information in the adjunct does not change the meaning of the main clause.

The kind of information just described is an example of what I mean by *literal* information being the proper target of a parser. On the other hand, knowing that the *plunge* by the dollar may have come to just 2 yen, or that *unexpectedly large* deficit may have been more than 120 billion dollars, is a very different matter, since this information is something that only someone who understood this subject matter would know. Further, they would have to already know it if it is to come to mind when they read this text. Since it is not given literally, but is inferred, it is not the parser's problem. These would be instances of the first problem, bringing general and situational knowledge to bear to understand more than the literal content of a text.

---

[5]Labels such as *information extraction* or *message processing* are often used to distinguish this research from what had been done before.

5.3.2 Goal 2: Coping with Unknown Words

As just defined, a partial parser is targeted for a specific kind of information and is designed to identify and analyze such information even when it appears embedded within a text that covers many more kinds of information than just that target. What this means is that we will have on the one hand a set of one or more algorithms and text processing mechanisms that are hopefully fairly general, and on the other a body of rules, a *grammar*, that embodies the parser's knowledge of the target information and how it appears in a text.

The greater part of a topic-specific grammar will consist of rules about words, the *content words* that convey concepts and relationships that can be quite specific to the domain of interest. This will include not only the technical vocabulary that may be unique to the domain, but also subtle shadings to the meanings of ordinary words, such as *old* and *new*. [6]

If it has good coverage, the parser will also know most of the *function words*—e.g., *to, does, who*, and *a*—whose role in the language is not so much to identify concepts as to indicate grammatical relations. It may also know words from the vocabularies of very common subjects such as dates, measures, numbers, money, etc. These words are *known* to the parser in the sense that it has specific rules that it applies when they appear in a text: starting a certain kind of phrase, retrieving a certain concept, establishing a certain relationship, etc. By this token, a word is *unknown* if the parser has no rules for handling it. Today, given what subjects are tractable for a parser to extract and what actually appears in a general text source like a newspaper or newswire, the vast bulk of the words a parser will encounter will be unknown. [7]

If all the unknown, off-topic words clustered together into their own portion of the text, then the partial parser's job would be simple: just skip over those parts. Unfortunately, this is anything but the case. Unknown words can appear anywhere, as unknown verbs between known noun phrases, unknown adjectives within noun phrases, etc. Even if all the content words in a sentence are unknown, it will still contain function words (an average of one every 3.5 words in the corpus described in Section 5.4), and these may activate the parser's mechanisms even though ultimately nothing will be ex-

---

[6] In the domain of employment, consider the differences between *the new position of assistant vice chairman* and *A new president wasn't named*. The new position is one that didn't exist before in the company's job roster. The new president will be new to the position but nothing about him or her per se will be new.

[7] Of course, if all one wants from a parser is a description of the text's syntactic structure, then a machine-readable dictionary can supply information about part of speech (noun, verb, adjective, adverb) and a number, possibly a large number, of general definitions in natural language. But this leaves the parser with very large problem of ambiguity, and it does not provide meanings for the words in the form in which information-extraction systems need them, since their goal is invariably to feed another computer program, today a database, but tomorrow an intelligent text-based system. Moreover, a great many unknown words will not be in a dictionary, some because of their rarity, but most because they are proper names—an open, seldom-cataloged set.

tracted. How a partial parser copes with unknown works will tell a lot about the quality of its algorithms.

5.4   A Multi-Algorithm Partial Parser

In keeping with this goal of having a parser that can accurately extract literal information from unrestricted texts, I have developed a system called SPARSER that is designed to extract selected information from unrestricted text sources, such as news articles in the *Wall Street Journal.*

I began work on this kind of parsing system in late 1987. An in-house production version using different techniques was used extensively at MAD Cambridge from mid-1988 through early September of 1989. The current version is a complete reimplementation done during the summer of 1990 in the course of about three months on a Mac II. SPARSER is written in CommonLisp and has been ported to several unix platforms and several different vendors' CommonLisps. On the Mac II, it presently runs at between 20 and 200 words per second depending on what layers of the system are being used.

As one would imagine, the design of this parser has much in common with other systems with similar goals, in particular the systems of Rau and Jacobs [1988], Martin and Riesbeck [1986], sublanguage-based systems like Sager's [1981], and in certain respects systems that produce a succession of phrases rather than sentences. such as Hindle's [1983] or O'Shaughnessy's [1989].

In the rest of this section, I will sketch the particular algorithms SPARSER uses and the motivations behind them. A thorough discussion of the special properties of the primary parsing algorithm can be found in [McDonald, 1992].

5.4.1   Why Multiple Algorithms

SPARSER has multiple parsing algorithms primarily because this makes it easier to write grammars. Information is distributed in a text in many different ways, and algorithms can be tailored to these differences according to the moments and forms with which the information becomes available and the way in which the rules for noticing the information are expressed.

An additional benefit comes from the ways a set of algorithms can be woven together. Given a careful control structure, there is no need to regiment them into a strict sequence or cascade; control can pass between the algorithms in reentrant loops, e.g., information that is found by a later algorithm can lead to a reexamination of the text by a normally early algorithm, causing it now to draw conclusions that were unavailable to it the first time through.

This is especially true when unknown words are involved. A first pass by one class of algorithm may make observations based on weak phrase-internal evidence, the boundaries of the phrasal segment are then established by a second class of algorithm, and the final classification is made only much later, once enough contextual evidence has been accumulated from other parts of the text for the judgment to be certain.

In the case of SPARSER, the algorithms are incorporated into six inter-leaved components: a tokenizer, a set of transition networks, a context-free phrase-structure parser, a context-sensitive parser, a conceptual analyzer, and a heuristic facility that hypothesizes phrasal boundaries using the grammatical properties of function words and partially-parsed phrases.

We will look at each in turn, starting with the simpler and more conventional, and then moving to the more heuristic algorithms designed specifically for coping with unknown words.

5.4.2 Tokenizing

Over all, a text parser is a transducer from the stream of characters that comprise the text to some abstract structured representation of the information it contains. Since characters are simply a means of representing words and punctuation, the first step in parsing is to segment the characters into orthographically sensible groups and look up the words that correspond to them, a process known as *tokenizing*.

SPARSER uses a very conservative tokenizing algorithm, grouping together contiguous sequences of characters of the same class, i.e., alphabetics, digits, or identical punctuation. Where most other tokenizers would see *$4.3 million* as two tokens or even one, SPARSER sees it as six (including a reified *word* representing the space), leaving it to later stages to combine the minimal tokens into phrases and to categorize them when context can be taken into account. This delay can have considerable advantages. For example, the string F-14 in one context could be the name of an airplane, in another a function key on a computer keyboard. Some systems make this judgment within their tokenizer, but I see that as a mistake since it commits the system prematurely, i.e., before any of the surrounding context can be taken into account. To SPARSER's tokenizer the string is just the capital letter *F*, a hyphen with no intervening spaces, and the number fourteen; to the next level of processing it is a still only a *hyphenated letter-number sequence* (in recognition of the fact that there are no spaces between the tokens), and it is left to the phrase structure components to apply contextual knowledge and make the substantive judgments.

The tokenizer is the level that first comes into contact with unknown words, i.e., any character sequence not already in its lookup table. Unknown does not mean without properties, however. The tokenizer notices capitalization and the presence of affixes (-*s*, -*ed*, -*ing*). These properties define artificial words that can be reacted to by later algorithms just like a known word.

5.4.3   Word-Level Transition Nets

When the words are known, most phrases will be built up by noticing pairs of adjacent elements: specific words, words labeled by their categories, or already formed labeled phrases. The question then arises as to what internal structure the phrases should have.

Most of the phrases linguists study are best described as binary branching trees where each lower constituent is well-founded semantically and makes a disciplined composition with its neighbor word or phrase. However, other, less studied but extremely frequent phrase types, such as proper names, numbers, and some word compounds involve little or no composition, and are best seen as flat structures. For parsing these, SPARSER provides hooks for a transition net facility that operates over the stream of words output from the tokenizer.

In principle, the phrase types could be handled with a minimal impact on efficiency by the phrase-structure rules that operate at the next stage. The transition nets are used because it is a more natural description for the grammar writer to choose. Similarly, other researchers have used much more elaborate pattern-matching facilities at the word level, [8] while I have judged that the kinds of things these complex patterns search for are more easily stated in terms of phrase-structure rules and handled at a later stage.

5.4.4   Phrase-Structure Parsing using Semantic Labels

The phrase-structure parser is driven by a grammar of conventional rewrite rules and constructs trees of phrases stored in a chart. Its algorithm [McDonald, 1992] is an unusually efficient deterministic variation on bottom-up parsing, and, like all phrase structure algorithms, it is reacting to patterns of adjacent labeled constituents.

What is unusual about SPARSER's rewrite rules is that they employ primarily semantic labels on phrases rather than syntactic. That is, rather than label the text *the dollar plunged* as a clause consisting of a noun phrase (consisting of a determiner and a noun) followed by a verb phrase consisting of a single verb, SPARSER's grammar will label the *dollar* as, e.g., *currency* and *plunged* as a verb of motion. [9]

---

[8]Often full regular expressions are allowed, with Boolean combinations, including optional elements, wildcards of stipulated length, variable bindings, etc., even multipass cascades, to resolve *metatokens*, e.g. [Masand and Duffey, 1985].

[9]Actually, SPARSER's labeling scheme is more complex than this. Every parse node has three *label* fields. The primary label is taken from a semantic vocabulary, but it is shadowed by a conventional syntactic label that is used in default rules, and there is also the category of the phrase's denotation. For the case of *dollar*, its primary label is *currency*, but it also has the label *head noun*, and a structured ambiguity in its denotation between *physical object*, *quantity of money worth 100 cents*, and *the value of U.S. currency on international money markets*. This ambiguity is resolved by the propagation of semantic constraints as phrases are formed, e.g., only a *value* is able to move and so the last sense is the one taken when a currency is combined with a verb like *plunged*.

The syntactic labeling is, of course, correct, but it is not to the point. SPARSER's goal is to extract semantically characterized information, not to produce a syntactic structural description. This approach to the choice of labels integrates the process of disambiguating word senses directly with the process of analyzing grammatical relations and forming phrases: A phrase will only be formed if its elements are semantically, as well as syntactically, consistent. This approach also dramatically reduces the number of structural ambiguities ever considered.

This kind of design was first worked out by Burton and Brown [Brown et al., 1982], and while considered an effective means of engineering a grammar for a small domain, it never gained support as a general strategy for syntactic parsers. This historical fact reflects the general trend in computational linguistics to see parsing as an isolated process just concerned with the recovery of a text's structure. In the context of text-based intelligent systems, however, this view is myopic. The purpose of a parser is to facilitate the recovery of the information a text contains, and any technique that speeds that effort is to the point. By folding interpretation and structural analysis together through the use of semantic labels, one is ensured that every phrase that is allowed to complete syntactically will never be rejected semantically: a dramatic savings in efficency at the cost of a multiplication in the number of rules in the grammar, which is a tradeoff easily made in today's computational architectures.

5.4.5   Context-Sensitive Phrase-Structure Parsing

In a context-free phrase-structure rewrite rule, a sequence of labels is matched against the labels of adjacent constituents in the text. If the match succeeds (*completes*), the entire sequence of constituents is composed into a new phrase and given the label that the rule dictates. A context-sensitive rule can be seen as a matching operation against a sequence of adjacent constituents, with the exception that now only one of those constituents is relabeled rather than the whole sequence.

Context-sensitive rules are used extensively in SPARSER's grammars. They allow information to be accumulated gradually. Early rules can be cautious in their assumptions about what a phrase denotes (as in *hyphenated letter-number sequence* or *name*), waiting for a context to accumulate around the phrase through the action of other rules. Once the context is established, a context sensitive rule will be triggered to enrich the categorization, e.g.:

```
name -> person  /  ____ <was named CEO>
```

5.4.6   Parsing Non-Adjacent Constituents with a Conceptual Analyzer

The conceptual analyzer algorithm is responsible for composing constituents that are not adjacent (and so are invisible to the phrase-structure algorithm), but that can be linked on semantic grounds based on how the constituents are labeled. The primary function of this component of the parser is to make it possible to *skip over* regions of the text that are outside of the system's competence.

Consider the following text from the perspective of a grammar of employment change. In bold are the text segments that the parser understands; a relative clause (plain text) intervenes between the person that is the subject of the sentence and the *appointment* verb phrase that it should combine with.

> ... **Robert A. Beck,** a 65-year-old former Prudential chairman who originally bought the brokerage firm, **was named chief executive of Prudential Bache**....

Even though the grammar contains a rule for it, the phrase structure algorithms cannot compose these segments because they are not adjacent. Instead, the conceptual analyzer algorithm, triggered by these *stranded* constituents, uses the grammar rule to define a search path to try and join them. In this case, the appointment verb phrase searches leftward through the partial constituents until it finds a person constituent to compose with. The search is constrained to fit the grammatical relation this rule instantiates, namely that of subject to predicate in a clause. This means that it will fail if the search extends beyond the current sentence or across constituents that could not be interposed between a subject and its predicate verb phrase.

The notion of a conceptual analyzer (CA) was developed by Roger Schank and his students during the 1970s at Yale (for a practical summary, see Birnbaum and Selfridge [1981]. SPARSER's version is based on the same philosophy: the composition of phrases based on their semantic (*conceptual*) characteristics rather than syntactic, with the significant difference that SPARSER's CA is operating in conjunction with a set of other parsing algorithms, and so is not also responsible for assembling the small, syntactically rich phrases where traditional techniques excel. In the traditional CA design, all parsing is done by searching for patterns of semantic elements. This leads to stating simple syntactic facts in a complicated semantic pattern language, again an unnecessary burden on the grammar writer.

5.4.7   Forming Phrases Heuristically

Working together, these algorithms can efficiently recover a description of the portion of a text where the words are known. Where they are not, a heuristic facility is drawn on to deduce as much as possible. This facility uses the linguistic properties of items such as inflectional and derivational morphemes (e.g., -**tion**, -**ed**) and function word vocabulary (e.g., *is, from, and*), to deduce the boundaries of phrases even though it does not recognize most of their words. For example, when the function word *the* is seen it knows that that must be the start of a noun phrase; an auxiliary verb like *does* or a preposition terminates whatever phrase came before it. This basis for segmenting a text can be combined with the phrase-structure rules to allow phrases to be formed that would otherwise be missed. Consider the real example ... *this gold mining company was* .... Two unknown words keep the conventional algorithms from forming this noun phrase, but in its context the function-word driven heuristics guarantee that all four words are in the same phrase. Given that there is a phrase-structure rule in the grammar that would have combined *this* and *company* had they been adjacent, we are entitled to span this entire phrase using that same rule. This will give us the label for the phrase, allowing it to be passed to the adjacency-driven algorithms for composition with its neighbors, even though we don't understand all of what it means. These techniques complement the conceptual analyzer, since they make constituents adjacent (and so, accessible to the phrase-structure rules, the backbone of SPARSER's operation) by allowing constituents to form even when they include unknown words, while the conceptual analyzer searches across unparsed text segments for which no analysis is possible.

Similar techniques are used by [Hindle, 1983] and [O'Shaughnessy, 1989] where, as in this case, the emphasis is on recovering a relatively robust parse of successive phrases, rather than insisting on a full parse of entire sentences, with the concomitant problems of structural ambiguities discussed above.

5.5 Results in Practice

The real test of any parser architecture is in how well the grammars written for it perform in realistic tests. Of course some of the results will be a function of the linguistic skills of the grammar writer, but the relative ease of use of the parser's rule notations will always be a key factor.

SPARSER was put to its first significant test in May of 1991 with a relatively large grammar for extracting information on people changing jobs. The parser analyzed 203 previously unseen articles from the *Wall Street Journal*, and the results were compared against a human analyst's judgments. The articles were literally the second half of all articles in the *Journal* that were labeled with the tag *WNEWS* during the month of February. They included short articles specifically about job changes, as well as long columns and even features where the information was incidental. Roughly three man-months had gone into preparing the grammar for this domain, resulting in approximately 2,300 rules, though these were known to be insufficient to account for many of the cases found in the training set.

The test was to identify all possible instances of the four-tuple: person, company or subsidiary, title, and type of event (e.g., appointment, retirement). In the texts, these corresponded to every clause with a relevant verb, as well as redundant cases of nominalizations and anaphoric references.

The results were strong, considering the amount of time invested. Four out of five of all possible events were correctly identified (597/735). Of the events identified, four out of five were completely correct in all four fields

(486/597), with the bulk of the deficit in omissions (empty fields) rather than actual mistakes. The false positive rate was 3%.

5.6   Directions

It is unlikely that, even with a great amount of work extending the present kind of grammar, the success rate on this task could be brought close to 100% (discounting, of course, texts that a person wouldn't understand either). Previously unseen verbs and new titles will always continue to be seen, and even the most carefully edited texts include occasional errors. The only way to surmount these problems would be by adding a new kind of component, one that deduced the category, if not the full meaning, of unknown or mistaken words.

This is not an intrinsically difficult problem (see, for example [Hirschman, 1986] and other papers in the same volume). But it can be very much easier or harder depending on the architecture of the parser. There must be an explicit model of the relationships among the grammar's rules, and the rules must be applied in a conservative, monotonic manner or else there will not be an adequate representation (the intermediate states of the parser) to run word-induction heuristics over. SPARSER is consistent with these properties, and some early experiments have been promising.

Another area of concern is the amount of labor needed to assemble a grammar for a new domain when using semantic instead of syntactic labels. Once the idiosyncratic constructions like dates or money are discounted, one syntactic grammar will cover nearly all texts, and it will need only hundreds of rules rather than the thousands required for each topic area when semantic labels are used as the lexical and phrasal categories.

However, to a certain extent, this is just a consequence of moving into the phrase-structure rules much of the apparatus that would have had to be in the total system anyway, though with a syntactic grammar it would have appeared in the *semantic interpretation component* rather than in SPARSER's rules. As the goal is to understand the text and not simply describe it, the full set of categorial distinctions and composition schemas of the domain is required, and having one or two orders of magnitude more rules is inevitable.

Nevertheless, one would like the process of adding a new domain to go more quickly, and we are investigating two possibilities. The first is to tightly couple the grammar writing process to the process of defining the concepts, relations, operations, etc. of the actual semantic model and reasoning methods of the new domain. We have taken some initial steps in this direction [McDonald, 1991], at the same time tying in the capability of reversing the process and generating texts from the objects of the conceptual model as well as parsing to them.

The second possibility is to collapse many of the rules of linguistic composition together by moving a certain class of the categorial distinctions into the semantic structures that accompany SPARSER's parse nodes (see note 10), having the differences that only affect interpretation without differentiating the possibilities for composition operate at a different level (though at the same time) as the parsing rules for assembling nodes out of constituents. This work is being done in collaboration with James Pustejovsky using his theory of the generative lexicon [Pustejovsky, 1991].

Bibliography

[Berwick and Weinberg, 1984] Robert C. Berwick and Amy Weinberg. *The Grammatical Basis of Linguistic Performance*. MIT Press, Cambridge, MA, 1984.

[Birnbaum and Selfridge, 1981] Lawrence Birnbaum and Mallory Selfridge. Conceptual analysis of natural language. In R. C. Schank and C. Riesbeck, editors, *Inside Computer Understanding*. Lawrence Erlbaum Associates, Hillsdale, NJ, 1981.

[Borning et al., 1983] A. Borning, Doug Lenat, David McDonald, Craig Taylor, and Steve Weyer. KNOESPHERE: Building expert systems with encyclopedic knowledge. In *Proceedings of the Eighth International Joint Conference on Artificial Intelligence*, Karslruhe, Germany, Aug 1983. Morgan Kaufmann.

[Brown et al., 1982]
John Seely Brown, Richard Burton, and Johan De Kleer. Pedagogical, natural language and knowledge engineering techniques in sophie I, II and III. In D. Sleeman and J. S. Brown, editors, *Intelligent Tutoring Systems*. Academic Press, New York, 1982.

[Clippinger et al., 1982] John H. Clippinger, Peter Szolovitz, David McDonald, Ken Church, and Glen Burke. Final report: Project to develop a prototype artificial intelligence system with a rapid automated intelligence gathering and analysis capability for natural language texts. Technical Report Contract No. DAAB07-82-J070, USACECOM, 1982.

[de Marcken, 1990] Carl G. de Marcken. Parsing the lob corpus. In *Proceedings of the 28st Annual Meeting of the Association for Computational Linguistics*, pages 243–251, Univ of Pittsburgh, PA, June 1990.

[Dyer, 1983] Michael G. Dyer. *In-Depth Understanding: A Computer Model of Integrated Processing for Narrative Comprehension*. MIT Press, 1983.

[Earley, 1970] Jay Earley. An efficient context-free parsing algorithm. *Communications of the Association for Computing Machinery*, 13(2):94–102, February 1970.

[Grosz *et al.*, 1985] Barbara Grosz, Douglas Appelt, Paul Martin, and Fernando Pereira. TEAM: An experiment in the design of transportable natural language interfaces. Technical Report 356, SRI International, 1985.

[Hindle, 1983] Don Hindle. Deterministic parsing of syntactic non-fluencies. In *Proceedings of the 21st Annual Meeting of the Association for Computational Linguistics*, pages 123–128, Cambridge, MA, June 1983.

[Hirschman, 1986] Lynette Hirschman. Discovering sublanguage structures. In Ralph Grishman and Richard Kittredge, editors, *Analyzing Language In Restricted Domains: Sublanguage Description and Processing*. Lawrence Erlbaum Associates, Hillsdale, NJ, 1986.

[Lenat and Guha, 1990] Doug Lenat and R. V. Guha. *Building Large Knowledge-Based Systems*. Addison-Wesley, Reading, MA, 1990.

[Marcus, 1980] Mitchell Marcus. *A Theory of Syntactic Recognition of Natural Language*. MIT Press, Cambridge, MA, 1980.

[Martin and Riesbeck, 1986] Charles Martin and Chris Riesbeck. Uniform parsing and inference for learning. In *Proceedings of the Fifth National Conference on Artificial Intelligence*, Philadelphia, PA, August 1986. Morgan Kaufmann.

[Masand and Duffey, 1985] Brij Masand and Roger Duffey. A rapid prototype of an information extractor and its application to database table generation. Technical Report working paper, Brattle Research Corporation, Cambridge, MA, 1985.

[McDonald, 1980] David D. D. McDonald. *Language Production as a Process of Decision-making Under Constraints*. PhD thesis, MIT, 1980.

[McDonald, 1991] David D. McDonald. Reversible NLP by deriving the grammars from the knowledge base. In *Proceedings of the Workshop on Reversible Grammar in NLP*, pages 40–44, Berkeley, CA, June 1991. (Available from the ACL.)

[McDonald, 1992] David D. McDonald. An efficient chart-based algorithm for partial parsing of unrestricted texts. In *Third Conference on Applied Natural Language Processing*, Trento, Italy, April 1992.

[O'Shaughnessy, 1989] O'Shaughnessy. Parsing with a small dictionary for applications such as text to speech. *Computational Linguistics*, 15(3):97–108, June 1989.

[Pustejovsky, 1991] James Pustejovsky. The generative lexicon. *Computational Linguistics*, 17(4):409–441, 1991.

[Rau and Jacobs, 1988] Lisa F. Rau and Paul S. Jacobs. Integrating top-down and bottom-up strategies in a text processing system. In *Proceedings of Second Conference on Applied Natural Language Processing*, pages 129–135, Austin, TX, February 1988. ACL.

[Rieger, 1975] Charles Rieger. Conceptual memory and inferences. In R. C. Schank, editor, *Conceptual Information Processing*. American Elsevier, New York, 1975.

[Riesbeck, 1975] Christopher Riesbeck. Conceptual analysis. In R. C. Schank, editor, *Conceptual Information Processing*. American Elsevier, New York, 1975.

[Sager, 1981] Naomi Sager. *Natural Language Information Processing*. Addison-Wesley, Reading, MA, 1981.

Corpus-Based Thematic Analysis [*]

Uri Zernik
GE Research and Development Center
Schenectady, NY 12301

Abstract

Thematic analysis is best manifested by contrasting collocations[1] such as "shipping pacemakers" vs. "shipping departments". In the first pair, the pacemakers are being shipped, while in the second one, the departments are probably engaged in some shipping activity, but are not being shipped.

Text pre-processors, intended to inject corpus-based intuition into the parsing process, have blurred the distinction between such cases. Although statistical tagging has attained impressive results overall, the analysis of multiple-content-word strings (i.e., collocations) has presented a weakness, and caused accuracy degradation.

In this paper we present a tagging algorithm designed to serve as a front end for a syntactic parser. Training over a large corpus, and exploiting distributional properties of collocations, the tagger performs accurate thematic analysis.

The critical advantage of this algorithm is the fact that training can be performed over raw (i.e., no need for manual tagging) corpus, thus enabling instantaneous training over any new corpus that requires text processing.

We provide empirical results: NLcp (NL corpus processing) acquired a 250,000 thematic-relation database through the 85-million word *Wall Street Journal* Corpus. Tested over a 66,000-word financial news stories, it drastically improved tagging of content words. The integration of the tagger with a parser is now under way, in a system that extracts joint venture date from newspapers.[2]

---

[*]This research was sponsored (in part) by the Defense Advanced Research Project Agency (DOD) and other government agencies. The views and conclusions contained in this document are those of the authors and should not be interpreted as representing the official policies, either expressed or implied, of the Defense Advanced Research Project Agency or the U.S. Government.

[1]In this discussion, a collocation is defined as a pair of co-occurring content words.

[2]I thank ACL/DCI (Data Collection Initiative), the Collins Publishing Company, and the *Wall Street Journal*, for providing invaluable on-line data.

101

6.1   Pre-Processing: The Bigger Picture

Sentences in a typical newspaper story include idioms, ellipses, and ungrammatical constructs. Since authentic language defies textbook grammar, we must re-think our basic unification-parsing paradigm, and tune it to the nature of the text under analysis.

Hypothetically, parsing could be performed by one huge unification mechanism [Kay, 1985; Shieber, 1986; Tomita, 1986], which would receive its tokens in the form of words, characters, or morphemes, negotiate all given constraints, and produce a full chart with all possible interpretations.

However, when tested on a real corpus, e.g., *Wall Street Journal* (WSJ) news stories, this mechanism collapses. For a typical well-behaved 33-word sentence it produces hundreds of candidate interpretations.

To alleviate problems associated with processing real text, a new strategy has emerged. A pre-processor, capitalizing on statistical data [Church, 1988; Zernik and Jacobs, 1990; Dagan *et al.*, 1991], and trained to exploit properties of the corpus itself, could highlight regularities, identify thematic relations, and in general, feed digested text into the unification parser.

Pre-processing research so far has addressed the use of statistical methods to perform part-of-speech tagging of free text. Such taggers have produced apparently impressive empirical results, with several systems showing accuracy beyond 95%. The impact of these results comes in part from the fact that this percentage *seems* so high, and in part from results that show that statistical methods do better even than full-scale parsing.

Parsing, and in particular data extraction, relies on thematic analysis, best manifested by contrasting collocations such as *shipping pacemakers* vs. *shipping departments*. The first pair indicates that the pacemakers are being shipped, while in the second one, the departments are probably engaged in some shipping activity, but are not being shipped.

Existing stochastic taggers [Church, 1988; Meteer *et al.*, 1991; Cutting *et al.*, 1992] have blurred this distinction, and consequently, for collocations, produced highly inaccurate tags. This weakness has rendered statistical tagging ineffective in the context of parsing.

At an overall rate of 95% accuracy *per word* existing statistical taggers are not accurate enough to serve in real text-processing configurations. For one thing, 95% accuracy *per word* can yield a meager 10% accuracy *per sentence*. For another, accuracy is much less than 95% in the parts of the sentence that matter – content words.

In this paper we present a tagging algorithm that overcomes this hurdle. The underlying analysis exploits distributional properties of collocations: Fixed phrases show little variability, while thematic relations show large variability. The method performs accurate thematic analysis and improves overall tagging.

The rest of the paper:

1. Motivates the linguistic phenomena and its manifestation in parsing

accuracy.

2. Describes a text-processing architecture in which a tagger serves as a pre-processor to a unification parser.

3. Gives an overview of how statistical analysis has been used in text processing so far, and explains why a new method is required to boost tagging accuracy.

4. Present our new tagging algorithm which exploits distributional differences to build a thematic database.

5. Presents the results and their implications.

6.1.1   The Linguistic Phenomenon

Consider the following *Wall Street Journal* (WSJ; August 19, 1987) paragraph processed by the NLcp pre-processor [Zernik *et al.*, 1991].

> Separately, Kaneb Services spokesman/nn said/vb holders/nn of its Class A preferred/jj stock/nn failed/vb to elect two directors to the company/nn board/nn when the annual/jj meeting/nn resumed/vb Tuesday because there are questions as to the validity of the proxies/nn submitted/vb for review by the group.
>
> The company/nn adjourned/vb its annual/jj meeting/nn May 12 to allow/vb time/nn for negotiations and expressed/vb concern/nn about future/jj actions/nn by preferred/vb holders/nn.

Strings of content words (boldfaced in the text above) present a major problem for existing HMM-based taggers. Those taggers rely to a large extent on syntactic "sugar". Function words such as *the* (a determiner), *from* (a preposition), and *are* (an auxiliary verb) help anchor the tagging strings. In the absence of such sugar, accuracy deteriorates.

The task under investigation in this work is the analysis of content-word strings. This analysis amounts to the classification of content-word pairs into one of three categories.

1.	negotiations and	expressed/VB concern/NN	about
2.	Kaneb Services	spokesman/NN said/VB	holders
3.	its class A	preferred/JJ stock/NN	*comma*

Expressed concern and *spokesman said* are tagged verb-object and subject-verb, respectively. *Preferred stock*, on the other hand, is tagged as a fixed adjective-noun construct.

6.1.2   Philosophical Underpinnings

Two resources, semantics and corpus, suggest certain linguistic preferences, and can be used for thematic-role assignment. Traditionally, NLP practice has followed the Fregean paradigm [Frege, 1967].

This paradigm relies on three questionable assumptions: (1) perfect semantic compositionality, (2) a complete ontology, and (3) a complete set of predicates over this ontology. Under these assumptions, thematic roles can be computed by so-called semantic analysis.

Thus, *shipping pacemakers* could be taken as verb-object since *pacemakers* belong in some *can-be-shipped* semantic category. *Shipping departments* is taken as verb-subject since *departments* belong in some *can-ship* category.

Although completeness is the obvious flaw in this thinking, it is consistency that causes its total collapse. Attempts to scale up the ontology and the knowledge base to cover wide domains lead to representational conflicts.

Recent efforts to scale up text processing beyond limited domains, have motivated the use of corpus-based methods. This trend realizes Wittgenstein's paradigm [Wittgenstein, 1921], where attention is focussed on *word usage* rather than *word meaning*.

A phenonmenon that highlights the contrast between semantics and usage is lexical selection. The collocation *strong tea* is much more plausible than *powerful tea*. Similarly, *powerful car* is preferred over *strong car*. As argued by Halliday [Halliday, 1966] (see also discussions by [Smadja, 1991; Church *et al.*, 1991]), there are no pure syntactic or semantic constraints that can account for this preference. These are lexical constraints that need to be introduced in order to filter out oddities when producing English.

Recent studies (see [Miller, 1969; Justeson and Katz, 1991]) have shown that such lexical constraints can be learnable from a corpus.

These observations can lead to practical results. Consider, for example, thematic analysis. In a closed domain, a system designer can dictate thematic role bindings by manually coding selectional restrictions. However, selectional restrictions fall apart when the domain is scaled up.[3] By relying on corpus-based acquisition, computer programs can attain appropriate linguistic performance over open-ended text.

6.2   The Text-Processing Architecture

Text processing in the [Jacobs, 1992a] system proceeds through the following stages:

Thematic Analysis (training-time): Collect and analyze collocations from a large corpus. Construct a thematic-relation database (250,000 items).

Tagging (processing-time):

- Perform lexical analysis based on the Collins on-line dictionary [Sinclair *et al.*, 1987].

- Perform initial tagging based on a fixed set of knowledge-based rules.

---

[3] Selectional restrictions fare well when applied to action verbs that take physical objects in a narrow and neatly represented domain. They prove problematic when applied to verbs that take abstract nouns, e.g., *delay the hearing*, *prefer stock*, etc.

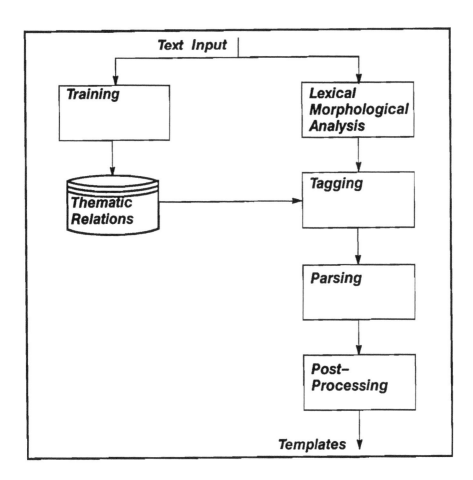

Figure 6.1: The text-processing architecture

Kaneb	NM		Services	NN VB		spokesman	NN
said	JJ VB		holders	NN		of	PP
its	DT		Class	JJ NN		A	DT JJ
preferred	JJ VB		stock	NN VB		failed	AD VB
to	PP		elect	VB		two	JJ NN
directors	NN		to	PP		the	DT
company	NN		board	NN VB		when	CC
annual	JJ		meeting	NN VB		resumed	JJ VB
tuesday	NM		questions	NN VB		validity	NN
proxies	NN		submitted	JJ VB		group	NN VB

Figure 6.2: Lexical analysis of sentence: words plus parts of speech

- Tag collocations based on the thematic-relation database.

Parsing: Perform syntactic analysis of the tagged text by a unification parser [Tomita, 1986].

Post-processing: Select the appropriate parse tree using semantic constraints.

The stages involving training and tagging are addressed in this paper.

6.2.1   The Output: A Parse Tree

Consider the following sentence:

> Separately, Kaneb Services spokesman said holders of its Class A preferred stock failed to elect two directors to the company board when the annual meeting resumed Tuesday because there are questions as to the validity of the proxies submitted for review by the group.

Without the use of pre-processing, the unification parser [Tomita, 1986] generates about 600 interpretations for this 44-word *Wall Street Journal* sentence. The parser has a grammar of constructs that are *allowed* in English. It does not have a notion of what constructs are *preferred* in a particular corpus.

To bring to bear these corpus preferences at an early stage, and so to prune out as many as possible of these candidate parse trees, we have employed corpus-based pre-processing. Early results indicate a reduction in the order of 10 to 20 in the number of interpretations due to corpus-based thematic analysis.

6.2.2   The Input: Ambiguous Lexical Tags

The complex scope of the pre-processing task is best illustrated by the input to the pre-processor shown in Figure 6.2, in the form of lexical tokens..

Lexical analysis is based on the Collins on-line dictionary (about 49,000 lexical entries extracted by NLcp) plus morphology. Each word is associated with *candidate* parts of speech, and almost all words are ambiguous. The tagger's task is to resolve this ambiguity further.

Ambiguous words such as *services, preferred,* and *expressed,* should be resolved as noun (*nn*), adjective (*jj*), and verb (*vb*), respectively. While some pairs (e.g., *annual meeting*) can be resolved easily, other pairs (e.g., *preferred stock* and *expressed concerns*) are more difficult, and require statistical training.

6.2.3   Part-Of-Speech Resolution

A program can bring to bear three types of clues in resolving part-of-speech ambiguity:

Local context: Consider the following two cases where local context dominates:

> 1. the preferred stock rose
> 2. he expressed concern about

The words *the* and *he* dictate that preferred and expressed are adjective and verb, respectively. This kind of inference, due to its local nature, is captured and propagated by existing pre-processors.

Global context: Global-sentence constraints are shown by the following two examples:

> 1. and preferred stock sold yesterday was ...
> 2. and expressed concern about ... *period*

In case 1, a main verb is found (i.e., *was*), and *preferred* is taken as an adjective; in case 2, a main verb is not found, and therefore *expressed* itself is taken as the main verb. This kind of ambiguity requires full-fledged unification, and it is not handled by pre-processors. Fortunately, only a small percent of the cases (in newspaper stories) depend on global reading.

Thematic Analysis: Corpus analysis provides certain preferences [Beckwith *et al.,* 1991]:

	collocation	total no.	vb-nn	jj-nn
1.	preferred stock	2314	100	0
2.	expressed concern	318	1	99

The construct *expressed concern,* which appears 318 times in the corpus, is almost always (99%) a verb-noun construct; on the other hand, *preferred stock,* which appears in the corpus 2,314 times, is 100% an adjective-noun construct.

However, this manually-prepared thematic data is not readily available in general. We need to resort to statistical methods that will extract internal collocation structure based on corpus analysis.

6.3   Statistical Text Processing: An Overview

Thematic analysis impinges on two statistical methods, which so far were unrelated: part-of-speech (POS) tagging and collocation analysis.

6.3.1   Part-of-Speech Tagging: The N-Gram Model

Although almost all English words possess more than one *lexical* part of speech, in context human readers are able to resolve this ambiguity. For example, we can easily tell that *kisses* in *Mary kisses John* is a verb and not a noun.

Accordingly, the tagging problem is phrased as follows: Given an in-sentence word, how can the part of speech for that word be determined by its sentential context?

The n-gram model provides a simplified statistical answer. Given, a word sequence W, and a tag sequence T, Bayes' rule dictates the *a posteriori* probability:

$$P(T|W) = \frac{P(T)P(W|T)}{P(W)}$$

The task at hand is to find a tagging sequence T which attains the highest *a posteriori* probability among all possible tagging sequences.

Since W is given, and is the same for all possible T's, this probability can be expressed as a product of dependencies on previous words and tags.

$$P(T|W)P(W) = \prod_{p(w_i|t_i...,w_{i-1}...)} p(t_0)p(t_1|t_0)p(t_i|t_{i-1}, t_{i-2}...)$$

At this point the simplifying *Markov independence assumption* is applied. Namely we assume that the tag of a word i (t_i) depends solely on the tags of the n preceding words $t_{i-1} \ldots t_{i-n}$. This model is called the n-gram model. The tri-gram model provides a feasible and relatively accurate approximation:

$$P(T|W)P(W) = p(t_0)p(t_1|t_0) \prod_{p(w_i|t_i)} p(t_i|t_{i-1}, t_{i-2})$$

This model requires a transition table, where each transition expresses the probability of a tag t_i given the current word and the two preceding tags t_{i-1} and t_{i-2}.

With this kind of transition table, statistical taggers have required relatively small training texts: A database of single-word statistics can be collected from a 1-million word corpus [Brill, 1992]; a database of state transitions for part-of-speech tagging can also be collected from a 1-million word corpus ([Church, 1988]), or even from a smaller 60,000-word corpus ([Meteer *et al.*, 1991]).

The fact that state transitions do not depend on individual constituent words is the main advantage of this model. Unfortunately, while this simplification greatly reduces the size of the state-transition table, and reduces the size of the required training corpus, it poses inherent limitations on accuracy. Since individual collocations are not explicitly accounted for, the algorithm cannot distinguish between *preferred stock* and *expressed concern*. This issue (i.e., tagging words that form collocations) remains the major source of tagging inaccuracy.

Accordingly, existing statistical taggers [Church, 1988; Meteer *et al.*, 1991; Brill, 1992; Cutting *et al.*, 1992], which rely on bigrams or trigrams, but which do not employ thematic analysis of individual collocations, fare poorly on this linguistic aspect. [4]

6.3.2   Collocation Identification

The mutual information formula calculates the significance of the co-occurrence of a pair of events. This formula has been employed in tasks such as collocation analysis [Church *et al.*, 1991], speech recognition [Jelinek, 1985], and categorization [Jacobs, 1992b]. It is best described in [Church *et al.*, 1991]:

> Mutual information, $MI(x; y)$, compares the probability of observing word x and word y *together* (the joint probability) with the probabilities of observing x and y *independently* (chance).
>
> $$MI(x; y) \equiv log_2 \frac{P(x, y)}{P(x)P(y)}$$
>
> If there is a genuine association between x and y, then the joint probability $P(x, y)$ will be much larger than chance $P(x)P(y)$, and consequently $MI(x; y) \gg 0$. If there is no interesting relationship between x and y, then $P(x, y) \sim P(x)P(y)$, and thus, $MI(x; y) \sim 0$. If x and y are in complementary distribution, then $P(x, y)$ will be much less than $P(x)P(y)$, forcing $MI(x; y) \ll 0$. Word probabilities, $P(x)$ and $P(y)$, are estimated by counting the number of observations of x and y in a corpus, $f(x)$ and $f(y)$, and normalizing

---

[4] The univariate-analysis strategy [Brill, 1992] of using default single-word probability is not successful in this case. All cases of *operating* would by default be tagged incorrectly as verb since the noun/verb ratio for *operating* is 454/331 in the 2-million word portion of WSJ manually tagged by the TreeBank project [Santorini, 1990].

by N, the size of the corpus. Joint probabilities, $P(x,y)$, are estimated by counting the number of times that x is followed by y, $f(x,y)$, and normalizing by N.

Four lists of collocations sorted by MI are given in Figure 6.3.

6.3.3   Thematic Analysis: Where Is the Evidence?

Mutual information enables the ranking of collocations by significance. Accordingly both *preferred stock* and *expressed concern* are found to be significant (MI of 8.72 and 10.85, respectively see Figure 6.3). However, the following questions regarding internal collocation structure remain unanswered:

1. What is the modification structure of a collocation? When is it a *post-modification* (e.g., $<< cat\ food > container >$), and when is it a *pre-modification* (e.g., $< yellow < food\ container >>$)?

2. What are the parts of speech within the collocation? Is it a *noun group* (e.g., *preferred*/**JJ** *stock*) or is it a *verb-noun phrase* (e.g., *expressed*/**VB** *concern*)?

3. How are thematic roles assigned in the collocation? Is it Subject-Verb-Object (e.g., *student teaching programs* or is it Object-Verb-Subject (e.g., *student-teaching programs*)? Unfortunately hyphens and punctuation are not very regular in written English and cannot be the sole indicator.

Unfortunately, mutual information does not address internal collocation structure. Indeed at the very high end (MI over 16) almost all collocations are noun groups, but for the bulk of the cases, namely, MI between 4 and 16, the classes are thoroughly mixed. Consider the collocations in Figure 6.3. High-MI collocations can potentially be verb-noun (taking advantage), adjective-noun (*preferred stock*), verb-adverb (*operate efficiently*), or even verb-adjective (taking drastic), which is a part of a longer collocation (*taking drastic measures*).

Can the text itself support part-of-speech analysis? A glance at Figures 6.4 and 6.5, does not reveal any clues that can distinguish *expressed concern* (which is a verb-noun) from *preferred stock* (which is an adjective-noun).

Since neither MI figures, nor text-based clues can systematically address the problem, we have widened the scope of our search to include also variants of collocations. Consider Figure 6.6, which includes variants of *expressed* collocations. *Expressed concern* shows a wide variability: express, expresses, expressing and expressed. On the other hand, an analogous figure does not exist for *preferred stock* since it does not take any variability.

Another similar comparison is shown (Figure 6.7) between the pairs *operating-system* and *taking-advantage*. The verb-noun collocation shows a diverse distribution while the adjective-noun collocation is fixed.

12.55	expressed-puzzlement	9.07	preferred-dividend
12.49	expressed-bewilderment	8.74	preferred-provider
12.08	expressed-astonishment	8.72	preferred-stock
12.05	expressed-disappointment	8.00	preferred-depositary
11.57	expressed-skepticism	7.65	preferred-share
11.41	expressed-dismay	7.35	preferred-stockholder
11.38	expressed-displeasure	7.03	preferred-holder
11.14	expressed-amazement	6.94	preferred-method
11.02	expressed-reservation	6.05	preferred-shareholder
10.96	expressed-sadness	6.00	preferred-via
10.85	expressed-concern	5.62	preferred-unit
10.82	expressed-outrage	5.31	preferred-auction
10.78	expressed-optimism	5.27	preferred-payable
10.76	expressed-satisfaction	4.98	preferred-redemption
10.64	expressed-unhappiness	4.92	preferred-convertible
10.58	expressed-gratitude	4.91	preferred-issue
10.48	expressed-delight	4.64	preferred-absorbed
10.18	expressed-uneasiness	4.56	preferred-outstanding
10.18	expressed-surprise	4.31	preferred-become
10.17	expressed-doubt	4.23	preferred-portion
10.02	taking-precedence	10.49	operating-efficiency
9.60	taking-advantage	9.84	operating-officer
9.43	taking-pain	9.39	operating-philosophy
9.40	taking-placebo	9.24	operating-profit
9.31	taking-erased	8.59	operating-expense
9.24	taking-precaution	8.36	operating-commercially
9.24	taking-bribe	8.01	operating-certificate
9.11	taking-deposition	8.00	operating-profitably
8.73	taking-step	7.68	operating-division
8.26	taking-place	7.67	operating-margin
8.16	taking-trimmed	7.59	operating-lose
8.15	taking-shape	7.50	operating-license
7.97	taking-aspirin	7.35	operating-system
7.62	taking-pared	7.28	operating-loss
7.52	taking-possession	7.13	operating-earnings
7.52	taking-aim	7.00	operating-result
7.19	taking-drastic	6.98	operating-subsidiary
7.19	taking-cooled	6.98	operating-cost
7.08	taking-wiped	6.96	operating-differential
7.05	taking-bet	6.94	operating-unit

Figure 6.3: Significant *expressed*, *preferred*, *taking*, and *operating* collocations

GE for the 585,000 shares of its   preferred   stock outstanding *period* The e
ume payments of dividends on the   preferred   stock in January *period* It sus
ohawk but lowered ratings on its   preferred   stock and commercial paper *comm
n* 3 from BAA *hyphen* 2 *comma*   preferred   stock to ba *hyphen* 2 from BAA
llar* 26.65 a share *period* The   preferred   is convertible until 5 P.M.. EDT
0 *pc* of Varity *ap* common and   preferred   shares outstanding *period* The
ng of up to *dollar* 250 million   preferred   shares *period* Terms of the tra
erms of the transaction call for   preferred   holders *comma* who previously a
sal *comma* to swap one share of   preferred   stock for 1.2 shares of common s
i *dollar* 2 million annually in   preferred   dividends *period* Artra owns 68
p* notes and 7,459 Lori series C   preferred   shares with a carrying value of
a share of newly issued series A   preferred   stock with a value equal to *dol
ance an adjustable *hyphen* rate   preferred   stock whose auction failed recen

Figure 6.4: *Preferred* phrases in context

id he told the house Mr. Dingell   expressed   concern *comma* sources said *co
ggested that the U.S. Mr. Harper   expressed   confidence that he and Mr. Baum
ne tax *period* Some legislators   expressed   concern that a gas *hyphen* tax
soybeans and feed grains *comma*   expressed   outrage over the case *comma* sa
bid *dash* *dash* *dash* GE unit   expressed   interest in financing offer for
hallenge *period* Mr. Wright has   expressed   dismay that a foreign company co
bt about their bank one also had   expressed   interest in Mcorp *ap* mvestment
italy *ap* President Cossiga and   expressed   concern about an Italian firm su
comma saying warner executives   expressed   surprise at Sony *ap* move but d
 secretary Robert Mosbacher have   expressed   concern about the EC *ap* use of
thor on the nature paper *comma*   expressed   disappointment that he was not i
eber who *comma* he said *comma*   expressed   support for the idea *period* Ca

Figure 6.5: *Expressed* phrases in context

ving gold in the street and then   expressing surprise when thieves walk by t
said that National Pizza Co. has   expressed renewed interest in acquiring th
r. nixon *comma* Chinese leaders   expressed no regret for the killings *comm
e Bay Area *ap* pastry community   express concern that Ms. Shere kept on act
 presidents also are expected to   express support for the Andean nations whi
its predecessor *period* It also   expressed its commitment to a free *hyphen
 related Services Co. people who   express interest in the certificates recen
c chairman Seidman *comma* while   expressing concerns *comma* also said ther
* on a tour of asia *comma* also   expressed a desire to visit China *period*
ponsored the senate plan *comma*   expressed some confidence that his plan we
 the nine supreme court justices   expressed varying degrees of dissatisfacti
nd primerica in his eagerness to   express his linguistic doubts to American
st few weeks alone *dash* *dash*   expressing their relief after crossing int
iterally flipped his wig *comma*   expressing delight at having an excuse to
 that the newspaper company said   expresses confidence in the outcome of a
who no longer feel they have to   express their zeal on the streets *comma*
icans writing to the hostages to   express their concern and support *period*
en summoned to chairman Gonzalez   expresses sympathy for Sen. Riegle *comma
riod* Frequently *comma* clients   express interest in paintings but do not

Figure 6.6: Variants of *express* in context

This property of collocations is exploited by our algorithm.

6.4   Acquiring Thematic Relations from a Corpus

In this section, I describe a statistical method called *variational analysis*
[Zernik, 1992] that capitalizes on the difference between the distributions of
fixed and variable phrases.

6.4.1   Identifying Collocation Variability

A view of variation across the corpus is presented in Figure 6.8. It provides
the frequencies found for each variant in the WSJ corpus. For example, *joint
venture* takes three variants totaling 4,300 instances, out of which 4,288 are
concentrated in two patterns, which in effect (stripping the plural −s suffix),
are a single pattern. For *produce car*, no single pattern holds for more than
21% of the cases. Thus, when more than 90% of the phrases are concentrated
in a single pattern, we classify it as a fixed adjective-noun (or noun-noun)
phrase. Otherwise, it is classified as a noun-verb (or verb-noun) thematic
relation.

```
e latest version of the UNIX V   operating   system software and some
th Microsoft 's MS *slash* DOS   operating   system *period* Microsoft
ties obtained licenses for the   operating   system *period* With the
nths before IBM can provide an   operating   system that taps its mach
 *comma* much as Microsoft 's    operating   system software is now th
r *colon* eta systems inc. its   operating   system has not been debug
cyber uses an unusual internal   operating   system *s-colon* to sell
*hyphen* Telegraph Co. 's UNIX   operating   system *comma* fast becom
willing to suffer with a crude   operating   system *period*
at someday the Macintosh II 's   operating   system would be enhanced
phen* compatible computers and   operating   systems has created an op
```

```
 allow the equity investors to   take    advantage of federal tax benef
spect that some countries will   take    advantage of the option to pay
 *comma* probably will want to   take    advantage of an option such as
  scheduling *comma* some might  take    advantage of the opportunity t
ed that rotated 360 degrees to   take    advantage of the view *period*
th cheap local deposits and by   taking  advantage of its low overhea
ins by nimbly trading zeros to   take    advantage of short *hyphen* te
dexes and futures contracts to   take    advantage of various differenc
itional financing *s-colon* to   take    advantage of future business o
pendent publishers *comma* and   take    advantage of our considerable
olon* but if brazil decides to   take    advantage of any price rally *
that some practical jokers had   taken   advantage of the offer *dash*
onent systems on time *period*   Taking  advantage of changing demogr
ravel plans by a few months to   take    advantage of the low fares *pe
tic producers can successfully   take    advantage of the tax to eke ou
ing lobbyists and scurrying to   take    advantage of the current hosti
 homeowners 's refinancing to    take    advantage of lower interest ra
g complete pc systems *period*   Taking  advantage of their lower *hy
 rally came from investors who   took    advantage of rising stock pric
n part by investors rushing to   take    advantage of britain 's high c
*comma* stayed long enough to    take    advantage of the amenities tha
ber of institutional investors   took    advantage of the rally to roll
mma* mo *period* Companies are   taking  advantage of that to rebuild
for example *dash* *dash* have   taken   advantage of the strong yen t
```

Figure 6.7: Fixed and variable phrases in context

Verb-Noun Relations

2	produced-car	387	expressed-concern	72	taken-advantage
9	produced-cars	25	expressed-concerns	22	takes-advantage
5	produces-cars	10	expresses-concern	995	take-advantage
4	produce-car	31	expressing-concern	2	take-advantages
13	produce-cars	3	expressing-concerns	260	taking-advantage
17	producing-cars	33	express-concern	159	took-advantage
2	production-cars				

Noun-Verb Relations

947	companies-said	118	analysts-note	51	spokesman-acknowledged
242	companies-say	192	analysts-noted	8	spokesman-acknowledges
13	companies-saying	192	analysts-noted	2	spokesman-acknowledging
135	companies-says	13	analysts-noting		
14146	company-said	79	analyst-noted		
43	company-say	6	analyst-notes		
20	company-saying	6	analyst-notes		
698	company-says	6	analyst-notes		
		9	analyst-noting		

Adjective-Noun Constructs

3491	joint-venture	3558	preferred-stock	2	operates-systems
807	joint-ventures	11	preferred-stocks	627	operating-system
2	joint-venturing			86	operating-systems
				2	operational-systems
				2	operates-system

Figure 6.8: Fixed and variable collocations across the corpus: Fixed phrases (e.g., *preferred stocks*) allow only a narrow variance. Full-fledged thematic relations (i.e., *produced cars*) appear in a wide variety of forms.

6.4.2   Training-Time Thematic Analysis

Training over the corpus requires inflectional morphology. For each collocation P the following formula is applied to calculate P's Variability Factor:

$$VF(P) = \frac{fW(plural(P)) + fW(singular(P))}{fR(stemmed(P))}$$

where fW(plural(P)) means the word frequency of the plural form of the
collocation; fW(singular(P)) means the frequency of the singular form of
the collocation; and fR(stemmed(P)) means the frequency of the stemmed
collocation. Applying this formula to *produced cars*, we obtain:

$$VF(produced - cars) = \frac{fW(produced - cars) + fW(produced - car)}{fR(produce - car)} =$$

$$\frac{2 + 9}{2 + 9 + 5 + 4 + 13 + 17 + 2} = \frac{11}{52} = 0.21$$

Accordingly, $VF(producing - car) = VF(producing - cars) = 0.32$; and
VF(produce-car) is (by coincidence) 0.32. In contrast, VF(joint-venture) is
1.00. A list of the first 38 content-word pairs encountered in the the Joint-
Venture corpus is shown in Figure 6.9. The figure illustrates the frequency
of each collocation P in the corpus relative to its stem frequency. The ratio,
called VF, is given in the first column. The second and third columns present
the collocation and its frequency. The fourth and fifth column present the
stemmed collocation and its frequency. The sixth column presents the mutual
information score.

Notice that fixed collocations are easily distinguishable from thematic
relations. The smallest VF of a fixed collocation has a VF of .86 (finance
specialist); the largest VF of a thematic relation is .56 (produce concrete).
Thus, a threshold, of say .75, can effectively be established.

6.4.3   Processing-Time Tagging

Relative to a database such as in Figure 6.9, the tagging algorithm proceeds
as follows, as the text is read word by word:

1. Use local-context rules to tag words. When no rule applies for tagging
   a word, **then** tag the word "??" ("untagged").

2. **If** the last word pair is a collocation (e.g., *holding companies*), **and**
   one of the two words is tagged "??",
   then generate the S-stripped version (i.e., *holding company*), and the
   affix-stripped version (i.e., *hold company*).

3. Look up database.

   (a) **If** neither collocation is found, **then** do nothing;

VF(P)	P	fW(P)	stemmed(P)	fR(st'd(P))	MI(P)
1.00	business-brief	10083	business-brief	10083	9.95
1.00	joint-ventures	4298	joint-venture	4300	12.11
1.00	aggregates-operation	9	aggregate-operation	9	5.84
0.56	produce-concrete	5	produce-concrete	9	4.59
1.00	crushed-stones	12	crush-stone	12	11.08
0.00	forming-ventures	2	form-venture	44	5.50
0.00	leases-equipment	2	lease-equipment	12	4.35
1.00	composite-trading	10629	composite-trade	10629	9.41
1.00	related-equipment	65	relate-equipment	65	5.28
0.17	taking-advantage	260	take-advantage	1510	9.25
0.99	electronics-concern	482	electronic-concern	485	6.87
1.00	work-force	2014	work-force	2014	7.79
0.00	beginning-operation	3	begin-operation	160	4.11
1.00	makes-additives	5	make-additive	5	4.39
1.00	lubricating-additive	4	lubricate-additive	4	14.66
0.18	showed-signs	62	show-sign	339	6.28
1.00	telephone-exchange	66	telephone-exchange	66	5.56
0.95	holding-company	7752	hold-company	8124	6.21
1.00	phone-equipment	51	phone-equipment	51	6.02
1.00	phone-companies	572	phone-company	572	5.56
0.93	venture-partner	140	venture-partner	150	6.17
0.26	report-net	283	report-net	1072	6.10
1.00	net-income	9759	net-income	9759	10.54
1.00	home-appliance	96	home-appliance	96	11.01
0.99	brand-name	683	brand-name	687	8.98
0.96	product-lines	965	product-line	1009	7.12
1.00	equity-stake	266	equity-stake	266	6.65
1.00	earning-asset	46	earn-asset	46	4.46
1.00	problem-loans	252	problem-loan	252	5.10
0.86	finance-specialists	30	finance-specialist	35	5.06
1.00	finished-products	93	finish-product	93	5.79
1.00	mining-ventures	18	mine-venture	18	5.03
1.00	gas-industry	154	gas-industry	154	5.05
0.18	began-talks	27	begin-talk	152	4.56
0.55	produce-electricity	27	produce-electricity	49	6.14
1.00	power-plants	1353	power-plant	1353	8.12
1.00	oil-heating	14	oil-heat	14	4.01

Figure 6.9: Thematic-relations database: each collocation is associated with a Variability Factor (VF). A high VF indicates a fixed construct while a low VF (under 0.75) indicates a verb-noun thematic relation.

(b) **if** only affix-stripped collocation is found, or
    if VF (variability factor) is smaller than threshold, **then**
    tag first word a verb

(c) **If** VF is larger than threshold, **then** tag adjective-noun or noun-
    noun (depending on lexical properties of word, i.e., running vs.
    meeting).

Notice that local-context rules override corpus preference. Thus, although
preferred stocks is a fixed construct, in a case such as *John preferred stocks*,
the algorithm will identify *preferred* as a verb.

6.5   Evaluation

The database was generated over the WSJ corpus (85 million words). The
database retained about 250,000 collocations (collocations below MI of 3.5
are dropped). The count was performed over the TIPSTER Joint-Venture
1988 corpus (66,186 words). In the evaluation, only content words (i.e., verbs,
nouns, adverbs, and adjectives, totaling 36,231 words) are observed.

Out of 36,231 content words, 1,021 are left untagged by the tagger due
to incomplete coverage.

Of the words in the text, 12,719 fall into collocations (of 2 or more content
words). Tags for 6,801 of these are resolved by local context rules. Thematic
analysis resolves tags for 4,652 words. The remaining 1,266 remain untagged.

Estimated part-of-speech accuracy is 97%, calculated by checking 1,000
collocations. A mismatch between adjective and noun was not counted as an
error.

6.5.1   Problematic Cases

Our algorithm yields incorrect results in two problematic cases:

Ambiguous Thematic Relations: Collocations that entertain both subject-
verb and verb-object relations, i.e., *selling-companies* (as in "the company sold its subsidiary ..." and "he sold companies ...").

Interference: Coinciding collocations such as: *market-experience* and *marketing
experience*, or *ship-agent* and *shipping-agent*.

Fortunately, these cases are very infrequent.

6.5.2   Limitations

Adjectives and nouns are difficult to distinguish in raw corpus (unless they
are marked as such lexically). For example, since the lexicon marks *light* as
both adjective and noun, there is no visible difference in the corpus between
light/JJ beer and *light/NN bulb*. Our algorithm tags both *light* cases as nouns.

6.5.3   Corpus Size vs. Database Size

Two parameters are frequently confused when assessing tagging effectiveness: training-time corpus size and run-time database size.

Increasing the training corpus improves both coverage (the number of cases that are tagged), since more collocations have been encountered, and precision (the number of cases that are tagged correctly), since for each collocation more variations have been analyzed.

In order to accommodate the tagger to a specific architecture (20M-byte SPARC, in our case), the program might be linked with only a partial database (low-frequency collocations are removed). Cutting down on run-time database does not reduce precision. In the configuration evaluated above, the run-time tagger used only the most frequent 200,000 collocations out of the entire collection of 250,000.

6.6   Conclusions

We have presented a mechanism for injecting corpus-based preference in the form of thematic relations into syntactic text parsing. Thematic analysis (1) is crucial for semantic parsing accuracy, and (2) helps correct the weakest link of existing statistical taggers.

The algorithm presented in this paper capitalizes on the fact that text writers draw fixed phrases, such as *cash flow, joint venture*, and *preferred stock*, from a limited vocabulary of collocations, which can be captured in a database. Human readers, as well as computer programs, are successful in interpreting the text since they have previously encountered and acquired the embedded collocations.

Although the algorithm identifies fixed collocations as such, it allows local-context rules to override those corpus-based preferences. As a result, exceptional cases such as *he is operating systems*, or *he preferred stocks* are handled appropriately. It turns out that writers of a highly-edited text such as WSJ know how to avoid potential false readings by making sure that exceptions are marked by local context "sugar".

Our general line of thinking follows [Church *et al.*, 1991; Beckwith *et al.*, 1991; Dagan *et al.*, 1991; Zernik and Jacobs, 1990; Smadja, 1991]: In order for a program to interpret natural language text, it must train on and exploit word connections in the text under interpretation.

Bibliography

[Beckwith *et al.*, 1991] R. Beckwith, C. Fellbaum, D. Gross, and G. Miller. Wordnet: A lexical database organized on psycholinguistic principles. In U. Zernik, editor, *Lexical Acquisition: Exploiting On-Line Dictionary to Build a Lexicon*. Lawrence Erlbaum Associates, Hillsdale, NJ, 1991.

[Brill, 1992] Eric Brill. A simple rule-based part of speech tagger. In *Proceedings of the Third Conference on Applied Natural Language Processing*, Trento, Italy, 1992. Association for Computational Linguistics.

[Church et al., 1991] K. Church, W. Gale, P. Hanks, and D. Hindle. Using statistics in lexical analysis. In U. Zernik, editor, *Lexical Acquisition: Using On-Line Resources to Build a Lexicon*. Lawrence Erlbaum Associates, Hillsdale, NJ, 1991.

[Church, 1988] K. Church. A stochastic parts program and noun phrase parser for unrestricted text. In *Proceedings of the Second Conference on Applied Natural Language Processing*, Austin, TX, February 1988. Association for Computational Linguistics.

[Cutting et al., 1992] D. Cutting, J. Kupiee, J. Pedersen, and P. Sibun. A practical part-of-speech tagger. In *Proceedings of the Third Conference on Applied Natural Language Processing*, Trento, Italy, 1992. Association for Computational Linguistics.

[Dagan et al., 1991] I. Dagan, A. Itai, and U. Schwall. Two languages are more informative than one. In *Proceedings of the 29th Annual Meeting of the Association for Computational Linguistics*, Berkeley, CA, 1991.

[Frege, 1967] Gottlob Frege. *The Basic Laws of Arithmetic*. University of California, Berkeley, CA, 1967.

[Halliday, 1966] M.A.K. Halliday. Lexis as a linguistic level. In C.E. Bazell, J.C. Catford, M.A.K Halliday, and R.H. Robins, editors, *In memory of J.R. Firth*, pages 148–162. Longmans Linguistics Library, London, 1966.

[Jacobs, 1992a] Paul S. Jacobs. Parsing run amok: Relation-driven control for text analysis. In *Proceedings of the 11th National Conference on Artificial Intelligence*, San Jose, CA, 1992.

[Jacobs, 1992b] Paul S. Jacobs. Joining statistics with NLP for text categorization. In *Proceedings of the Third Conference on Applied Natural Language Processing*, Trento, Italy, 1992. Association for Computational Linguistics.

[Jelinek, 1985] Frederick Jelinek. Self-organized language modeling for speech recognition. Technical report, IBM, 1985.

[Justeson and Katz, 1991] J.S. Justeson and S.M. Katz. Co-occurrence of antonymous adjectives and their contexts. *Computational Linguistics*, 17(1):1–20, 1991.

[Kay, 1985] Martin Kay. Parsing in Functional Unification Grammar. In D. Dowty, L. Kartunnen, and A. Zwicky, editors, *Natural Language Parsing: Psychological, Computational, and Theoretical Perspectives*. Cambridge University Press, Cambridge, England, 1985.

[Meteer *et al.*, 1991] M. Meteer, R. Schwartz, and R. Weischedel. POST: Using probabilities in language processing. In *Proceedings of the 12th International Joint Conference on Artificial Intelligence (IJCAI-91)*, 1991.

[Miller, 1969] George A. Miller. The organization of lexical memory: Are word associations sufficient? In G. A. Talland and N. C. Waugh, editors, *The Pathology of Memory*. Academic Press, New York, 1969.

[Santorini, 1990] Beatrice Santorini. Annotation manual for the pen tree-bank project. Technical report, University of Pennsylvania, Computer and Information Science, Philadelphia, PA, 1990.

[Shieber, 1986] Stuart Shieber. *An Introduction to Unification-Based Approaches to Grammar*. Center for the Study of Language and Information, Palo Alto, CA, 1986.

[Sinclair *et al.*, 1987] J. Sinclair, P. Hanks, G. Fox, R. Moon, and P. Stock, editors. *Collins Cobuild English Language Dictionary*. Collins, London, 1987.

[Smadja, 1991] Frank Smadja. Macrocoding the lexicon with co-occurrence knowledge. In U. Zernik, editor, *Lexical Acquisition: Using On-Line Resources to Build a Lexicon*. Lawrence Erlbaum Associates, Hillsdale, NJ, 1991.

[Tomita, 1986] Masaru Tomita. *Efficient Parsing for Natural Language*. Kluwer Academic Publishers, Hingham, MA, 1986.

[Wittgenstein, 1921] Ludwig Wittgenstein. *Tractatus Logico-Philosophicus*. Routledge, London, 1921.

[Zernik and Jacobs, 1990] U. Zernik and P. Jacobs. Tagging for learning. In *COLING 1990*, Helsinki, Finland, 1990.

[Zernik *et al.*, 1991] U. Zernik, A. Dietsch, and M. Charbonneau. IMToolset programmer's manual. GE-CRD technical report, Artificial Intelligence Laboratory, Schenectady, NY, 1991.

[Zernik, 1992] U. Zernik. Shipping departments vs. shipping pacemakers: Using thematic analysis to enhance tagging accuracy. In *Proceedings of the 11th National Conference on Artificial Intelligence*, San Jose, CA, 1992.

Part II

"Traditional" Information Retrieval

Part II: "Traditional" IR

While Part I emphasized text interpretation, "traditional" Information Retrieval (IR) emphasizes text retrieval. The label ascribed to this group of papers is a bit of an oxymoron, because each of the papers describes an approach that's quite different from current practice.

What's traditional about this work, aside from the fact that these are some of the leaders in the field of IR research, is the rigid emphasis on user-centered evaluation. The methodology of information retrieval forces a "bottom-line" evaluation of every result: If a technique does not significantly increase the percentage of relevant text that a user sees, or significantly decrease the amount of irrelevant text, it is considered altogether unproven. This puts most natural language interpretation work on shaky ground, since it's generally aimed at getting something out of text rather than helping the user find a particular text. Also, most natural language systems simply can't process the range of broad texts and user queries that information retrieval experiments require. The papers by Lewis and Sparck Jones especially challenge the assumption that NL can help IR in its current form, detailing what hasn't worked in the past and what has to work in order for the methods to be truly proven.

Along with IR's skepticism about the role of natural language, there is genuine optimism about improving IR in general. The paper by Croft and Turtle proposes a very new model for retrieval that is firmly rooted in artificial intelligence methods, and the Salton and Buckley paper shows that IR is far from a static discipline, looking at large documents in the context of current on-line text management systems (where most of IR historically has looked at abstracts and smaller texts).

Taken as a group, these papers summarize some of the approaches that have been tried in the past, show the current direction of information retrieval as a field, and pose a challenge for what natural language must do in order to advance IR performance.

Text Retrieval and Inference

W. Bruce Croft
Computer Science Department
University of Massachusetts
Amherst, MA 01003
and
Howard R. Turtle
West Publishing Company
50 West Kellogg Blvd.
St. Paul, MN 55164

Abstract

The basic processes in a text retrieval system are text representation, representation of a user's information need, and comparison of these two representations. These processes are complementary, and improving the effectiveness of text retrieval will involve improving them all. Retrieval models provide the theoretical frameworks for integrating research in these areas. In this paper, we give an overview of the basic text retrieval models and then describe a recent model that is based on probabilistic inference. This model has been tested successfully in a variety of retrieval environments and can potentially make effective use of complex text representations produced by natural language processing techniques.

7.1 Introduction

Information retrieval (IR) is concerned with techniques that can provide effective access to large collections of objects containing primarily text. Objects in the collection may take many forms, for example, scientific journal articles, messages in an electronic mail archive, medical reports, encyclopedia articles, or user manuals. Objects may also exhibit complex structure in which one object is formed by combining several others (e.g., chapters may be viewed as objects that make up a book). In most of what follows, we will assume that the objects of interest are documents.

Information retrieval techniques that facilitate access to document collections have a history that dates back to at least the third century B.C. when the first libraries with large cataloged collections (>100,000 documents) began to appear [Hessel, 1955]. Our interest, however, is in retrieval techniques that can be applied under program control to select items from machine-readable collections. For these machine-readable collections, we have descriptions of the objects in the collection rather than the objects themselves (for objects that exist only in machine readable form, e.g., electronic mail messages, we may have the actual objects). These descriptions usually consist of text describing various attributes of the objects, but may also include descriptors assigned by the creator of the object or some other indexing agent (e.g., controlled vocabulary terms assigned by a human indexer or some automatically assigned classification), or used to describe relationships between objects in the collection (e.g., citations or hypertext links).

Another important aspect of retrieval systems is acquiring a description of the information need. The searcher is our most reliable source of information about whether objects are of interest. We will restrict decisions about "interest" to the context of a single "information need." The idea here is that the searcher has some more or less well defined purpose for seeking items in the collection and will make decisions about interest based on that purpose rather than in the more general context of all objects that may be interesting. If, for example, a searcher is looking for documents that deal with the computational complexity of inference networks, we expect that a document on experimental aircraft would not be judged interesting, even if the searcher finds it to be interesting in another context. This information need is internal to the searcher and we will have only an incomplete description of the information need. This description (a query) is often expressed in natural language, but other forms are possible (e.g., sample documents, Boolean expressions). We also expect that the user's understanding of the information need will change during the search.

We will assume that the description of an information need is a description (albeit imprecise and incomplete) of characteristics that will be found in documents that match the information need. This is a major assumption that is implicit in most information retrieval research (indeed, many retrieval models essentially assume that the description of the information need is a sample document). The expected query form distinguishes information retrieval from closely related activities such as database query processing, question answering, or fact retrieval (e.g., database queries are similar to IR queries in that they represent a description of the characteristics of objects that will match the information need, but the description is entirely in terms of attributes that have a well defined semantics and no true natural language component).

Given a text description of an object and a text description of an information need, a human can generally (but not always) decide if the object would satisfy the information need. The kind of understanding that would allow us to make this decision under program control is, however, well beyond current natural language understanding techniques and our decision about the likelihood that a document matches an information need will be based on the fairly crude representations of the meaning or content that we can currently extract from these descriptions.

Information retrieval, then, can be seen as comprising three basic steps. Given a set of descriptions for objects in the collection and a description of an information need, we must:

1. generate a representation of the meaning or content of each object based on its description,

2. generate a representation of the meaning of the information need, and

3. compare these two representations to select those objects that are most likely to match the information need.

When we fix the details of these representations, how they are generated, and how they are compared we have defined a retrieval model.

Given this three step view of information retrieval, the major IR research issues fall into four broad categories:

1. What makes a good document representation? What are retrievable units and how are they organized? How can a representation be generated from a description of the document?

2. How can we represent the information need and how can we acquire this representation either from a description of the information need or through interaction with the user?

3. How can we compare representations to judge likelihood that a document matches an information need?

4. How can we evaluate the effectiveness of the retrieval process?

These categories are not independent. We cannot, for example, develop a good representation of an information need without considering the document representation and the matching process.

In this paper, we concentrate on the formal foundations for techniques that will improve the process of comparing representations. No current representation technique completely captures the meaning of a document or information need and there is little reason to believe that truly adequate representations will be developed in the near future. Indeed, the notion of a single representation of meaning may not be practical since the meaning of a body of text is so heavily dependent upon the context in which it is to be interpreted.

There are, however, many representation techniques that capture at least some aspects of meaning in text. The artificial intelligence (AI) community, particularly that portion interested in natural language understanding, has developed a number of techniques for representing the meaning of a text [Allen, 1987]. The most successful representations make fairly specific assumptions about the way in which the text should be interpreted (e.g., as a story about one of a small number of topics) and about the kinds of questions that might be asked about the text (e.g., questions about actor's intentions). Some work has been done to adapt the natural language understanding techniques to an information retrieval setting, but there is little near-term hope that these techniques could be used to represent large document collections and arbitrary queries [Sparck Jones and Tait, 1984].

Within the information retrieval community, a number of techniques have been developed that can represent the content of documents and information needs. These representations have a much different flavor than NLP representations. They are generally based on simple, very general, features of documents (e.g., words, citations) and represent simple relationships between features (e.g., phrases) and between documents (e.g., two documents cite the same document). The focus here is on simple, but general, representations that can be applied to most texts rather than on specialized techniques which capture more information but are applicable only in narrow contexts. Information retrieval representations also make extensive use of the statistical properties of representation features and attempt to make use of information produced by human analysis (e.g., manual indexing) when available.

Over the last decade there has been considerable interaction between the AI and information retrieval communities; AI techniques have been adapted to an IR setting and the IR focus on "real" document collections and on thorough experimental evaluation has helped to expand the focus of AI research.

Given the availability of a number of representation techniques that capture some of the meaning of a document or information need, our basic premise is that decisions about which documents match an information need should make use of as many of the representation forms as practical. The remainder of this paper develops a theoretical framework for retrieval that allows multiple representations to be combined.

In the next section, we describe the major types of retrieval models. Section 7.3 presents the motivation for a retrieval model based on inference. In Section 7.4, we review related research on inference and network models. Sections 7.5 and 7.6 describe the basic inference network model and how it is used. Section 7.7 addresses the issue of causality in a network model. The final section discusses recent results and research directions.

7.2   Current Retrieval Models

A retrieval model fixes the details of the representations used for documents and information needs, describes how these are generated from available descriptions, and how they are compared. If the model has a clear theoretical basis we call it a formal retrieval model; if the model makes little or no appeal to an underlying theory we call it *ad hoc*. We use the terms theory and model here in the mathematical or logical sense in which a theory refers to a set of axioms and inference rules that allow derivation of new theorems. A model is an embodiment of the theory in which we define the set of objects about which assertions can be made and restrict the ways in which classes of objects can interact.

Four retrieval models are particularly important in IR research: the Boolean, cluster-based, probabilistic, and vector-space models. Most of the commercial and prototype IR systems currently available are based on some variation of these models, and some understanding of them is necessary for our discussion of the inference net model in the next sections.

Boolean. Boolean retrieval forms the basis of most major commercial retrieval services, but is generally believed to be difficult to use and has poor recall and precision performance[1] since the model does not rank documents. In the Boolean model we have a finite set of representation concepts or features $R = \{r_1, \ldots, r_k\}$ that can be assigned to documents. A document is simply an assignment of representation concepts and this assignment is often represented by a binary-valued vector of length k. The assignment of a representation concept r_i to a document is represented by setting the ith element of the vector to *true*. All elements corresponding to features not assigned to a document are set to *false*.

An information need is described by a Boolean expression in which operands are representation concepts. Any document whose set of representation concepts represents an assignment that satisfies the Boolean expression is deemed to match the information need, all other documents fail to match the information need. This evaluation partitions the set of documents, but provides no information about the relative likelihood that documents within the same partition will match the information need.

Relevance in Boolean retrieval, then, is defined in terms of satisfiability of a first-order logic expression given a set of document representations as axioms. Several attempts have been made to extend the basic Boolean model to provide document ranking.

Cluster-based retrieval. Cluster-based retrieval is based on the Cluster Hypothesis which asserts that similar documents will match the same information needs [van Rijsbergen, 1979]. Rather than comparing representations of individual documents to the representation of the information need, we first form clusters of documents using any of several clustering algorithms and similarity measures. For each cluster, we then create an "average" or representative document and compare this cluster representative to the information need to determine which clusters best match. We then retrieve the clusters that are most likely to match the information need rather than

---

[1] We use the measures precision and recall when describing retrieval performance. Precision is the proportion of a retrieved set that is actually relevant. Recall is the proportion of all relevant documents that are actually retrieved. These and other measures are discussed in [van Rijsbergen, 1979].

the individual documents. There are several ways to identify the clusters to be retrieved, particularly when using hierarchical clustering techniques that allow navigation of the cluster hierarchy.

Since many techniques are used to compare the query with the cluster representative, there is no single definition of relevance for cluster-based retrieval. Rather, relevance is partially defined by the model that forms the basis of the comparison. The similarity measures used to define clusters and the method used to create the cluster representatives also play a part in defining relevance since they determine which documents will be judged similar to a cluster representative that matches the information need.

Vector-space retrieval. In the vector-space model, we have a set of representation concepts or features $R = \{r_1, \ldots, r_k\}$. Documents and queries are represented as vectors of length k in which each element corresponds to a real-valued weight assigned to an element of the representation set. Several techniques have been used to compute these weights, the most common being *tf.idf* weights which are based on the frequency of a term in a single document (*tf*) and its frequency in the entire collection (*idf*). These *tf.idf* weights are discussed in more detail in [Salton and McGill, 1983].

Documents and queries are compared using any of several similarity functions, the most common function being the cosine of the angle between their representation vectors.

Since several techniques have been used to compute weights for the vector elements, the vector-space model has no single form of document or query representation, although all representations have a common form. Similarly, since several similarity functions have been used, relevance has no single definition.

The vector-space model is historically important since it forms the basis for a large body of retrieval research that can be traced back to the 1960's. The vector-space model has been criticized as an *ad hoc* model since there is relatively little theoretical justification for many of its variations.

Probabilistic retrieval. Probabilistic retrieval is based on the Probability Ranking Principal which asserts that the best overall retrieval effectiveness will be achieved when documents are ranked in decreasing order of probability of relevance [Robertson, 1977].

There are several different probabilistic formulations which differ mainly in the way in which they estimate the probability of relevance. Using a representative model, a document d_i and an information need f_j are represented as the now familiar vectors of length k in which each element is true if the corresponding representation concept is assigned to the document or query. If we let F represent the set of representations for information needs and D represent the set of document representations, then we can define an event space $F \times D$ and our task becomes one of determining which of these document-request pairs would be judged relevant, that is, estimating $P(R|d_i, f_j)$. We then use Bayes' theorem and a set of independence assumptions about the distribution of representation concepts in the documents and queries to derive a ranking function that computes $P(R|d_i, f_j)$ in terms of the probabilities that individual representation concepts will be assigned to relevant and non-relevant documents. Different independence assumptions lead to different forms of the model. Given estimates for these two probabilities (say, from a sample of documents judged relevant and from the entire collection), we can compute $P(R|d_i, f_j)$.

Probabilistic models are in many ways similar to the vector-space model [Bookstein, 1982; Turtle and Croft, 1992]. Both can be considered to be generalizations of the Boolean model in that they can support partial matching using Boolean queries. Probabilistic models, however, provide a sounder theoretical base for the design of IR systems, and have significantly contributed to our understanding of some aspects of IR, such as term weighting, ranking, and relevance feedback.

7.3 Retrieval Based on Inference and Networks

Recent retrieval research has suggested that significant improvements in retrieval performance will require techniques that, in some sense, "understand" the content of documents and queries [van Rijsbergen, 1986; Croft, 1987] and can be used to infer probable relationships between documents and queries. In this view, information retrieval is an inference or evidential reasoning process in which we estimate the probability that a user's information need, expressed as one or more queries, is met given a document as "evidence."

The idea that retrieval is an inference or evidential reasoning process is not new. Cooper's logical relevance [Cooper, 1971] is based on deductive relationships between representations of documents and information needs. Wilson's situational relevance [Wilson, 1973] extends this notion to incorporate inductive or uncertain inference based on the degree to which documents support information needs. The techniques required to support these kinds of inference are similar to those used in expert systems that must reason with uncertain information. A number of competing inference models have been developed for these kinds of expert systems and several of these models can be adapted to the document retrieval task.

In this paper, we describe a retrieval model based on inference networks. This model is intended to

- Support the use of multiple document representation schemes. Research has shown that a given query will retrieve different documents when applied to different representations, even when the average retrieval performance achieved with each representation is the same. Katzer, for example, found little overlap in documents retrieved using seven different representations, but found that documents retrieved by multiple representations were likely to be relevant [Katzer *et al.*, 1982]. Similar results have been obtained when comparing term- with cluster-based representations [Croft and Harper, 1979] and term- with citation-based representations [Fox *et al.*, 1988].

- Allow results from different queries and query types to be combined. Given a single natural language description of an information need, different searchers will formulate different queries to represent that need and will retrieve different documents, even when average performance is the same for each searcher [McGill *et al.*, 1979; Katzer *et al.*, 1982]. Again, documents retrieved by multiple searchers are more likely to be relevant. A description of an information need can be used to generate several query representations (e.g., probabilistic, Boolean), each using a different query strategy and each capturing different aspects of the information need. These different search strategies are known to retrieve different documents for the same underlying information need [Croft, 1987].

- Facilitate flexible matching between the terms or concepts mentioned in queries and those assigned to documents. The poor match between the vocabulary used to express queries and the vocabulary used to represent documents appears to be a major cause of poor recall [Furnas *et al.*, 1987]. Recall can be improved using domain knowledge to match query and representation concepts without significantly degrading precision.

The resulting formal retrieval model integrates several previous models (probabilistic, Boolean, and cluster-based) in a single theoretical framework [Turtle, 1990]. Moreover, retrieval results produced by these disparate models can be combined to form an overall assessment of relevance. In the network model, multiple document and query representations are treated as evidence which is combined to estimate the probability that a document satisfies a user's information need.

Before describing the details of the inference net retrieval model, we will summarize related research in the areas of uncertain inference and networks in IR.

7.3.1   Uncertain Inference

A number of automated inference mechanisms have been proposed, principally in the context of expert systems. Of particular interest are inference techniques that deal with uncertain information or evidence and with inference based on this evidence. Early approaches tended to be ad hoc (e.g., MYCIN's certainty factors [Shortliffe, 1976] or PROSPECTOR's use of probability [Duda *et al.*, 1976; Duda *et al.*, 1978]). The development of more formal techniques has led to heated debate among several competing schools. We will not review the debate in detail (see [Kanal and Lemmer, 1986; Lemmer and Kanal, 1988] for surveys), but three main approaches have emerged.

The first approach relies on symbolic reasoning [Cohen, 1985; Fox, 1986; Doyle, 1979] in which degrees of certainty are encoded using a discrete set of values (certain, somewhat certain, ...) that are then used with a deductive reasoning system. The second approach uses fuzzy set theory [Zadeh, 1983; Zadeh, 1986a]. The third approach, and the one we will concentrate on, is based on probabilistic methods.

Two main probabilistic approaches are in use. The first uses conventional probabilistic methods [Pearl, 1988; Lauritzen and Spiegelhalter, 1988; Andersen et al., 1989] and the second uses the Dempster-Shafer theory of evidence [Dempster, 1968; Shafer, 1976; Shafer, 1987; Zadeh, 1986b]. The two approaches are similar; the Dempster-Shafer approach represents an attempt to generalize Bayesian methods in order to cope with the fact that a complete probability distribution is rarely available. Spiegelhalter [Spiegelhalter, 1986] compares the Dempster-Shafer and Bayesian methods. Pearl [Pearl, 1988] compares Dempster-Shafer with Bayesian inference networks and describes conditions under which they are equivalent.

Other probabilistic approaches have been developed but have not been as widely accepted. Nilsson's probabilistic logic [Nilsson, 1986] represents an alternative method of dealing with incomplete probability models by estimating bounds for probabilities rather than point estimates. Quinlan's INFERNO [Quinlan, 1983] incorporates these kinds of probability bounds.

The same three inference approaches (symbolic, fuzzy set, probabilistic) are evident in information retrieval research. Symbolic approaches include those based on Boolean logic and on relational algebra [Blair, 1988] or calculus. Retrieval models based on fuzzy sets have been proposed (for example, [Bookstein, 1985; Radecki, 1979]) and a wide variety of probabilistic models have been explored [Maron and Kuhns, 1960; Robertson and Sparck Jones, 1976; Cooper and Maron, 1978; van Rijsbergen, 1979; Fuhr, 1989].

Van Rijsbergen [van Rijsbergen, 1986; van Rijsbergen, 1989] discusses the nature of inference in information retrieval and has proposed the use of non-classical logics for determining the degree to which a document implies or matches a query. Croft [Croft, 1987; Croft et al., 1989] has developed the notion of plausible inference in information retrieval and suggested that multiple sources of evidence should be combined to infer the probability that a document matches a query.

7.3.2   Network Models in Information Retrieval

Graph and network structures have been widely used in information retrieval. Salton [Salton, 1968] describes early use of tree and graph models in information retrieval and describes implementation of many of the basic structures used in retrieval systems (e.g., inverted files, dictionaries) in graph theoretic terms. Salton and McGill [Salton and McGill, 1983] and van Rijsbergen [van Rijsbergen, 1979] provide more current introductions to common retrieval structures, many of which are graph or network based. Other uses of networks in information retrieval can be loosely categorized as support for clustering, rule-based inference, structure matching, browsing, spreading activation, and connectionist approaches.

Clustering. Networks arise naturally in the representation of document and term clusters. Willett [Willett, 1988] reviews document clustering techniques and Sparck Jones [Sparck Jones, 1971; Sparck Jones, 1974] reviews term clustering techniques.

Rule-based inference. In RUBRIC [Tong *et al.*, 1983; Tong and Shapiro, 1985], Tong represents queries as a set of rules in an evaluation tree that specifies how individual document features can be combined to estimate the certainty that a document matches the query. One of the objectives of the RUBRIC design was to allow comparison of different uncertainty calculi and RUBRIC has recently been reformulated to use inference networks [Fung *et al.*, 1990]. Rule-based inference using network structures has been used with thesaurus information to improve the match between document and query vocabularies [Croft and Thompson, 1987; Shoval, 1985]. Semantic networks have also been used to represent thesaurus-like information [Smith *et al.*, 1989; Monarch and Carbonell, 1987].

Structure matching. Structure matching forms the basis of most retrieval techniques based on semantic networks. Early work by Salton [Salton, 1968] describes the use of graphs to represent the syntactic structure of text and graph matching to identify similar text content. Lewis, Croft, and Bhandaru [Lewis *et al.*, 1989] discuss the use of frame-based networks produced by natural language parsers to represent documents and queries and network matching functions that can be used for retrieval. Structure matching also underlies the simpler network structures used by Belkin *et al.* to represent anomalous states of knowledge (ASK) [Belkin and Kwasnik, 1986; Oddy *et al.*, 1986] regarding document and query content.

Browsing. When networks are used to represent documents and indexing information, browsing can be used to help users locate relevant material. Browsing is common in thesaurus systems. Oddy's THOMAS system [Oddy, 1977] uses browsing in a simple network of documents and terms to build a model of the user's information need. Croft and Thompson use browsing in a more complex network as one search strategy in I^3R [Croft and Thompson, 1987].

Browsing is an important technique for accessing text in hypertext networks. Croft and Turtle [Croft and Turtle, 1989] and Frisse and Cousins [Frisse and Cousins, 1989] describe retrieval models for hypertext networks.

Spreading activation. Spreading activation is a search technique in which a network representation of a document collection is used to retrieve documents that are "similar" to a query. The query is used to activate a set of nodes in a representation network which, in turn, activate neighboring nodes. Halting conditions and weighting functions vary, but the pattern of activation is used to rank documents for presentation to the user. Croft [Croft *et al.*,

1989] used spreading activation in a network based on document clustering. Cohen and Kjeldson [Cohen and Kjeldsen, 1987] used spreading activation in a more complex representation network with typed edges.

Connectionist approaches. Connectionist approaches are similar to spreading activation. They differ in that the connectionist links do not have a clear semantic interpretation (they simply characterize the "association" between network nodes) and the weights associated with links are learned from training samples or user guidance. Croft and Thompson [1984] use a connectionist network in an attempt to learn to select a query strategy. Brachman and McGuiness [1988] use a connectionist approach to retrieve facts from a knowledge base on programming languages. Other connectionist approaches to information retrieval are described by Belew [1989] and Kwok [1989].

The connectionist retrieval approaches that have been reported use simple networks with no hidden units and thus learn simple linear discriminant functions. The inference network model supports dependence structures that require nonlinear functions and require more complex learning strategies.

7.4 The Inference Network Model

Probabilistic methods are among the most effective tools known for improving retrieval effectiveness and information retrieval research has produced a substantial body of knowledge about the statistical properties of text. In this section, we will describe how Bayesian inference networks can be used to extend this line of research.

A Bayesian inference network is a directed, acyclic dependency graph in which nodes represent propositional variables or constants and edges represent dependence relations between propositions. If a proposition represented by a node p "causes" or implies the proposition represented by node q, we draw a directed edge from p to q. The node q contains a matrix (a *link matrix*[2]) that specifies $P(q|p)$ for all possible values of the two variables. When a node has multiple parents, the matrix specifies the dependence of that node on the set of parents (π_q) and characterizes the dependence relationship between that node and all nodes representing its potential causes. Given a set of prior probabilities for the roots of the DAG, these networks can be used to compute the probability or degree of belief associated with all remaining nodes.

Different restrictions on the topology of the network and assumptions about the way in which the connected nodes interact lead to different schemes for combining probabilities. In general, these schemes have two components which operate independently: a *predictive* component in which parent nodes provide support for their children (the degree to which we believe a proposition depends on the degree to which we believe the propositions that might

---

[2] The link matrix is actually a link *tensor* [Turtle, 1990].

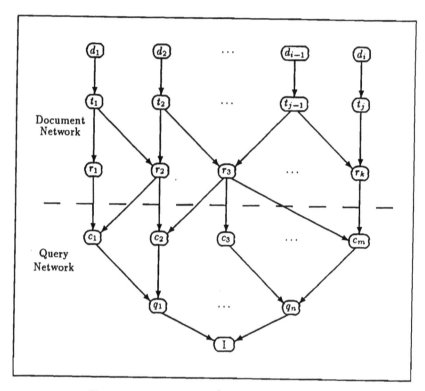

Figure 7.1: Basic document inference network

cause it), and a *diagnostic* component in which children provide support for their parents (if our belief in a proposition increases or decreases, so does our belief in its potential causes). The propagation of probabilities through the net can be done using information passed between adjacent nodes.

Bayesian inference networks provide a framework for describing complex joint probability distributions. To apply this framework to IR, we must use it to describe the important propositional variables and dependence relations in the retrieval process. There are many ways of doing this, and each network topology represents a different probabilistic retrieval model. The following model was designed to be a generalization of previous models and computationally efficient.

The basic document retrieval inference network, shown in Figure 7.1, consists of two component networks: a document network and a query network. The document network represents the document collection using a variety of document representation schemes. The document network is built once for a given collection, and its structure does not change during query processing. The query network consists of a single node, which represents the user's information need and one or more query representations, which express that information need. A query network is built for each information need and is modified during query processing as existing queries are refined or new queries are added in an attempt to better characterize the information need. The document and query networks are joined by links between representation concepts and query concepts. All nodes in the inference network are binary-valued and take on values from the set $\{false, true\}$.

7.4.1 Document Network

The document network consists of document nodes (d_i's), text representation nodes (t_j's), and concept representation nodes (r_k's). If we let D be the set of documents, T be the set of text representations, and R be the set of representation concepts, where the cardinality of these sets is n_d, n_t, and n_r, respectively, then the event space represented by the document network is $E_d = D \times T \times R$. Since all propositions are binary-valued, the size of the event space is $2^{n_d} \cdot 2^{n_t} \cdot 2^{n_r}$.

Each document node represents an actual document in the collection. A document node corresponds to the event that a specific document has been observed. The form of the document represented depends on the collection and its intended use, but we will assume that a document is a well defined object and will focus on traditional document types (e.g., monographs, journal articles, office documents, ...).

Document nodes correspond to abstract documents rather than their physical representations. A text representation node or text node corresponds to a specific text representation of a document. A text node corresponds to the event that a text representation has been observed. We will focus here on traditional document texts, but one can easily imagine other content types for documents (e.g., figures), and multi-media documents might have several content representations (e.g., audio or video). In these cases, a single document might have multiple physical representations. Similarly, a single text content might be shared by more than one document. While this sharing is rare (an example would be a journal article that appears in both a serial issue and in a reprint collection) and is not generally represented in current retrieval models, it is common in hypertext systems. For clarity, we will only consider text representations and will assume a one-to-one correspondence between documents and texts. The dependence of a text upon the document is represented in the network by an arc from the document node to the text node.

The content representation nodes or representation nodes can be divided into several subsets, each corresponding to a single representation technique that has been applied to the document texts. For example, if a collection has been indexed using automatic phrase extraction and manually assigned index terms, then the set of representation nodes will consist of two distinct subsets or content representation types with disjoint domains. Thus, if the phrase "information retrieval" has been extracted and "information retrieval" has been manually assigned as an index term, then two representation nodes with distinct meanings will be created. One corresponds to the event that "information retrieval" has been automatically extracted from a subset of the collection, the second corresponds to the event that "information retrieval" has been manually assigned to a (presumably distinct) subset of the collection. We represent the assignment of a specific representation concept to a document by a directed arc to the representation node from each text node corresponding to a document to which the concept has been assigned. For now we assume that the presence or absence of a link corresponds to a binary assigned/not assigned distinction; that is, there are no partial or weighted assignments.

In principle, the number of representation schemes is unlimited. In addition to phrase extraction and manually assigned terms, we would expect representations based on natural language processing and automatic keyword extraction. Refinements that can be applied to multiple representations (e.g., thesauri, term clustering, or inference rules) are discussed in [Turtle, 1990]. For any real document collection, however, the number of representations used will be fixed and relatively small. The potential domain of each representation scheme may also be unlimited, but the actual number of primitive representation concepts defined for a given collection is fixed by the collection. The domain for most automated representation schemes is generally bounded by some function of the collection size (e.g., the number of keywords cannot exceed the number of words in a collection). For manual representation schemes the domain size is limited by the number of documents and the amount of time a human expert can invest to analyze each document.

The basic document network shown in Figure 7.1 is a simple three-level directed acyclic graph (DAG) in which document nodes are roots, text nodes are interior nodes, and representation nodes are leaves. Document nodes have exactly one text node as a child and each text node has one or more representation nodes as children.

Each document node has a prior probability associated with it that describes the probability of observing that document; this prior probability will generally be set to 1/(collection size) and will be small for reasonable collection sizes. Each text node contains a specification of its dependence upon its parent; by assumption, this dependence is complete: A text node is observed ($t_i = true$) exactly when its parent document is observed ($d_i = true$).

Each representation node contains a specification of the conditional probability associated with the node given its set of parent text nodes. This specification incorporates the effect of any indexing weights (e.g., term frequency for each parent text) or term weights (e.g., inverse document frequency) associated with the representation concept. While, in principle, this would require $O(2^n)$ space for a node with n parents, in practice we will generally use canonical representations that will allow us to compute the required conditional probabilities when needed. These canonical schemes are described in

[Turtle, 1990] and require $O(n)$ space if we need to weight the contribution of each parent or $O(1)$ space if parents are to be treated uniformly.

7.4.2   Query Network

The query network is an "inverted" DAG with a single leaf, that corresponds to the event that an information need is met and multiple roots, that correspond to the concepts that express the information need. As shown in Figure 7.1, a set of intermediate query nodes may also be used in cases where multiple query representations are used to express the information need. These nodes are a representation convenience; it is always possible to eliminate them by increasing the complexity of the distribution specified at the node representing the information need.

If we let C represent the set of query concepts and Q represent the set of queries, where n_c and n_q are the cardinalities of these sets, then the event space represented by the query network is $E_q = C \times Q \times I$. Since we can always eliminate query nodes, $|E_q| \leq 2^{n_c+1}$. The event space represented by the entire inference network is then $E_d \times E_q$.

In general, the user's information need is internal to the user and is not precisely understood. We attempt to make the meaning of an information need explicit by expressing it in the form of one or more queries that have a formal interpretation. It is unlikely that any of these queries will correspond precisely to the information need, but some will better characterize the information need than others, and several query representations taken together may be a better representation of the information need than any of the individual queries.

The roots of the query network are query concepts, the primitive concepts used to express the information need. A single query concept node may have several representation concept nodes as parents. A query concept node contains a specification of the probabilistic dependence of the query concept on its set of parent representation concepts. The query concept nodes define the mapping between the concepts used to represent the document collection and the concepts that make up the queries. In the simplest case, the query concepts are constrained to be the same as the representation concepts and each query concept has exactly one parent representation node. In a slightly more complex example, the query concept "information retrieval" may have as parents both the node corresponding to "information retrieval" as a phrase and the node corresponding to "information retrieval" as a manually assigned term.

As we add new forms of content representation to the document network and allow the use of query concepts that do not explicitly appear in any document representation, the number of parents associated with a single query concept will tend to increase. In many ways, a query concept is similar to a representation concept that is derived from other representation concepts, and in some cases it will be useful to "promote" a query concept to a representation concept. For example, suppose that a researcher is looking for information on a recently developed process that is unlikely to be explicitly identified in any existing representation scheme. The researcher is sufficiently motivated, however, to work with the retrieval system to describe how this new concept might be inferred from other representation concepts. If this new concept definition is of general interest, it can be added to the collection of representation concepts. The process of defining new representation concepts is similar to that used in RUBRIC [Tong et al., 1983; Tong and Shapiro, 1985], where a user might add a rule that asserts that the concept "car bomb" should be inferred with some level of certainty if the term "car" and "bomb" occur in the same sentence. The RUBRIC approach differs in that all representation concepts are manually defined, whereas most representation concepts in an inference network are created automatically.

The attachment of the query concept nodes to the document network has no effect on the basic structure of the document network. None of the existing links need change and none of the conditional probability specifications stored in the nodes are modified.

A query node represents a distinct query representation and corresponds to the event that the query representation is satisfied. Each query node contains a specification of the dependence of the query on the query concepts it contains. The content of the link matrices that contain the conditional probabilities is discussed further in [Turtle, 1990], but it is worth noting that the form of the link matrix is largely determined by the query type; a link matrix simulating a Boolean query is very different from a matrix simulating a probabilistic or weighted query.

Multiple query representations can be obtained from many sources. It is possible that the user might provide more than one form (e.g., a natural language description and a sample document), but it is more likely that additional forms will be generated automatically based on the original natural language query or using information obtained by an intelligent interface. In cases where a search intermediary is used, we may have multiple human-generated query representations.

The single leaf representing the information need corresponds to the event that an information need is met. In general, we cannot predict with certainty whether a user's information need will be met by an arbitrary document collection. The query network is intended to capture the way in which meeting the user's information need depends on documents and their representations. Moreover, the query network is intended to allow us to combine information from multiple document representations and to combine queries of different types to form a single, formally justified estimate of the probability that the user's information need is met. If the inference network correctly characterizes the dependence of the information need on the collection, the computed probability provides a good estimate.

7.4.3   Causation in Bayesian Inference Networks

The notion of causation, that one random variable can be perceived as causing another, is fundamental to Bayesian inference networks. By drawing an arc from node a to node b we are asserting that a in some sense causes b. If a is observed, then our belief in b is fixed by that observation (assuming b has no other parents). If we later observe b to have a value that conflicts with our computed belief we suspect that either the conditional probability $P(b|a)$ is incorrect or that the topology is wrong (either b has causes we haven't recognized or a does not, in fact, cause b). If, however, we first observe b then our belief in a changes because a is a potential explanation for b; that is, the observation of b constitutes evidence confirming or disconfirming a.

While in many cases the direction of causation is clear (e.g., most instances of physical causation), in many others it is difficult to distinguish between causal and evidential support. For example, our network in Figure 7.1 asserts that our belief in a set of query concepts causes our belief in the query that contains them. We could also have argued that our belief that the query is a representation of the information need causes our belief that the query concepts are useful. In this case we view the query concepts as evidence that supports our belief in the query.

In our network in Figure 7.1 we assert that the observation of a document (or a set of documents) causes our belief in a text representation, which causes our belief in a set of representation concepts, which in turn cause belief in a set of query concepts, which cause our belief in a set of queries, which finally cause our belief that the document supports the information need. In fact, there are (at least) two other topologies that have some intuitive appeal. In the first, we simply invert the entire network. This structure asserts that the information need causes our belief in the queries, which cause our belief in the query concepts they contain. While this chain of causation is at least plausible, the next step, in which query concepts cause our belief in representation concepts, is not very appealing. Since documents and their representations have an existence independent of any query network, the query concepts cannot cause the representation concepts; our belief that a representation concept is assigned to a set of documents is not altered by the processing of a query.

7.5   Use of the Inference Network

The inference network we have described is intended to capture all of the significant probabilistic dependencies among the variables represented by nodes in the document and query networks. Given the prior probabilities associated with the documents (roots) and the conditional probabilities associated with the interior nodes, we can compute the posterior probability or belief associated with each node in the network. Further, if the value of any variable represented in the network becomes known we can use the network to recompute the probabilities associated with all remaining nodes based on this "evidence."

The network, taken as a whole, represents the dependence of a user's information need on the documents in a collection where the dependence is mediated by document and query representations. When the query network is first built and attached to the document network we compute the belief associated with each node in the query network. The initial value at the node representing the information need is the probability that the information need is met given that no specific document in the collection has been observed and all documents are equally likely (or unlikely). If we now observe a single document d_i and attach evidence to the network asserting $d_i = true$ with all remaining document nodes set to $false$ (referred to as $instantiating\ d_i$), we can compute a new belief for every node in the network given $d_i = true$. In particular, we can compute the probability that the information need is met given that d_i has been observed in the collection. We can now remove this evidence and instead assert that some d_j, $i \neq j$ has been observed. By repeating this process we can compute the probability that the information need is met given each document in the collection and rank the documents accordingly.

In principle, we need not consider each document in isolation but could look for the subset of documents that produce the highest probability that the information need is met. While a general solution to this best-subset problem is intractable, in some cases good heuristic approximations are possible. Best-subset rankings have been considered in IR [Stirling, 1975; Bookstein, 1989], and similar problems arise in pattern recognition, medical diagnosis, and truth-maintenance systems. (See [Pearl, 1988] for a discussion of the best-subset or belief revision problem in Bayesian networks.) At present, we consider only documents in isolation since the approach is computationally simpler. This simplification is an important factor in reducing the exponential complexity of network evaluation.

The document network is built once for a given collection. Given one or more queries, we then build a query network that attempts to characterize the dependence of the information need on the collection. If the ranking produced by the initial query network is inadequate, we must add additional information to the query network or refine its structure to better characterize the meaning of the existing queries. This feedback process is similar to that used in current retrieval systems [Salton and McGill, 1983].

7.6   An Example

In this section, we present a simple example inference network and show how queries are evaluated.

The inference network fragment shown in Figure 7.2 contains two documents and four representation concepts. Document d_1 discusses the use of

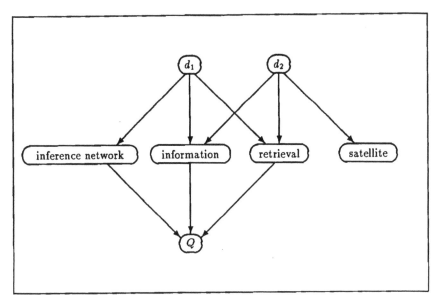

Figure 7.2: Inference network fragment

inference networks for information retrieval and is represented by the phrase *inference network* and the keywords *information* and *retrieval* (among others). Document d_2 discusses the retrieval of satellites from low-earth orbit and is represented by the keywords *information, retrieval,* and *satellite*. A single query has been attached containing the phrase *inference network* and the keywords *information* and *retrieval*. For the purposes of this example we are using only features of a simplified form of the basic model shown in Figure 7.1. We will use this network to estimate $bel(Q|d_1)$ and $bel(Q|d_2)$.

In a belief network the absence of any evidential support for or against a proposition is represented by $bel = 0.5$. Positive evidential support is represented by beliefs in the range $(0.5, 1.0]$ with $bel = 1.0$ representing certainty that the proposition is true. Similarly, negative evidential support is represented by beliefs in the range $[0.0, 0.5)$ with $bel = 0.0$ representing certainty that the proposition is false. Our first task, then, is to find estimates for belief that lie in the appropriate intervals.

Several weighting schemes have been proposed in which the belief in a representation concept depends on the frequency with which the concept occurs in a document and on the frequency of the concept in the collection (see, for example, [Edmundson and Wyllys, 1961]). We will assume that belief in a representation concept is proportional to the within-document frequency (*tf*) and inversely proportional to the frequency of the concept in the collection. The collection frequency component is generally expressed as

Table 7.1: Frequencies and idf and tf weights

	frequency	$nidf$ score	tf_{d_1}	tf_{d_2}	ntf_{d_1}	ntf_{d_2}
inference network	16	0.77	3	0	0.6	0.0
information	16461	0.18	3	2	0.6	0.5
retrieval	820	0.43	5	1	1.0	0.25
satellite	2675	0.33	0	4	0.0	1.0

the term's inverse document frequency (idf) which is given by

$$idf = \log(\frac{\text{collection size}}{\text{concept frequency}}).$$

We will normalize both tf and idf to the range $[0, 1]$ by dividing tf by the maximum tf value for any term in the document and dividing idf by the maximum possible idf value in the collection (the idf score for a term that occurs once). For concept i that occurs tf_{ij} times in document j and f_i times in the entire collection, we have

$$ntf_{ij} = \frac{tf_{ij}}{max\_tf_j} \qquad (7.1)$$

$$nidf_i = \frac{\log(\frac{\text{collection size}}{f_i})}{\log(\text{collection size})}. \qquad (7.2)$$

Techniques for estimating these beliefs are discussed in detail in [Turtle, 1990], but for the purposes of the example, we will assume that $P(r_i = \text{true}|d_j = \text{true})$ is given by

$$P(r_i = \text{true}|d_j = \text{true}) = 0.5 + (0.5 \cdot ntf_{ij} \cdot nidf_i) \qquad (7.3)$$

and that

$$P(r_i = \text{true}|\text{all parents false}) = 0.0. \qquad (7.4)$$

(As discussed in [Turtle, 1990], this is not a very good estimate, but it simplifies the example and is the estimate used in most probabilistic models.) Link matrices can be built directly from these estimates.

Arcs are drawn from a document only to representation concepts that have been assigned to that document. When a document is instantiated it provides equal support for all members of the set of assigned representation concepts; all other representation concepts receive no support (this is not the case in some extended forms of the model). Any representation concept with no support is believed to be false (not observed or $bel = 0$). Any representation concept that receives support is believed to the degree specified in equation 7.3.

Table 7.1 gives frequency and $nidf$ scores based on a small NTIS database ($n = 136,609$) and the tf and ntf values for the two documents. We assume that $max\_tf_{d_1} = 5$ and that $max\_tf_{d_2} = 4$.

7.6.1   Simple Query

If we interpret the query in Figure 7.2 as a simple combination of concepts, from equation (7.3) we have

$$
\begin{aligned}
P(inference\ network = true | d_1 = true) &= 0.5 + 0.5 \cdot 0.6 \cdot 0.77 \\
&= 0.731
\end{aligned}
$$

which results in a link matrix of

$$
L_{inference\ net} = \begin{pmatrix} 1.000 & 0.269 \\ 0.000 & 0.731 \end{pmatrix}.
$$

For the *information* node we must compute beliefs for both parents, so

$$
\begin{aligned}
P(information = true | d_1 = true) &= 0.5 + 0.5 \cdot 0.6 \cdot 0.18 \\
&= 0.554 \\
P(information = true | d_2 = true) &= 0.5 + 0.5 \cdot 0.5 \cdot 0.18 \\
&= 0.545
\end{aligned}
$$

which results in a link matrix of

$$
L_{information} = \begin{pmatrix} 1.000 & 0.455 & 0.446 & 0.446 \\ 0.000 & 0.545 & 0.554 & 0.554 \end{pmatrix}.
$$

The last column of this link matrix is unused since only one document can be instantiated at a time. It is set to the maximum of the individual document beliefs.

Using the same procedure, the link matrix for *retrieval* is

$$
L_{retrieval} = \begin{pmatrix} 1.000 & 0.285 & 0.446 & 0.285 \\ 0.000 & 0.715 & 0.554 & 0.715 \end{pmatrix}
$$

and for *satellite* we have

$$
L_{satellite} = \begin{pmatrix} 1.000 & 0.335 \\ 0.000 & 0.665 \end{pmatrix}.
$$

There are several ways to estimate the matrix at Q. We would generally estimate the matrix based on the frequency of each term in the query text, but for the example we will assume that the user has indicated that the probability that a document matches his information need if it contains none of the query terms is 0.1, that the probability for a document containing all of the terms is 0.9, that the phrase *inference network* is twice as important as either keyword, and that the probabilities for multiple terms are additive. The link matrix can then be estimated as

$$
L_Q = \begin{pmatrix} 0.9 & 0.7 & 0.7 & 0.5 & 0.5 & 0.3 & 0.3 & 0.1 \\ 0.1 & 0.3 & 0.3 & 0.5 & 0.5 & 0.7 & 0.7 & 0.9 \end{pmatrix}.
$$

Instantiating d_1 results in

bel(inference network)	=	0.731	bel(information)	=	0.554
bel(retrieval)	=	0.554	bel(satellite)	=	0.000

which gives

$$
\begin{aligned}
bel(Q|d_1) &= 0.1 \cdot 0.269 \cdot 0.446 \cdot 0.446 + 0.3 \cdot 0.269 \cdot 0.446 \cdot 0.554 \\
&\quad + 0.3 \cdot 0.269 \cdot 0.554 \cdot 0.446 + 0.5 \cdot 0.269 \cdot 0.554 \cdot 0.554 \\
&\quad + 0.5 \cdot 0.731 \cdot 0.446 \cdot 0.446 + 0.7 \cdot 0.731 \cdot 0.446 \cdot 0.554 \\
&\quad + 0.7 \cdot 0.731 \cdot 0.554 \cdot 0.446 + 0.9 \cdot 0.731 \cdot 0.554 \cdot 0.554 \\
&= 0.614.
\end{aligned}
$$

Instantiating d_2 results in

bel(inference network)	=	0.000	bel(information)	=	0.545
bel(retrieval)	=	0.715	bel(satellite)	=	0.665

which gives

$$
\begin{aligned}
bel(Q|d_2) &= 0.1 \cdot 1 \cdot 0.455 \cdot 0.285 + 0.3 \cdot 1 \cdot 0.455 \cdot 0.715 + 0.3 \cdot 1 \cdot 0.545 \cdot 0.285 \\
&\quad + 0.5 \cdot 1 \cdot 0.545 \cdot 0.715 + 0.5 \cdot 0 \cdot 0.455 \cdot 0.285 + 0.7 \cdot 0 \cdot 0.455 \cdot 0.71 \\
&\quad + 0.7 \cdot 0 \cdot 0.545 \cdot 0.285 + 0.9 \cdot 0 \cdot 0.545 \cdot 0.715 \\
&= 0.352.
\end{aligned}
$$

If relevance judgments were available, they could be used to adjust link matrix values at Q and to produce refined estimates of $bel(Q)$. As mentioned previously, in practice link matrices are replaced by a variety of canonical forms that are more efficient to store and compute [Turtle and Croft, 1991].

7.6.2   Boolean Query

If the query of Figure 7.2 is interpreted as the Boolean conjunction

"inference net" *and* information *and* retrieval

rather than a simple query, we would use the following link matrix form

$$
L_Q = \begin{pmatrix} 1 & 1 & 1 & 1 & 1 & 1 & 1 & 0 \\ 0 & 0 & 0 & 0 & 0 & 0 & 0 & 1 \end{pmatrix}.
$$

Using the same term weights as above, our beliefs in the representation concepts would be unchanged, and evaluation of the Boolean query would result in

$$
\begin{aligned}
bel(Q|d_1) &= 0 \cdot 0.269 \cdot 0.446 \cdot 0.446 + 0 \cdot 0.269 \cdot 0.446 \cdot 0.554 \\
&\quad + 0 \cdot 0.269 \cdot 0.554 \cdot 0.446 + 0 \cdot 0.269 \cdot 0.554 \cdot 0.554 \\
&\quad + 0 \cdot 0.731 \cdot 0.446 \cdot 0.446 + 0 \cdot 0.731 \cdot 0.446 \cdot 0.554 \\
&\quad + 0 \cdot 0.731 \cdot 0.554 \cdot 0.446 + 1 \cdot 0.731 \cdot 0.554 \cdot 0.554 \\
&= 0.224.
\end{aligned}
$$

and

$$bel(Q|d_2) = 0 \cdot 1 \cdot 0.455 \cdot 0.285 + 0 \cdot 1 \cdot 0.455 \cdot 0.715 + 0 \cdot 1 \cdot 0.545 \cdot 0.285$$
$$+0 \cdot 1 \cdot 0.545 \cdot 0.715 + 0 \cdot 0 \cdot 0.455 \cdot 0.285 + 0 \cdot 0 \cdot 0.455 \cdot 0.715$$
$$+0 \cdot 0 \cdot 0.545 \cdot 0.285 + 1 \cdot 0 \cdot 0.545 \cdot 0.715$$
$$= 0.0.$$

These examples illustrate the use of the inference networks and have been simplified to reduce the number of computational details. We have used simple estimates for the link matrices, and have not dealt with more complex network features described in [Turtle, 1990].

7.7 Summary and Future Directions

In this paper, we focused on the role of a retrieval model in an information retrieval system. The inherent uncertainty in text and information need representations means that IR models must deal with uncertain inference in some form. We described a probabilistic model based on inference networks and related it to other approaches to dealing with uncertainty.

The inference net model has been used successfully in a variety of retrieval experiments [Turtle and Croft, 1991; Croft *et al.*, 1991], and experiments with large test collections are continuing. These experiments are concentrating on the incorporation of better text representations, query formulation techniques, and learning strategies into the inference net framework. We are also using this framework as the basis for routing, filtering, and categorization experiments [Lewis, 1991]. The natural language processing techniques that are being used to produce text representations in these experiments are fairly simple and are restricted primarily to morphological and syntactic analysis [Lewis *et al.*, 1989]. It should be possible to use the inference net framework for representations based on semantic analysis, such as has been used in text extraction (described elsewhere in this book). Regardless of the text analysis tool used, the representations produced will be uncertain, and it will be necessary to combine knowledge-based representations with simpler word-based representations in order to get effective and robust retrieval performance.

Bibliography

[Allen, 1987] James Allen. *Natural Language Understanding.* Benjamin/Cummings, 1987.

[Andersen *et al.*, 1989] Stig K. Andersen, Kristian G. Olesen, Finn V. Jensen, and Frank Jensen. HUGIN–a shell for building Bayesian belief universes for expert systems. In N. S. Sridharan, editor, *Proceedings of the Eleventh International Joint Conference on Artificial Intelligence*, pages 1080–1085, August 1989.

[Belew, 1989] Richard K. Belew. Adaptive information retrieval: Using a connectionist representation to retrieve and learn about documents. In N. J. Belkin and C. J. van Rijsbergen, editors, *Proceedings of the Twelfth Annual International ACM SIGIR Conference on Research and Development in Information Retrieval*, pages 11–20, New York, NY, 1989. ACM.

[Belkin and Kwasnik, 1986] Nicholas J. Belkin and B. H. Kwasnik. Using structural representations of anomalous states of knowledge for choosing document retrieval strategies. In Fausto Rabitti, editor, *Proceedings of the ACM SIGIR Conference on Research and Development in Information Retrieval*, pages 11–22, 1986.

[Blair, 1988] David C. Blair. An extended relational retrieval model. *Information Processing and Management*, 24(3):349–371, 1988.

[Bookstein, 1982] Abraham Bookstein. Explanation and generalization of vector models in information retrieval. In *Proceedings of the Fifth ACM SIGIR International Conference on Research and Development in Information Retrieval*, pages 118–132. Springer-Verlag, 1982.

[Bookstein, 1985] Abraham Bookstein. Probability and fuzzy-set applications to information retrieval. In Martha E. Williams, editor, *Annual Review of Information Science and Technology*, pages 117–151. Knowledge Industries Publications, Inc., 1985.

[Bookstein, 1989] Abraham Bookstein. Set-oriented retrieval. *Information Processing and Management*, 25(5):465–475, 1989.

[Brachman and McGuiness, 1988] Ronald J. Brachman and Deborah L. McGuiness. Knowledge representation, connectionism, and conceptual retrieval. In *Proceedings of the Eleventh International Conference on Research and Development in Information Retrieval*, pages 161–174, New York, 1988. ACM.

[Cohen and Kjeldsen, 1987] Paul R. Cohen and Rick Kjeldsen. Information retrieval by constrained spreading activation in semantic networks. *Information Processing and Management*, 23(2):255–268, 1987.

[Cohen, 1985] Paul R. Cohen. *Heuristic Reasoning About Uncertainty: An Artificial Intelligence Approach*. Pitman, Boston, MA, 1985.

[Cooper and Maron, 1978] W. S. Cooper and M. E. Maron. Foundations of probabilistic and utility-theoretic indexing. *Journal of the ACM*, 25(1):67–80, January 1978.

[Cooper, 1971] W. S. Cooper. A definition of relevance for information retrieval. *Information Storage and Retrieval*, 7:19–37, 1971.

[Croft, 1987] W. Bruce Croft. Approaches to intelligent information retrieval. *Information Processing and Management*, *23*(4):249–254, 1987.

[Croft and Harper, 1979] W. Bruce Croft and D. J. Harper. Using probabilistic models of document retrieval without relevance information. *Journal of Documentation*, *35*:285–295, 1979.

[Croft et al., 1989] W. Bruce Croft, T. J. Lucia, J. Cringean, and P. Willett. Retrieving documents by plausible inference: An experimental study. *Information Processing and Management*, *25*(6):599–614, 1989.

[Croft and Thompson, 1984] W. Bruce Croft and Roger H. Thompson. The use of adaptive mechanisms for selection of search strategies in document retrieval systems. In C. J. van Rijsbergen, editor, *Proceedings of the ACM/BCS International Conference on Research and Development in Information Retrieval*, pages 95–110, 1984.

[Croft and Thompson, 1987] W. Bruce Croft and Roger H. Thompson. I^3R: A new approach to the design of document retrieval systems. *Journal of the American Society for Information Science*, *38*(6):389–404, November 1987.

[Croft and Turtle, 1989] W. Bruce Croft and Howard Turtle. A retrieval model incorporating hypertext links. In *Hypertext '89 Proceedings*, pages 213–224, 1989.

[Croft et al., 1991] W. B. Croft, H.R. Turtle, and D.D. Lewis. The use of phrases and structured queries in information retrieval. In *Proceedings of the ACM SIGIR Conference on Research and Development in Information Retrieval*, pages 32–45, 1991.

[Dempster, 1968] A. P. Dempster. A generalization of Bayesian inference. *Journal of the Royal Statistical Society B*, *30*:205–247, 1968.

[Doyle, 1979] John Doyle. A truth maintenance system. *Artificial Intelligence*, *12*(3):231–272, 1979.

[Duda et al., 1976] R. O. Duda, P. E. Hart, and N. J. Nilsson. Subjective Bayesian methods for rule-based inference. In *Proceedings of the National Computer Conference*, volume 45, pages 1075–1082, 1976.

[Duda et al., 1978] R. O. Duda, P. E. Hart, P. Barnett, J. Gaschnig, K. Konolige, R. Reboh, and J. Slocum. Development of the PROSPECTOR consultant system for mineral exploration. Technical report, SRI International Artificial Intelligence Center, 1978. Final report on SRI projects 5821 and 6915.

[Edmundson and Wyllys, 1961] H. P. Edmundson and R. E. Wyllys. Automatic abstracting and indexing survey and recommendations. *Communications of the ACM*, *4*:226–234, 1961.

[Fox et al., 1988] Edward A. Fox, Gary L. Nunn, and Whay C. Lee. Co-efficients for combining concept classes in a collection. In *Proceedings of the Eleventh Annual International ACM SIGIR Conference on Research and Development in Information Retrieval*, pages 291–308, New York, NY, 1988. ACM.

[Fox, 1986] John Fox. Three arguments for extending the framework of probability. In Laveen N. Kanal and John F. Lemmer, editors, *Uncertainty in Artificial Intelligence*, pages 447–458. North-Holland, Amsterdam, 1986.

[Frisse and Cousins, 1989] Mark E. Frisse and Steve B. Cousins. Information retrieval from hypertext: Update on the dynamic medical handbook project. In *Hypertext '89 Proceedings*, pages 199–212, 1989.

[Fuhr, 1989] Norbert Fuhr. Models for retrieval with probabilistic indexing. *Information Processing and Management*, 25(1):55–72, 1989.

[Fung et al., 1990] Robert M. Fung, Stuart L. Crawford, Lee A. Applebaum, and Richard M. Tong. An architecture for probabilistic concept-based information retrieval. In Jean-Luc Vidick, editor, *Proceedings of the 13th International Conference on Research and Development in Information Retrieval*, pages 455–467. ACM, September 1990.

[Furnas et al., 1987] G. W. Furnas, T. K. Landauer, L. M. Gomez, and S. T. Dumais. The vocabulary problem in human-system communication. *Communications of the ACM*, 30(11):964–971, November 1987.

[Hessel, 1955] Alfred Hessel. *A History of Libraries*. The Scarecrow Press, New Brunswick, NJ, 1955. Translated by Reuben Peiss.

[Kanal and Lemmer, 1986] Laveen N. Kanal and John F. Lemmer, editors. *Uncertainty in Artificial Intelligence*. North-Holland, Amsterdam, 1986.

[Katzer et al., 1982] J. Katzer, M. J. McGill, J. A. Tessier, W. Frakes, and P. DasGupta. A study of the overlap among document representations. *Information Technology: Research and Development*, 1:261–274, 1982.

[Kwok, 1989] K. L. Kwok. A neural network for probabilistic information retrieval. In N. J. Belkin and C. J. van Rijsbergen, editors, *Proceedings of the 12th International Conference on Research and Development in Information Retrieval*, pages 21–30, June 1989.

[Lauritzen and Spiegelhalter, 1988] S. L. Lauritzen and D. J. Spiegelhalter. Local computations with probabilities on graphical structures and their application to expert systems. *Journal of the Royal Statistical Society B*, 50(2):157–224, 1988.

[Lemmer and Kanal, 1988] John F. Lemmer and Laveen N. Kanal, editors. *Uncertainty in Artificial Intelligence 2*. North-Holland, Amsterdam, 1988.

[Lewis, 1991] David D. Lewis. *Representation and Learning in Information Retrieval*. PhD thesis, University of Massachusetts at Amherst, 1991.

[Lewis *et al.*, 1989] David Lewis, W. Bruce Croft, and Nehru Bhandaru. Language-oriented information retrieval. *International Journal of Intelligent Systems*, *4*:285–318, 1989.

[Maron and Kuhns, 1960] M. E. Maron and J. L. Kuhns. On relevance, probabilistic indexing and information retrieval. *Journal of the ACM*, *7*:216–244, 1960.

[McGill *et al.*, 1979] Michael McGill, Mathew Koll, and Terry Noreault. An evaluation of factors affecting document ranking by information retrieval systems. Technical report, Syracuse University, School of Information Studies, 1979.

[Monarch and Carbonell, 1987] I. Monarch and Jaime Carbonell. Coal-SORT: A knowledge-based interface. *IEEE Expert*, pages 39–53, 1987.

[Nilsson, 1986] Nils J. Nilsson. Probabilistic logic. *Artificial Intelligence*, 28(1):71–87, 1986.

[Oddy *et al.*, 1986] Robert N. Oddy, Ruth A. Palmquist, and Margaret A. Crawford. Representation of anomalous states of knowledge in information retrieval. In *Proceedings of the 1986 ASIS Annual Conference*, pages 248–254, 1986.

[Oddy, 1977] Robert N. Oddy. Information retrieval through man-machine dialogue. *Journal of Documentation*, *33*:1–14, 1977.

[Pearl, 1988] Judea Pearl. *Probabilistic Reasoning in Intelligent Systems: Networks of Plausible Inference*. Morgan Kaufmann, 1988.

[Quinlan, 1983] J. R. Quinlan. INFERNO: A cautious approach to uncertain inference. *The Computer Journal*, *26*:255–269, 1983.

[Radecki, 1979] Tadeusz Radecki. Fuzzy set theoretical approach to document retrieval. *Information Processing and Management*, *15*:247–259, 1979.

[van Rijsbergen, 1979] C. J. van Rijsbergen. *Information Retrieval*. Butterworths, 1979.

[van Rijsbergen, 1986] C. J. van Rijsbergen. A non-classical logic for information retrieval. *Computer Journal*, *29*(6):481–485, 1986.

[van Rijsbergen, 1989] C. J. van Rijsbergen. Towards an information logic. In N. J. Belkin and C. J. van Rijsbergen, editors, *Proceedings of the Twelfth Annual International ACM SIGIR Conference on Research and Development in Information Retrieval*, pages 77–86, New York, 1989. ACM.

[Robertson and Sparck Jones, 1976] S. E. Robertson and K. Sparck Jones. Relevance weighting of search terms. *Journal of the American Society for Information Science*, 27:129–146, May-June 1976.

[Robertson, 1977] S. E. Robertson. The probability ranking principle in IR. *Journal of Documentation*, 33(4):294–304, December 1977.

[Salton, 1968] Gerard Salton. *Automatic Information Organization and Retrieval*. McGraw-Hill, 1968.

[Salton and McGill, 1983] Gerard Salton and Michael J. McGill. *Introduction to Modern Information Retrieval*. McGraw-Hill, 1983.

[Shafer, 1976] Glen Shafer. *A Mathematical Theory of Evidence*. Princeton University Press, 1976.

[Shafer, 1987] Glen Shafer. Belief functions and possibility measures. In J. Bezdek, editor, *Analysis of Fuzzy Information, Volume 1: Mathematics and Logic*, pages 51–58. CRC Press, Boca Raton, FL, 1987.

[Shortliffe, 1976] Edward H. Shortliffe. *Computer-based Medical Consultation: MYCIN*. Elsevier, New York, 1976.

[Shoval, 1985] Peretz Shoval. Principles, procedures and rules in an expert system for information retrieval. *Information Processing and Management*, 21(6):475–487, 1985.

[Smith et al., 1989] Philip J. Smith, Steven J. Shute, and Deb Galdes. Knowledge-based search tactics for an intelligent intermediary system. *ACM Transactions on Information Systems*, 7(3):246–270, July 1989.

[Sparck Jones and Tait, 1984] Karen Sparck Jones and J. Tait. Automatic search term variant generation. *Journal of Documentation*, 40(1):50–66, 1984.

[Sparck Jones, 1971] Karen Sparck Jones. *Automatic Keyword Classification for Information Retrieval*. Archon Books, 1971.

[Sparck Jones, 1974] Karen Sparck Jones. Automatic indexing. *Journal of Documentation*, 30(4):393–432, 1974.

[Spiegelhalter, 1986] David J. Spiegelhalter. A statistical view of uncertainty in expert systems. In W. Gale, editor, *Artificial Intelligence and Statistics*, chapter 2, pages 17–55. Addison-Wesley, Reading, MA, 1986.

[Stirling, 1975] K. H. Stirling. The effect of document ranking on retrieval system performance: A search for an optimal ranking rule. *Proceedings of the American Society for Information Science*, 12:105–106, 1975.

[Tong and Shapiro, 1985] Richard M. Tong and Daniel Shapiro. Experimental investigations of uncertainty in a rule-based system for information retrieval. *International Journal of Man-Machine Studies*, *22*:265–282, 1985.

[Tong et al., 1983] Richard M. Tong, Daniel G. Shapiro, Brian P. McCune, and Jeffrey S. Dean. A rule-based approach to information retrieval: Some results and comments. In *Proceedings of the National Conference on Artificial Intelligence*, pages 411–415, 1983.

[Turtle, 1990] Howard R. Turtle. *Inference Networks for Document Retrieval*. PhD thesis, University of Massachusetts at Amherst, 1990.

[Turtle and Croft, 1991] H.R. Turtle and W.B. Croft. Evaluation of an inference network-based retrieval model. *ACM Transactions on Information Systems*, *9*(3):187–222, 1991.

[Turtle and Croft, 1992] H.R. Turtle and W.B. Croft. A comparison of text retrieval models. *Computer Journal*, 1992. In press.

[Willett, 1988] Peter Willett. Recent trends in hierarchic document clustering: A critical review. *Information Processing and Management*, *24*(5):577–598, 1988.

[Wilson, 1973] Patrick Wilson. Situational relevance. *Information Storage and Retrieval*, *9*:457–471, 1973.

[Zadeh, 1983] Lotfi A. Zadeh. The role of fuzzy logic in the management of uncertainty in expert systems. *Fuzzy Sets and Systems*, *11*:199–228, 1983.

[Zadeh, 1986a] Lotfi A. Zadeh. Is probability theory sufficient for dealing with uncertainty in AI? A negative view. In Laveen N. Kanal and John F. Lemmer, editors, *Uncertainty in Artificial Intelligence*, pages 103–116. North-Holland, Amsterdam, 1986.

[Zadeh, 1986b] Lotfi A. Zadeh. A simple view of the Dempster-Shafer theory of evidence and its implication for the rule of combination. *AI Magazine*, *7*(2):81–90, 1986.

Assumptions and Issues in Text-Based Retrieval

Karen Sparck Jones
Computer Laboratory, University of Cambridge
New Museums Site, Pembroke Street
Cambridge CB2 3QG, UK

8.1 Introduction

This paper is intended to provide an analytical background for those seeking effective text retrieval systems, and more specifically for those advocating the application of techniques drawn from artificial intelligence (AI) and natural language processing (NLP) for this purpose. A new wind is blowing through the world of information retrieval, and it seems that some of the apparent limitations of existing methods for characterizing and retrieving text-based information can be overcome. These existing methods refer primarily to information retrieval in the sense of document retrieval. Much of what is proposed falls, explicitly or implicitly, under this broad heading; and it is also useful to approach other forms of information retrieval from document retrieval, to make their distinctive properties and implications clear.

My aim is therefore to lay bare the nature and conditions of document retrieval as these have hitherto appeared, in order to provide the context within which new and hopefully better retrieval strategies can be defined and developed. The experience of the past shows that information, i.e., document, retrieval in general is an intractable task, and thus also an intractable task for automation seeking a high level of performance. This implies that it may be harder than expected, in the general case, to make radical improvements with new techniques. But these techniques should certainly be investigated, and they may, as indicated in my conclusion, provide real payoffs in some types of context or in individual applications.

8.2 Motivation

My starting point is therefore that developments in computing technology, and in artificial intelligence and natural language processing, have stimulated interest in information retrieval from those outside the established library and information science community, and have led to suggestions that the time

is ripe for new approaches to retrieval. These are particularly associated
with the use of the full texts of documents, which are typically not available
in conventional retrieval services, and with the idea that AI and NLP offer
distinctively new approaches to text characterization and searching not found
in conventional systems. There is also an interest in types of material—for
instance, news stories—not generally covered by conventional bibliographic
services, and in direct searching by end users, typically armed with high-class
workstation facilities.

It is often assumed that what is done conventionally, or has been done in
past information retrieval research, is inadequate or irrelevant in these new
contexts. But as this assumption may well be based on lack of knowledge or
experience, it is most important that, when approaches are claimed as new,
they should be related to important distinctions and justified accordingly.
In this case, these distinctions are between doing something automatically
that has hitherto been done manually, producing the same type of output
intended for the same type of use; doing something automatically which is
quite different from what has hitherto been done manually or automatically,
but is still intended for the same sort of use; and doing something novel
automatically which is also intended for novel uses. In the present context,
these distinctions are crucial for document characterization, i.e., indexing.
In the first case novelty is only in the means, not the end, and can only be
justified by better (or cheaper) retrieval performance. In the second case
novelty is in the means as well as in the end, but has still to be justified
in the same way, by better (or cheaper) performance in the same generic
context. In the third case the nature of the new context, and especially the
nature of new information uses rather than just of new materials, has to
be understood. It is further necessary, in this case, to establish appropriate
methods of performance evaluation, and also to check the performance of
new indexing and searching resources designed for the new contexts against
older approaches rejigged for the new contexts.

This paper spells out properties of, issues for, and experience with, document retrieval, to provide a background for developing and evaluating new
approaches to information retrieval, and specifically approaches that stem
from the application of NLP and the use of full text. It therefore considers
the findings of past retrieval research and the potential role for NLP in document and text indexing; the implications of past retrieval experience and
of retrieval constraints for NLP-based indexing; the consequences of alternative applications of NLP to create autonomous information bases; and the
requirements to develop the necessary evaluation techniques for retrieval performance in novel contexts, and especially those involving highly interactive
searching and mixes of different information-seeking activity.

8.3   Automatic Indexing Research

Information retrieval (IR) has conventionally referred to document retrieval, and specifically to automatic document retrieval. It has normally excluded searching for known items, like finding the storage location of a known book using an author or title catalogue, and has thus focused on finding documents relevant to information needs as expressed by subject or topic requests.

In the initial development of automatic retrieval systems, the basic assumption was that documents would be *indexed*, i.e., would be represented by brief subject or topic characterizations on which searching is actually carried out. Intellectually, the essentials of an automatic system were the same as those of manual ones, focusing on indexing as the summary indication of key document content, and hence on strategies for providing good descriptions and for finding document descriptions appropriately matching request ones. Automation nevertheless allowed two practical novelties, with long-term intellectual consequences. One was the ability to permute and select, so descriptions could be decomposed and reconstructed to allow multiple views of topics. The other was the ability was to search text directly, for instance abstract texts, so document descriptions could be formed, through matching, at search time.

Operational automatic retrieval systems have developed in two ways. One has been to retain manual indexing using subject heads or thesaurus descriptors, i.e. controlled language terms, combining this with the search time exploitation of Boolean request structure, and providing support for the selection of indexing and search terms through index language classification schemes embodying hierarchical and other relational structure. The other development has been in free text searching on keywords, though normally again with requests constructed using Boolean operators. The perceived, and real, problems of both of these have been associated on the one hand with the opacity of controlled index languages, on the other with the weakness of uncontrolled natural language, and on both hands with the rigidity of Boolean requests.

Information retrieval research over the last two decades has suggested, indeed demonstrated to the limit in non-trivial experiments, that controlled and natural language indexing and searching are competitive in fair comparisons, achieving the same middling level of performance [Cleverdon, 1967; Cleverdon, 1977; Salton, 1986; Salton, 1991; Salton and McGill, 1983; Sparck Jones, 1981; Willett, 1988]. This research has also indicated the value of much more flexible request formats than conventional Boolean formulae, with free term coordination offering ranked output, and has shown that statistically-based keyword weighting is useful. The research has further demonstrated that relevance feedback techniques of an essentially statistical kind can also be very valuable [Salton and Buckley, 1990; Sparck Jones, 1980; Sparck Jones and Webster, 1980]. Iterative searching is, of course, normal in conventional contexts, but this research has shown that it can be effective with little effort on the user's part. This is important because it is hard to provide effective support in search development for the end user.

These superior techniques stemming from research have begun to be implemented, though not widely in conventional system contexts [Debili *et al.*, 1989; Doszkocs, 1983; Harman and Candela, 1991; Porter and Galpin, 1988; Sanderson and van Rijsbergen, 1991; Stein, 1991; Willett, 1988]. It is essential to recognize that all the experiments done so far have shown that the research methods are superior to those implemented in normal operational Boolean keyword systems, which have given natural language in information retrieval a bad name. It has, however, to be accepted that these newer natural language techniques have not been rigorously tested on a really large scale. Thus, the largest serious experiments have been with data of order 150 requests and 30,000 documents, and most comparative testing has been with much smaller sets.

8.4   Opportunity and Challenge

The main new development of recent years has been the growth of full text sources. This is taken to open up striking new possibilities for improvements in information retrieval. Thus, it is widely believed that searching full text directly, without the impediment of index descriptions, will provide both immediate and superior access to the information the text embodies, and is thus naturally to be preferred to working with index descriptions instead.

At the same time developments in both NLP and in AI appear to offer appropriate strategies for capturing this text information and making it accessible to the topic or concept-hunting user. The approaches stemming from NLP and AI can be broadly labelled *meaning-oriented* and *fact-oriented*, respectively. This paper is primarily concerned with the first, i.e., with meaning-oriented information management, so it considers fact-oriented information retrieval only later, where the comparison is important.

The starting assumption is therefore that what is required is to determine and represent the meaning of a text, so retrieval, operating on a similar representation of request meaning, is a matter of establishing sameness or similarity or some other relationship of meaning between document and request representations. Thus to take a not very extreme example, a document might be represented as a structure of syntactically normalized, semantically resolved propositions, and a request as a similar but much smaller set.

8.4.1   Indexing

The crucial issue here (assuming that this sort of NLP can be done) is apparent in the question: What does a request-document match imply? That is to say, suppose a request sentence and one of the document sentences convey the same or sufficiently similar propositions: What does this tell us about the relevance of the document to the request? It may seem obvious that the document is relevant, but this is not necessarily so.

The reason why things are not so simple became apparent when full text was offered for keyword searching. Word matching on titles or even abstracts could be as effective as matching previously-constructed index descriptions consisting of lists of manually selected words because, on the whole, words in titles or abstracts reflect the importance of the concepts they refer to in the underlying full document. This is not the case with matches straight against the text. A word can occur in a text but be very unimportant for it. The same holds, though somewhat less disastrously, for a proposition. Thus, those engaged in keyword indexing were obliged to invoke statistical selectivity measures designed to distinguish important from unimportant word occurrences with respect to individual texts. For instance, a word occurring with medium frequency in a collection of documents as a whole, but with very high frequency for a single text, may be taken as a significant content indicator for that text [van Rijsbergen, 1979].

The important point about index descriptions, in other words, is that their function is not simply negative. They are not a regrettable substitute for full text, which can be jettisoned with more and cheaper machine storage. They have a vital positive function which is to indicate the important, main concepts or message of a text. This still leaves open what exactly is meant by this, how much is selection, how much generalization, and so forth, questions that can similarly be asked about abstracts. The major difficulty about indexing, illustrated by comparing indexing done by different human indexers, is that what is important is not unequivocal or permanent.

Index descriptions are thus reductive, simply because not everything in a text is important. But index descriptions were formerly, and still are, also reductive for the simple good reason that human beings cannot read every text to find out what it is about, i.e. index descriptions have the same vital filtering function as titles. They will still have this function in any system involving significant user interaction and non-trivial amounts of material. Moreover even where users are happy themselves to work directly on full texts without prior filtering, there may be a subsequent or supportive role for abbreviated descriptions in internal file structuring linking one document with another. Thus even if users always want in the end to access a full document text, not just to read it for its information content but (possibly at the same time) to assess it, in fine detail, for relevance to their need, index descriptions have an essential role as prior filters embodying a condensed characterization of a document. At the same time, index descriptions may need different forms for human and machine consumption. This may be a matter simply of presentation, for instance, offering keywords in phrasal rather than alphabetical order; but real differences may be justified by the intrinsic differences between the ways humans and machines manipulate information.

There is, however, a further constraint on index description, which the earlier work on the full-text keyword indexing served to establish, though it was also recognized in keyword operations with e.g., title terms. This is that it is not enough for a document description to be a good description of the document itself. It also has to be discriminating. Thus, given that descriptions are reductions, they naturally reduce the difference between documents, in just the way that the same two or three words may be used as the title for very different books. However, as the need the user has will often, though not necessarily, be for relevant information at the more detailed level of the full text, descriptions should, as far as possible, balance accuracy of description with distinctions between descriptions.

What all this implies, for those who believe that what is needed in information retrieval is a "one-for-one" representation of a text established by using NLP, is as follows. Full representations are required either in their own right, or as a means to the end of reductive indexing. In the first case, as defined by data properties or search purposes, retrieval means retrieval on full representations. This may be done directly or in two stages via reductive descriptions derived from the full ones; but either way, it is necessary to show that the file data or the search purposes force the use of full representations in order to serve retrieval needs adequately (utilizing them because they are cheap and good enough). That selectivity for extra performance is too costly, is a separate matter that has to be justified in its own terms. In the second case, full representations are the necessary precursors to reductive index descriptions. However it is then essential, if the full representation is only a means to the end of reductive indexing and is not preserved, to demonstrate that the desired nature and/or quality of the indexing cannot be obtained without going through the full representation.

In this context it must also be emphasized that if the user is directly involved in searching, he must either be able to understand the form of a representation or have it translated for him, and that this is especially critical with full representations.

8.5   Potential Roles for NLP

Now consider the case where indexing is explicitly accepted as the goal of the full-text NLP, so intermediate representations of whatever sort, and not just full ones, are jettisoned when they have been exploited to provide index descriptions. The presumption is that NLP will give better indexing than the current keyword standard. But it is essential here to be clear about the exact nature of the claim that is being made.

One form of the claim is that NLP analysis (and perhaps generation) will give better indexing (and associated searching) than, for example, conventional Boolean keyword systems. But this is misconceived goal, since while these systems for a variety of reasons do not perform well, they can be improved on by the superior word-based strategies of information retrieval research. Thus, the correct comparison is with these research-based techniques for term selection and weighting (just as new cars should be designed to work better than this year's cars, not last year's).

It is also necessary in these comparisons to make proper checks on the starting points. Thus sensible request formulation is vital for reasonable performance: This is part of the controlled language operation with a skilled intermediary, and needs to be provided for in other ways (even with relevance feedback as a bootstrap) with text-based approaches - as it was not obviously provided with Blair and Maron's STAIRS investigation [Blair and Maron, 1985]. These points are general ones: There may be circumstances where, given an institutional Boolean system, performance might be improved by using NLP to give better keywords for Boolean searching which explicitly combines different search fields [Rau and Jacobs, 1991].

Another possible, though less frequently encountered, claim is that NLP on full text will provide better index descriptions than the conventional ones using thesaurus descriptors or subject headings, given the underlying presumption that this sort of indexing is better than raw or even improved keyword indexing. This claim may be associated either with the same degree of reduction as in conventional indexing, when this is in fact done from full-text rather than abstracts, or with less reduction, yielding fuller or more complex descriptions. In the second case the value of more extensive or exhaustive descriptions would have to be demonstrated, taking into account the various factors like increased matching potential which have already been investigated for manual indexing. But these descriptions would still be reductions on their sources, and in general, the advocates of NLP for indexing have not considered how reduction is to be achieved.

However, the main thrust of the argument for NLP is either that applying NLP, whether more shallowly or more deeply, would deliver the same sort of result as conventional manual indexing, but a better quality one, or alternatively that it would deliver a different and better kind of index description. (Of course these claims could also be made for abstract or even title processing.) These claims are normally based on the view that NLP, perhaps supplemented by AI-style inference, can provide a better concept *identification* and better concept *representation* than has so far been achieved.

The identification claim is typically associated with the view that the component terms of a description can only be properly recognized by using information about syntactic/semantic structure in the text, i.e., about constituent relationships and/or functional roles. The representation claim is typically associated with the view that the representation itself has to have a syntactic or semantic structure indicating the constituent relationships and/or functional roles of its terms. The representation claim may also be associated with the view that description involves normalization, not just of structure but of vocabulary, for the same reason that in conventional thesaurus indexing ordinary language words are replaced by controlled language terms.

These two aspects of description are quite independent, and conventional indexing can vary along both structure and vocabulary dimensions, covering both more or less syntactic structure, more or less regularized syntax, and more or less explicit syntax, with varying degrees of vocabulary control [Chan et al., 1985; Lancaster, 1972; Lancaster et al., 1989]. Thus, when proposals for more sophisticated indexing based on NLP techniques refer to representation, i.e., the nature of the index descriptions for documents, they can refer to different possibilities. They can refer to complex natural language descriptions of the same kind as, e.g., titles, or to descriptions combining natural language words with constrained or artificial syntax, as in PRECIS [Austin and Digger, 1985] or to descriptions with both vocabulary and syntax in a specialized artificial indexing language. Clearly there are quite different implications for the user in these different types of description, and particularly in the use of indexing languages imposing artificial constraints on the form and content of descriptions. However, what follows to a large extent applies whichever of these styles of index language is adopted.

The crucial point now is that the view that NLP (with or without AI) is needed to deliver sophisticated descriptions, for the uses that ordinary indexing descriptions are put to, cannot properly be based on hoary examples of the kind in which syntax is needed to distinguish blind Venetians from Venetian blinds. Nor should it be based on the assertion that keyword searching of the kind often implemented in legal services delivers poor results and that more sophisticated indexing would obviously deliver better results.

8.6   Past Retrieval Experience

Assertions like these may be based on an inadequate grasp of the facts, on the one hand about the realities of retrieval and on the other about the history of retrieval testing. Thus for example, and just to begin with, a collection may not have documents about both physical disabilities and interior decoration. In any case, search descriptions with the necessary discrimination can be very readily achieved simply by adding further terms to the request, like "sight" or "curtains"; this is useful anyway since increasing the number of term matches increases the chance of relevant retrieval. Equally, quite apart from the fact that simple natural language indexing can be used more effectively than in conventional keyword services using Boolean queries, information retrieval research since the late fifties has been largely concerned with index language design and performance, and specifically with the design and performance of manual indexing languages and descriptions. The range of languages and methods developed and investigated has been very large, subsuming both approaches applied in serious or large-scale operational services and in more experimental ones. These performance evaluations have covered not only the nature of the indexing resources themselves, but also relevant matters like the effects of care in indexing, and a host of other issues like indexing exhaustivity. One of the major features in particular of the research has been comparisons between different indexing languages and forms of description [Sparck Jones, 1981] (especially Chapter 12) [Salton, 1986].

This work is relevant to current proposals for automated indexing and retrieval using NLP and AI techniques for two sorts of good reason.

The first reason is that these earlier proposals and tests referred to indexing notions of the same general kind as nowadays proposed, i.e., with relationally motivated and structured compound terms or complete descriptions, and also studied them in many individual particular forms covering a very wide range of possibilities. Some were indeed implemented automatically, see, e.g., [Bely et al., 1970], but this is not the important point. The important point is that the end indexing styles were the same as those now proposed, so whether they were effective in use is what really matters, not how they were achieved. Thus, those advocating modern versions of these methods have the obligation to look at what was advocated in this work as a necessary preliminary to claims for superiority or difference. Moreover even if implementation quality and consistency has also to be taken into account, the quality achieved in the past has to be established as inferior to that likely to be achieved now, meaning, notably, that past human indexing has to be shown to be less effectively executed than the proposed automatic indexing.

The many studies done in the past showed, in particular, both that performance for quite different techniques, when seriously applied, was much the same, and thus that simple techniques were very competitive with more sophisticated ones, and that absolute performance is not high [Sparck Jones, 1981]. Those who want to make legitimate claims about the superiority and novelty of their approaches to indexing need to look much more carefully at conventional indexing in all its variety and in all its aspects - philosophy, implementation, index language design, indexing description principles and so forth [Chan et al., 1985].

This is particularly important because the current focus of attack is on indexing and, more particularly, on the way documents are described. The evaluation tests done in the past showed how important other factors are, and in particular how important requests are. It is more helpful to devote attention to determining the user's *need* and to expressing this as a request than to fiddling with individual documents, particularly when searching can be iterative, so that if relevant documents are not found first off in one way they may be found later in another. The details of indexing languages may thus not be particularly important. For example, how much does recall (getting all the available relevant documents) matter to the average user? Languages and descriptions may or may not be designed to promote recall. Thus the real challenge of information retrieval is the indeterminacy, complexity, and variety of users' needs, and the correct approach to developing indexing and searching techniques is to relate these firmly to the properties of users [Belkin and Vickery, 1985; Hewins, 1990; Saracevic et al., 1988].

The second good reason for taking past research on board in the context of current interests in NLP-driven indexing is that this research has served to establish investigative methods and evaluation techniques. Performance testing in information retrieval is far in advance of that in NLP, so those moving from NLP to information retrieval need to know what is involved, for example, in choosing measures or gathering data samples [Sparck Jones, 1981]. It is true that even the largest tests have been limited, given the size of major operational services, so the results obtained may not scale up. But this is a problem for new NLP-based techniques as much as for older ones, whether conventional or the products of earlier research with, e.g., simple natural language term approaches. Even so, major research projects have conducted many hundreds of runs just to establish quite basic propositions [Salton and Buckley, 1990; Sparck Jones and Webster, 1980; Willett, 1988].

It may, however, be that NLP is advocated not as a means of generating sophisticated descriptions as wholes, but as a means of making more sophisticated choices of simple NL terms than the research-based statistical ones. For example, it may be thought necessary, given a simple coordinated-term style of indexing, still to allow for terms that are multi-word units, although with implicit rather than explicit relationships. Here again, past research investigating the relative merits of syntactically motivated units, statistical phrases, and simple de facto coordination at search time is relevant [Fagan, 1987; Keen, 1991; Lewis *et al.*, 1989; Salton and McGill, 1983]. The same applies to the most limiting case of NLP, where analysis is used to identify individual words satisfying conditions like, e.g., being nominal heads. This again has to be compared with cruder approaches (e.g., all content words), and like all the other techniques, has to be related to the statistical properties of terms that are relevant in indexing, whether for the whole text, or for the collection. One of the important challenges for any NLP-based indexing is to combine it effectively with statistical information. This may seem simple if collection-based information is used for selection or weighting of individual terms, but is more complex in phrase identification, where the components of a phrase have different statistical properties.

8.7   Retrieval Constraints

All of the foregoing has been concerned with indexing aimed at meeting retrieval needs of the usual sort, i.e., for documents relevant to some topic, and has been aimed at reducing ignorance about this. Indexing here has to be based on an understanding of the intrinsic problem character of this situation and so, whether applied to documents or requests, has to address the problems of the choice of descriptive items, the internal structure these descriptors have and the structural relations between them, and the lexical normalization that is required. In general, the closer to the actual text the indexing is, the more matching requirements have to be met by the orthogonal provision of a vocabulary normalization apparatus in the form of a thesaurus or whatever. This again has to be grounded either in the view of vocabulary organization characteristic of conventional thesauri or in more recent approaches based on statistical or relevance associations. Without this apparatus to support matching, the user has to contribute more, by explicitly indicating alternative expressions for the same content.

Finally, it is increasingly important to address the user interface, and specifically the end user, as opposed to professional search intermediary. Modern technology offers great opportunities here, but those engaged with online public access catalogues (OPACs) have already learned how hard it is to make sure that the non-professional and particularly occasional user is able to search effectively [Borgman, 1986; Mischa and Lee, 1987]. This is an active area of research, but it is as necessary for those offering supposedly superior types of indexing as for those offering traditional forms (whether automatically obtained or not), to show how end users can deploy the indexing information that is supplied effectively. Thus the more complex indexing is, the more difficult it may be to understand and use. This is true even though there are also issues about helping the end user enough, for example, to find alternative words, when simple natural language techniques are used, whether these are of a conventional or a research-based kind.

It is therefore necessary to demonstrate that end users are able to manage more sophisticated forms of indexing and their associated retrieval operations, which has not proved easy with conventional subject headings, classification schemes or thesauri, whether of an older fashioned or newer associative kind [Keen, 1977]. This is an area where expert systems methods have been applied, since these may be used (as in [Pollitt, 1987] and [Vickery et al., 1987] to hide the technical complexities of the actual indexing required for the search specifications from the user, while helping him to formulate his need. At the same time, modern interactive technology, with windows and so forth, can make displays more effective and housekeeping during searching more efficient. But though it may, for example, be easier to display classifications with modern technology, they may still not be easy to understand and use. Thus one important area of information retrieval research has been in extracting search information painlessly from users by exploiting relevance feedback, simple judgments of whether documents are acceptable or not without any indication of why, since the system infers this.

So far, I have been concerned not only with retrieval of the "usual" sort as far as topic specification and matching are concerned, but also with what may be described as typical retrieval contexts, for instance, involving retrieval from masses of journal articles. Indexing and retrieval schemes have, of course, in the past been designed for more specialized situations, whether these refer to the type of material, or to the form of usage (i.e., properties of the user community and its "requests"). One example is the use of facetted classifications for company libraries. Thus, while it may be argued that the need for sophisticated and deep indexing in general contexts has not been demonstrated, this may be required in special contexts. This may follow from the nature of the material or the nature of the needs, but the case has to be carried through, not just taken for granted. Moreover, the point just mentioned, about whether end users can manage sophisticated, and especially constrained and artificial, indexing language and descriptions, still applies.

The essential issues with full text retrieval are therefore as follows. Direct searching on full text, when there is a great deal of text, is either not practical for the human user because he will be swamped, or not sensible because he will fail to reach items that matter. There has to be a means of access, i.e., indexing (and whether this is best, or has to be, done at file or search time is irrelevant here). If there has to be indexing, does better retrieval performance require sophisticated indexing going beyond simple NLP strategies, and especially essentially statistical ones? If it does, how easy is it for the end user to work with descriptive terms and structures which are not ordinary natural language ones, but are only more or less arbitrarily related to natural language? If the user cannot work with descriptions of this sort, how well can he operate with plain natural language terms, given the mass of data available for them, and the size of the files he is searching? All the evidence is that complex natural language expressions are of no material use as units for searching, however important whole phrases or sentences may be, as they are in the case of titles, as supports for search output assessment. But if the user is left starting from words, how can the user manage, e.g., extensive collocational or associative information about words, so as to be able to improve a search specification? The real challenge with full text is how to benefit from the opportunity offered by direct, text-based searching without being overwhelmed by masses of easily retrieved material, which is precisely what relevance feedback techniques are designed to do.

Whether sophisticated indexing, to be applied in a way that is entirely hidden from the user, is required and can be supplied in a superior form through novel NLP techniques is a separate matter. It, of course, has to meet all the criteria already mentioned for overt rather than covert indexing, and has to be justified, as overt indexing does, by rigorous comparative evaluation. However, there is also the additional requirement that all of the system's description and search operations exploiting the indexing have to be driven by automatic transformations of the natural language and text data the user sees, and formulating effective searches under these constraints is not obviously easy. This transformation job is what the professional librarian and intermediary does in ordinary information-seeking environments.

But, though I have so far been concerned with indexing, i.e., with meaning-oriented information description, it is also possible to see information retrieval in a quite different light, as not concerned with indexing for its conventional access purpose at all. Thus, the suggestion that complex indexing descriptions are required may stem from the belief that many information management activities are carried out solely with the document descriptions. This belief takes the traditional use of descriptions as scanning aids to identify source documents to the point where the descriptions can be seen directly as primary sources of information in their own right, just as abstracts may be.

8.8   Creating Information Bases

Using descriptions as information sources in their own right leads to the second major current line of work in NLP and AI-based information retrieval. This treats document descriptions not as access aids, but as substitutes for their sources, giving all the essential information of the sources in a more explicit, or regular, or other more convenient form.   Modern approaches to message processing, for example, where natural language originals are replaced by instantiated frames [Lehnert and Sundheim, 1991; Young and Hayes, 1985], sometimes illustrate this strategy, though it was followed much earlier in Sager's work [Sager, 1978]. In some message processing applications there is no or very little reduction, so the representation can, for many purposes, be taken as a substitute for the original. Effective reduction is more difficult to achieve (see [DeJong, 1982]'s summarizing) and it also follows that the sources must remain available. (In some message processing cases, as in Sager's work, the frame fillers may be only slightly normalized, and preserve much of their original natural language character.)

These message processing examples illustrate the case where the set of descriptions can be treated as an aggregated knowledge base, in the way many record catalogues constitute an aggregate base. The base may, however, be integrated not just in the minimal sense represented by having common fillers for slots in different frames, but in the more thorough sense represented by the explicit definition of frame relationships, as in a hierarchy. It is easy to see that a natural progression from here to full integration would occur when all reference to the particular sources of whole frames or of individual fillers was abandoned. At this point the interest of NLP or AI techniques for document processing is just that of knowledge base derivation, on the assumption that the knowledge base is appropriate for information retrieval, which is now interpreted in a rather different way and in turn leads to fact retrieval and full-blown AI.

It is important to recognize explicitly that this step is being taken, and that it is assumed that source documents are of no interest in their own right, e.g., for their expressive properties or character as individual wholes [Sparck Jones, 1991]. It is possible to combine having a knowledge base with access to backup documents, but this is difficult to manage—i.e., what points to what—and, like the full abandonment of the sources, has to be justified by particular information needs. Thus, when proposals are made to apply NLP or AI methods to produce text representations or replacements, a proper case has to be made that the specific retrieval needs to be met really require this. It has to be shown, that is, that these needs are not of the usual generic topic kind that indexing in the ordinary sense is designed to meet. Indexing of this sort for document retrieval has developed because long experience has been taken to show that, given the many sorts of imprecision involved in retrieval, combined with the fundamental lack of information that retrieval presupposes, descriptive refinement is unnecessary, and what is needed rather is proper support for the user in searching. This imprecision stems, in document retrieval in the ordinary sense, from the multi-facetted nature of any topic, the analogous property of ordinary language, and the indirection of access; it has to be counterbalanced by redundancy in indexing and searching, not by pared-to-the-bone accuracy, especially as allowance has also to be made for the imprecision of the user's need.

This is not to imply that retrieval from information or knowledge bases does not allow for non-specific or partial queries. It is rather that if the form the base takes is independently justifiable on good grounds, as it is in the similar case of conventional databases, it may imply correspondingly different forms of interrogation. In general, if the assumption behind having a knowledge base is that the base can directly provide answers to questions in the shape of facts then, as with conventional databases, the inquiry situation is functionally different from the document and text retrieval case we are concerned with here, where the user's constructive interpretation of the retrieval materials is essential and central. It is, however, also possible to envisage information and text bases being used directly for searching with imprecise needs provided, as mentioned earlier, the user fully understands the form of knowledge representation used.

8.9 Evaluation Problems

The current opportunity is that there are new contexts for information retrieval in the broad sense; and these are interesting because they may justify new approaches to information extraction and representation. But with new approaches the concomitant challenge is to devise and conduct appropriate system evaluations.

The root problem here is dealing with interaction. As mentioned earlier, those working in document retrieval over the last thirty years have painfully acquired a set of techniques for evaluating retrieval system performance that are far in advance, methodologically, of anything normally used in NLP apart from machine translation, at least until the recent Message Understanding Conferences [Lehnert and Sundheim, 1991] and similar projects (and the same holds for much of AI, cf. [Cohen, 1991]). These techniques were, however, originally developed for offline searching, and though they are still used (for example, in SMART-related work: cf. [Salton and McGill, 1983; Salton and Buckley, 1990]) and are useful, evaluation methods and standards need developing for online and interactive searching. Evaluation methods, especially for performance evaluation in operational contexts, are also specifically needed for retrieval from non-text information or knowledge bases; but while this is a tough problem in itself, the real challenge, as in the document and text-retrieval case, is in evaluating interactive search performance [Robertson and Hancock-Beaulieu, in press].

The essential point here is that the user is not responding passively to system output, but is revising his search specification in response. This may, and usually will, imply a redefinition of his information need, which has two consequences, one for the individual search, the other for testing in general.

With the individual search, the problem is that as the definition of the need may have changed, it is very difficult, at the end of searching, to evaluate performance for what has been retrieved in relation to what ought to have been retrieved. But while precision (the ratio of relevant retrieved to non-relevant retrieved) may be captured only from what has been retrieved (though even in this case this may involve a somewhat misleading aggregation over the whole search), it is also often important to evaluate performance for an indexing or searching method in relation to what was not retrieved.

The other problem is that whenever comparisons between methods are called for, the individual user has been corrupted by his past experience and so cannot be invited to search for the same need using different methods. That is to say, the user has been corrupted by the relevance assessments he has already made. In older-style investigations, searching was separated from assessment. This corruption problem implies much larger samples of searches to establish system performance properly.

Information retrieval systems, however intelligently adaptive to the individual user they are supposed to be, are essentially driven by averages: Indexing or searching devices are adopted because they have generally worked satisfactorily, over many searches, in the past, and can therefore be predicted to perform correspondingly in the future. In essence this also applies to systems offering tailoring to the individual. The prime requirement of retrieval system evaluation is thus to obtain reliable average performance data (whether for different users or for the same user at different times), using performance criteria and measures appropriate to the essential nature of the retrieval task.

8.9.1   Evaluation Techniques for Novel Systems

Performance criteria and measures thus need much more investigation in their own right, as a necessary preliminary to assertions of the value of novel approaches to retrieval. It is at the same time necessary to be careful about a particular point in connection with novel systems. With novel systems, the "feelgood" factor is important: Do people like using them? Asking people whether they do is perfectly legitimate, but the question must be clearly recognized for what it is and not misunderstood as an objective measure of success in retrieving relevant material, any more than saying food tastes good means it is nutritionally adequate.

Then with any novel NLP-based scenarios in the document and text retrieval case, it is necessary to develop monitoring and measurement techniques for interactive information management, perhaps using the experience being gained with OPACs. Although there have been studies of user search behavior [Keen, 1977; Mischa and Lee, 1987], and of notions of relevance as well as of, e.g., how their readers use scientific papers [Hewins, 1990], there has not been enough investigation of how users interact in an online computational context with end documents. This also applies where abstracts are effectively treated as if they were end documents. It is also necessary, where retrieval is from information or knowledge bases rather than text ones, but where the user's needs are imprecise, to establish the appropriate fundamental concepts analogous to relevance for document retrieval, or rather to give relevance an appropriate interpretation. For instance, if the user is interested in browsing through a frame knowledge base, to see what it can tell him, what exactly is his need and how therefore can success in meeting it be established? Finally, it is necessary to develop appropriate evaluation criteria and methodologies for the multi-purpose or "hybrid" information environments, combining many diferent types of resource, that are now being developed. Where the user switches not only from one resource to another but from one type of task to another, according to current contextual requirements, how are either the global system's performance, or that of its individual components, to be measured? Some first beginnings have been made for the elements of such systems [Croft *et al.*, 1990], but much more needs to be done.

But if it is essential to develop appropriate detailed evaluation methods to take account of the new working environment which combines modern interactive and display resources with novel, text-motivated techniques for representing and seeking information, it is also necessary to bear in mind what modern technology offers existing modes of indexing and searching. Modern technology is not the working environment just for novel NLP or AI-based approaches to information retrieval. It is also the context in which the strategies developed in earlier retrieval research are being applied [Harman and Candela, 1991; Sanderson and van Rijsbergen, 1991; Stein, 1991]. This may make these comparatively established technologies more effective from the point of view both of formal performance measures and of informal user satisfaction. Thus the advantages that modern technology, say, for screen displays, could give to these to these older approaches could lead to higher performance levels for them which would raise the competitive stake for the newer alternative, and putatively superior, approaches.

8.10   Conclusion

My first conclusion is thus that it is not clear that modern analytic, rather than statistical, NLP techniques can, of themselves, make a large contribution to "mainstream" document indexing and retrieval. They should certainly be tried for this, but better motivated in relation to exactly how they differ from conventional indexing and searching, as means or for ends, than they often are. They need, in particular, to be more fully considered from the point of view of request rather than document properties, and they need to be studied from the point of view of scale effects, not on processing, but on discrimination. One of the disconcerting findings of the past has been that quite different forms of indexing or retrieval have much the same effect in the little and the large. Thus, it is necessary not merely to show difference of method but difference of outcome.

My second conclusion, however, is that even for the "mainstream" case (and taking this as more homogeneous than it is), novel NLP techniques should be tried when they are to be applied within the framework of multi-level processing, for example, with coarse-grained and then fine-grained matching adopted as an intellectually rather than economically motivated search strategy. Although hybrid strategies are used in conventional systems, the particular forms that NLP would allow the system (rather than the user) to apply have not been a practical option in established systems.

My third conclusion is that modern NLP techniques call for trial within the working environment offered by current interface technology, where many different types of information objects and information management operations can be conveniently combined. This will not be easy, as any attempt to automate the production of hypertext links suggests, and it may also not be easy to establish that any particular device, like parsing, is making any noticeable contribution to overall performance. But the opportunities here should certainly be investigated.

Finally, and most importantly, there is every good reason to experiment with substantive NLP and AI methods for information determination and retrieval for special types of application context or in individual, currently non-standard, retrieval environments. This clearly applies to the case where an explicit information or knowledge base wholly or partly replaces source text, but it could clearly also hold in the document case where the nature of the material and user requirements demanded it. The manifest need, therefore, is to obtain a better idea of what these conditions justifying more than only statistical language processing actually are, and exactly how they should be met. Thus, if on the one hand, as Hayes (this volume) notes, effective routing may not call for syntactic text analysis, it would seem to be called for when an information request can be properly treated as a direct question for which an answer may be sought in the stored text. The pressing research need is thus to establish what the many data variables, from collection size or typical relevant/nonrelevant ratio to user experience and goal, imply not just for the feasibility but for the potential utility of NLP in new and different, as well as old and familiar, retrieval environments.

Bibliography

[Austin and Digger, 1985] D. Austin and J. A. Digger. PRECIS: the preserved context index system. In L.M. Chan, P.A. Richmond, and E. Svenonius, editors, *Theory of Subject Analysis: A Sourcebook*. Libraries Unlimited, Littleton, CO, 1985.

[Belkin and Vickery, 1985] N. J. Belkin and A. Vickery. Interaction in information systems. *Library and Information Research Report, 35*, 1985. The British Library, London.

[Bely et al., 1970] N. Bely et al. *Procedures d'analyse semantique appliques a la documentation scientifique*. Gauthier-Villars, Paris, 1970.

[Blair and Maron, 1985] D. C. Blair and M. E. Maron. An evaluation of retrieval effectiveness for a full-text document retrieval system. *Communications of the Association for Computing Machinery*, 28(3):289–299, 1985.

[Borgman, 1986] C. L. Borgman. Why are online catalogues hard to use? Lessons learned from information-retrieval studies. *Journal of the American Society for Information Science*, 37:387–400, 1986.

[Chan et al., 1985] L. M. Chan, P. A. Richmond, and E. Svenonius, editors. *Theory of Subject Analysis: A Sourcebook*. Libraries Unlimited, Littleton, CO, 1985.

[Cleverdon, 1967] C. W. Cleverdon. The Cranfield tests on index language devices. In *Aslib Proceedings 19*, pages 173–194, 1967.

[Cleverdon, 1977] C. W. Cleverdon. A comparative evaluation of searching by controlled language and controlled language in an experimental NASA database. Technical Report ESA 1-432, European Space Agency, Frascati, Italy, 1977.

[Cohen, 1991] P. R. Cohen. A survey of the Eighth National Conference on Artificial Intelligence: Pulling together or pulling apart? *AI Magazine*, 12(1):16–41, 1991.

[Croft et al., 1990] W. B. Croft, R. Krovetz, and H. Turtle. Interactive retrieval of complex documents. *Information Processing and Management*, 26:593–613, 1990.

[Debili et al., 1989] F. Debili, C. Fluhr, and P. Radasoa. About reformulation in full-text irs. *Information Processing and Management*, 25:647–657, 1989.

[DeJong, 1982] G. DeJong. An overview of the FRUMP system. In W.A. Lehnert and M.D. Ringle, editors, *Strategies for Natural Language Processing*. Lawrence Erlbaum Associates, Hillsdale, NJ, 1982.

[Doszkocs, 1983] T. E. Doszkocs. CITE NLM: Natural-language searching in an online catalogue. *Information Technology and Libraries*, *2*:364–380, 1983. (Reprinted in Willett, 1988.)

[Fagan, 1987] J. L. Fagan. *Experiments in Automatic Phrase Indexing for Document Retrieval: A Comparison of Syntactic and Non-Syntactic Methods*. PhD thesis, Cornell University, September 1987. (Computer Science Department Technical Report 87-868.)

[Hancock-Beaulieu et al., 1991] M. Hancock-Beaulieu, S. Robertson, and C. Nielson Evaluation of online catalogs: Eliciting information from the user. *Information Processing and Management*, *27*:523–532, 1991.

[Harman and Candela, 1991] D. Harman and G. Candela. Bringing natural language retrieval out of the closet. Technical report, National Institute of Standards and Technology, Gaithersburg MD, 1991.

[Hewins, 1990] E. T. Hewins. Information need and use studies. In M.E. Williams, editor, *Annual Review of Information Science and Technology*, volume 25. Elsevier, Amsterdam, 1990.

[Keen, 1977] E. M. Keen. The processing of printed subject index entries during searching. *Journal of Documentation*, *33*:266–276, 1977.

[Keen, 1991] E. M. Keen. The use of term position devices in ranked output experiments. *Journal of Documentation*, *47*:1–22, 1991.

[Lancaster et al., 1989] F. W. Lancaster, C. Elliston, and T.H. Connell. Subject analysis. In M.E. Williams, editor, *Annual Review of Information Science and Technology*, volume 24. Elsevier, Amsterdam, 1989.

[Lancaster, 1972] F. W. Lancaster. *Vocabulary control for information retrieval*. Information Resources Press, Washington, DC, 1972.

[Lehnert and Sundheim, 1991] W. G. Lehnert and B. M. Sundheim. A performance evaluation of text analysis technologies. *AI Magazine*, *12*(3):81–94, Fall 1991.

[Lewis et al., 1989] D. D. Lewis, W. B. Croft, and N. Bhandaru. Language-oriented information retrieval. *International Journal of Intelligent Systems*, *4*:285–318, 1989.

[Mischa and Lee, 1987] W.H. Mischa and J. Lee. End-user searching of bibliographic databases. In M.E. Williams, editor, *Annual Review of Information Science and Technology*, volume 22. Elsevier, Amsterdam, 1987.

[Pollitt, 1987] A.S. Pollitt. CANSEARCH: An expert systems approach to document retrieval. *Information Processing and Management*, *23*:119–138, 1987.

[Porter and Galpin, 1988] M.F. Porter and V. Galpin. Relevance feedback in a public access catalogue for a research library - MUSCAT at the Scott Polar Research Institute. *Program*, *22*:1–20, 1988. (Reprinted in Willett, 1988.)

[Rau and Jacobs, 1991] Lisa F. Rau and Paul S. Jacobs. Creating segmented databases from free text for text retrieval. In *Proceedings of the 14th International Conference on Research and Development in Information Retrieval*, pages 337–346, New York, October 1991. Association for Computing Machinery.

[van Rijsbergen, 1979] C. J. van Rijsbergen. *Information retrieval*. Butterworths, London, 2nd edition, 1979.

[Sager, 1978] N. Sager. Natural language information formatting: The automatic conversion of texts to a structured database. In M.C. Yovits, editor, *Advances in Computers*, volume 17. Academic Press, New York, 1978.

[Salton, 1986] G. Salton. Another look at automatic text-retrieval systems. *Communications of the Association for Computing Machinery*, *29*(7):648–656, 1986.

[Salton, 1991] G. Salton. Developments in automatic text retrieval. *Science*, *253*:974–980, 1991.

[Salton and Buckley, 1990] G. Salton and C. Buckley. Improving retrieval performance by relevance feedback. *Journal of the American Society for Information Science*, *41*(4):288–297, 1990.

[Salton and McGill, 1983] G. Salton and M. McGill. *An Introduction To Modern Information Retrieval*. McGraw-Hill, New York, 1983.

[Sanderson and van Rijsbergen, 1991] M. Sanderson and C.J. van Rijsbergen. NRT (News Retrieval Tool). Technical report, Computing Science Department, University of Glasgow, 1991.

[Saracevic et al., 1988] T. Saracevic et al. A study of information seeking and retrieving. Part I: Background and methodology. Part II: Users, questions, and effectiveness. Part III: Searchers, searches, and overlap. *Journal of the American Society for Information Science*, 39:161–216, 1988.

[Sparck Jones, 1980] K. Sparck Jones. Search term relevance weighting - Some recent results. *Journal of Information Science*, 1:325–332, 1980.

[Sparck Jones, 1981] K. Sparck Jones, editor. *Information Retrieval Experiment*. Butterworths, London, 1981.

[Sparck Jones, 1991] K. Sparck Jones. The role of artificial intelligence in information retrieval. *Journal of the American Society for Information Science*, *42*:558–565, 1991.

[Sparck Jones and Webster, 1980] K. Sparck Jones and C.A. Webster. Research on relevance weighting 1976-1979. Technical report, Computer Laboratory, University of Cambridge, 1980. British Library Research and Development Report 5553.

[Stein, 1991] R.M. Stein. Browsing through terabytes. *Byte*, pages 157–164, May 1991.

[Vickery *et al.*, 1987] A. Vickery *et al.* A reference and referral system using expert system techniques. *Journal of Documentation*, 43:1–23, 1987.

[Willett, 1988] P. Willett, editor, *Document Retrieval Systems*. Taylor Graham, London, 1988.

[Young and Hayes, 1985] S. Young and P. Hayes. Automatic classification and summarization of banking telexes. In *The Second Conference on Artificial Intelligence Applications*, pages 402–208. IEEE Press, 1985.

Text Representation for Intelligent Text Retrieval: A Classification-Oriented View

David D. Lewis
Center for Information and Language Studies
University of Chicago
Chicago, IL 60637

9.1 Introduction

Any text-based system requires some representation of documents, and the appropriate representation depends on the kind of task to be performed. Content-based text processing systems can be broadly classified into *classification* systems and *understanding* systems. Text classification systems have been the primary focus of information retrieval (IR) researchers. These systems include text retrieval systems, which retrieve texts in response to a user query, as well as text categorization systems, which assign texts to one or more of a fixed set of categories. Text understanding systems go beyond classification to transform text in some way, such as producing summaries, answering questions, or extracting data.

In this article we look at what the nature of classification tasks tells us about desirable properties of text representations for text retrieval. We begin by reviewing the major representations used in current text retrieval systems. We then discuss classification tasks, first in general, and then specifically classification as accomplished in text retrieval systems. Emphasizing the classification aspects of text retrieval systems leads to a list of desirable characteristics of text representations. We consider two text representation strategies, vocabulary control and precoordination, from the standpoint of these desirable characteristics. One or both of these strategies figure prominently in many recent text representation proposals, as well as in many text representations tested in past IR research, with disappointing results. However, the increasing capability of natural language processing (NLP) systems and the new emphasis on inference in text retrieval suggest some promising directions for research. We end by discussing some of these, as well as the role of text classification in text-based systems as a whole.

9.2   Current Major Text Representations

Most text representations in operational use today can be viewed as the result
of choices along two major dimensions:

- Assignment of indexing terms by humans (*I*) vs. assignment of indexing terms by computer software (*II*).

- An open-ended set of indexing terms corresponding to words or other
  natural language structures (*a*) vs. a fixed set of indexing terms
  created by experts (*b*).

We can illustrate these choices with an article by Kumar and Bjorn-
Andersen, which appeared in the May 1990 issue of *Communications of the
ACM*:

"A Cross-Cultural Comparison of IS Designer Values"

The most widely used form of text representation for text retrieval has
been human assignment of indexing terms from a fixed set (*Ib* above) or *controlled vocabulary indexing*. The authors of the above article assigned it the
following categories from the *Computing Reviews* controlled vocabulary:

K.4.m [Computers and Society]: Miscellaneous
K.6.1 [Management of Computing and Information Systems]: People and
Project Management

If the above terms had been assigned by automated text categorization (see
Hayes in this volume) instead of by the authors then the above would be the
result of *automated controlled vocabulary indexing* (*IIb*).

CACM authors are also asked to assign any additional words or phrases
they think would be used by people searching a text database for the topics
discussed in the article. This is called *free indexing* (*Ia*). The terms the
authors of the above paper chose were:

General Terms: Design, Management
Additional Key Words and Phrases: Cross-cultural comparisons,
designer values, information systems design, organizational issues, socio-
technical design

As more text and more kinds of text are available online, *natural language indexing*, the computer selection of indexing terms from text (*IIa*), has
become increasingly used. It has also long been the focus of most research
efforts in information retrieval. The simplest and most widely used form of
natural language indexing is to index on single words from the text. If only
the title of the above article was available online, then a natural language

indexing of this document might be:

> *A, Cross-cultural, Comparison, of, IS, Designer, Values*

or

> *cross-cultural, comparison, designer, values*

or

> *cross, cultur, compar, is, design, valu*

or any of a number of other possibilities, depending on the details of the indexing approach.

Surprisingly, experiments have found natural language indexing using individual words from text to be at least as effective as the other methods described above, and also as effective as a wide range of more complex and seemingly more descriptive representation methods [Sparck Jones, 1981; Keen, 1981; Salton, 1986; Croft, 1987]. If new representations (such as those proposed by several authors in this volume) are to improve on current ones, then careful attention will need to be paid to how the properties of text representations impact effectiveness.

9.3   Classification

One of the most basic intellectual tasks that we might hope to have a computer perform is the assigning of objects to one or more of a set of preexisting categories. This task has been studied in many disciplines and so goes by many names, of which *classification* is perhaps the most common [Clancey, 1985; James, 1985].

We can view a system that attempts to solve a classification task as computing a function whose domain is the set of all possible representations of objects, and whose range is the set of possible decisions about membership of an object in one or more classes. We use the term *classifier* to refer both to such a function and to instantiations, potentially imperfect, of that function in software or hardware. Classifiers can be built by machine learning, by human knowledge engineering, or by combinations of the two.

Objects to be classified are often (though, as we will see, not always) represented by ordered tuples or vectors of values, where the value on each dimension of the tuple is derived in some fashion from the object to be classified. We will refer to these dimensions as *features*. The decisions output by a classifier can usually also be viewed as tuples of values, one value for each of the classes under consideration. Typically these values are either binary (*True* vs. *False*, or 0 vs. 1), or are numeric values indicating a probability or degree of membership in a class.

The ability to accurately perform a classification task depends crucially on the representation of objects to be classified [Quinlan, 1983]. Research in machine learning has devoted considerable attention to both *feature selection* (choosing which of a set of features to use in a classifier) and *feature extraction*

or *constructive induction* (creating new features from more primitive ones)
([Kittler, 1986]; [James, 1985], ch. 7 and 8). Choosing what data to measure,
and what abstracted features of the data to generate are also crucial in the
knowledge engineering of classifiers [Buchanan *et al.*, 1983; Clancey, 1985].

9.4   Classification in Text Retrieval Systems

Text retrieval is the computer selection of a subset of a document database
to display in whole or summary form in response to a user request. A text
retrieval system, therefore, is a classifier. It sorts documents into two groups:
documents that will be displayed to the user, and those that will not. Many
advanced text retrieval systems not only select documents for display, but
also attempt to order displayed documents by importance. These systems
can be viewed as computing the degree of membership of a document in the
class of documents relevant to the user.

Interaction with a text retrieval system typically begins with the user en-
tering a query into the system. The form of query most widely supported in
commercial text retrieval systems is the *Boolean query*, of which the following
is an example:

(*parallel* AND *algorithms*) OR [*Knuth* IN AUTHORS]

An IR system interprets a Boolean query as a Boolean function, and
retrieves all texts for which the function takes on the value TRUE. The
system is therefore classifying texts into two categories: texts to be retrieved
and texts not to be retrieved. For the example above, all texts containing
the word *parallel* and the word *algorithms*, or which are authored by *Knuth*
will be retrieved.

In this case the classifier is a *d*-to-1, binary function supplied by the user.
The classifier is defined over a text representation which includes a binary
feature corresponding to every word that appears in the text database, and
a single nominal feature whose value for a text is the set of authors of the
text.

The choice of the sets of features to support in a text retrieval system
has a very strong impact on the ability of users to define classifiers capturing
their information needs. It would be extremely difficult, for instance, to enter
a Boolean query retrieving all and only the documents authored by Knuth if
the only features available corresponded to words appearing in the document
title.

While most commercial systems allow only Boolean querying, the main
focus of IR research has been on text retrieval systems that allow arbitrary
natural language requests for documents, as in:

I'm interested in algorithms for parallel computers.

To produce a classification function that truly captures the intent of this user request is beyond the capabilities of current natural language analysis and user modeling technology. Text retrieval systems allowing natural language requests instead use the request to do feature selection, i.e., to identify a set of features likely to be associated with relevant texts. The text retrieval system then uses any of a variety of methods to construct a classification function using these features. The request above might be converted into a function such as:

$$f(\mathbf{x}) = c_1 x_{interested} + c_2 x_{parallel} + c_3 x_{algorithms} + c_4 x_{computers}$$

This classification function computes a numeric score for each document. The text representation is a set of numeric features. The feature $x_{parallel}$, for instance, might take one the value 1 for a text if the word *parallel* appeared in the text, and 0 otherwise. If each of the c_i was equal to 1, then the above function would assign a score to a text equal to the number of content words it had in common with the original query. The system might then retrieve all texts with a score higher than some threshold or, more commonly and more usefully, display to the user a ranking of documents in order of score.

A wide variety of methods for converting natural language queries into effective text classification functions have been explored. Some methods correspond to using different forms of classification functions. The most effective methods use statistics on word occurrences to set the coefficients of the classifier [Croft, 1983; Salton, 1986]. The best results are obtained when learning from examples, in the guise of *relevance feedback*, is used [Salton and Buckley, 1990; Croft and Das, 1990]. In this method, the user is shown an initial set of documents and asked to judge whether each document should or shouldn't have been retrieved. These judgments are then used to determine the form and/or coefficients of a new classification function.

Other variations in translating a natural language request into a system query are actually choices in how to use the request for feature selection. For instance, the classification function $f(x)$ above does not contain features for the words *I'm* or *in* from the corresponding textual request. These and other grammatical words are viewed as poor features on which to base a classification function, and so are often omitted from text representations. A more sophisticated method might recognize that *interested* is also a low quality feature for this query, and thus not select it for use in a classification function, even though that feature may be part of the indexing language for documents, and may even be a useful feature for some other user's information need.

9.5   The Nature of Good Text Representations for Text Classification

IR researchers have learned a good deal about what characteristics are important in text representations used with classification functions. A large body of empirical and theoretical results about classification function learning from statistics and machine learning are also relevant. Elsewhere I have reviewed this research and presented a theoretical model of text classification systems, the *Concept Learning model*, which attempts to explain the effect of different text representations on text classification effectiveness [Lewis, 1992].

On statistical grounds it can be argued that text features should be:

1. Relatively few in number.

2. Moderate in frequency of assignment.

3. Low in redundancy.

4. Low in noise (distortion or inconsistency in feature values).

Features that deviate from these characteristics make it more difficult to use machine learning methods to produce classification functions for retrieval, categorization, and other text classification tasks. It is not unreasonable to assume that the same characteristics impact the effectiveness of classification functions produced from natural language user requests, although this is less well understood.

Taking word-based natural language indexing as an example, we find many ways in which it is a less than ideal text representation. Indexing any significant body of text on words will result in tens of thousands of features, far more than will usually be optimal from the standpoint of statistical classification. Most of these words will occur in only one or two documents. This low frequency means they have little effect on most retrievals, and are difficult to use effectively in a statistical model. There is considerable redundancy in a word-based representation, in the sense that many synonymous or nearly synonymous sets of features are present. Furthermore, if two words are synonymous then, from the standpoint of classification, they should appear in the same documents. The fact that this often does not happen can be viewed as a kind of noise (distortion of feature values) afflicting a word-based representation.

Somewhat separate from statistical concerns, the particular way in which a representation groups documents together has a strong impact on its appropriateness. The ideal text representation for a particular classification task would be one that had a single feature taking on a unique value for exactly the texts that should be assigned to each class. The challenge in text retrieval systems is to produce a set of features such that most user needs can be expressed by simple classification functions. Text features should be:

5. Related in semantic scope to the classes to be assigned.

There are a few nontrivial things that can be said about such a relationship. One is that in most text retrieval tasks we are interested in learning multiple classifiers over the same feature set and data. The quality of a set of terms must be considered with respect to a distribution of possible user classes, rather than with respect to a single class. A word-based natural language indexing has the advantage of including a wide variety of distinctions, though perhaps at a more broad level than desired by most users. Note that there is a tension between the desire to have a small feature set and the desire to have a feature set that contains good features for a wide variety of user information needs.

The problem of finding the appropriate set of concepts to use in indexing documents has been studied by librarians and information scientists for centuries, but there is still a great deal that is not known [Svenonius, 1986]. However, one issue on which there is substantial agreement is ambiguity. Text features should be:

6. Relatively unambiguous in meaning.

Ambiguity is hard to define explicitly beyond the rather vague notion of a word or other linguistic structure having more than one meaning. From a text classification standpoint, an ambiguous word or phrase might be viewed as a disjunction over two or more unrelated concepts. This is an undesirable characteristic in a text representation because the members of a set of unrelated concepts are unlikely to all be of interest to a particular user. For instance, the word *plant* may mean a factory, a growing thing, or a spy, to give only three examples. A user wishing to retrieve documents where *plant* has one of these meanings is unlikely to also desire documents where it has the others.

Ambiguity has long been recognized as a problem in text retrieval. Direct approaches, i.e., attempting to define linguistic criteria for recognizing which sense of a word is being used, are receiving increasing interest, as I discuss in the next section. Indirect approaches to dealing with ambiguity in text retrieval have included both term clustering [Sparck Jones, 1971] and phrase formation (see Section 9.7.1). Ambiguity of words has been mentioned as a major problem for builders of text categorization systems as well [Vleduts-Stokolov, 1987; Hayes *et al.*, 1988]. (In some cases, characteristics of text representations can be more easily studied via text categorization systems than text retrieval systems [Lewis, 1992a].)

We have illustrated the above discussion with examples from word-based natural language indexing. If ideally designed and applied, a controlled vocabulary would be superior to word-based indexing on all six characteristics discussed. However, while dimensionality is almost always reduced, controlled vocabulary representations vary widely on the other five characteristics. Controlled vocabularies are at the very least meant to eliminate ambiguity and synonymy of terms, but these properties are subjective. From the standpoint of one user, a category **Artificial Intelligence** may be terribly ambiguous, conflating practical applications of AI with, for instance, cognitive modeling. To another user the presence of the categories **Artificial Intelligence** and **Pattern Recognition** might constitute redundancy.

Similarly, the semantic fit between categories and user needs can vary greatly. A medical vocabulary that makes fine-grained distinctions between diseases may be useless or even a hindrance to someone interested in dietary treatments of all diseases. The same vocabulary might fail to distinguish private vs. public hospitals, a distinction crucial to another user. This is an area in which natural language indexing has an advantage, by including, in its limited way, all the distinctions made in the original document texts.

Even if a category set is perfectly designed, the way in which categories are chosen to be assigned to documents may be noisy or otherwise suboptimal. Indexing by human effort can draw upon large amounts of knowledge and subtle clues in deciding whether a document falls into a category. On the other hand, variations in skill and training, as well as economic considerations, mean that in practice manual indexing is plagued by considerable inconsistency.

The other two representations I mentioned in the introduction have characteristics intermediate between the two discussed above. In free indexing, the human indexers can to some degree avoid ambiguous words and phrases, and can try to assign synonymous terms to all appropriate documents. However, if important terms are ambiguous, there is little that can be done about this. Free indexing is also, to an even larger degree than manually controlled vocabulary indexing, limited by human inconsistency and expense.

Most work on automated assignment of controlled vocabulary categories has attempted to duplicate the choices that human indexers would make. To the extent that this is successful, the properties of the two representations are identical. Any differences are best characterized as increased noise, in the form of inappropriately assigned or unassigned categories.

Having discussed some important characteristics of text representations, and how the most widely used representations stack up on them, we turn in the next section to some recently proposed representations. Two broad strategies, vocabulary control and precoordination, are fundamental to many of the recent proposals. These methods have been widely investigated in the IR literature, but recent proposals use these methods in novel ways.

9.6   Vocabulary Control

We have already discussed vocabulary control in traditional controlled vocabulary indexing. The replacing or aiding of manual controlled vocabulary indexing with automated text categorization is one very active area of research in text representation.

Vocabulary control is also implicit in a number of other recent approaches to text representation. One broad direction of research here is the use of *term categorization*, the assignment of categories not to documents but to words or phrases from the document text. Manual term categorization, in the form of *roles*, was an early enhancement to free indexing and manual controlled vocabulary indexing. One set of roles, developed by the Engineers Joint Council, was ([Lancaster, 1972], p. 126):

0. Bibliographic data
1. Input
2. Output
3. Undersirable component; waste
4. Uses or applications
5. Environment
6. Cause
7. Effect
8. Main topic
9. Passively receiving an operation
10. Means to accomplish primary topic

Note that while several of the above roles are conceptually relationships between two or more items, they were used in indexing not to connect two or more terms but as tags on single terms. In this representation, the natural language query, *Is there any information on the synthesis of benzene from cyclohexane?* might be expressed using roles as ([Vickery, 1970], pp. 131–132):

synthesis-8, cyclohexane-1, benzene-2

with the expectation that document words would be similarly tagged.

Recent proposals have focused on automated term categorization methods. For instance, word sense disambiguation [Krovetz and Croft, 1989] (also Zernik, this volume) seeks to replace or augment an uncontrolled vocabulary of words with a controlled one of predefined word senses. The segmented indexing system of Rau and Jacobs [1991] lets users restrict matches on natural language terms to those terms assigned to a limited set of categories. A number of recent proposals associate numeric-valued semantic feature vectors with words. A document is represented as the vector sum (or similar combination) of the feature vectors for its words [Sutcliffe, 1991; Wendlandt and Driscoll, 1991].

The effect that term categorization methods have on representation characteristics varies with how they are used. In one approach, represented by traditional role assignments, the Rau and Jacobs method, and some word sense disambiguation schemes, the representation consists of all combinations of the original words with each of their possible categories. In these cases, the new representation will necessarily have more features than the original word-based one, and features will be lower in frequency of assignment, and higher in redundancy and noise, for reasons similar to those holding for syntactic phrase indexing (see next section). They will, as desired, also be less ambiguous.

An alternative approach is to represent the text only by term categories, ignoring the original words. The semantic vector approaches, and some proposals for word sense disambiguation, have this flavor. The characteristics of such a representation depend on the set of categories used, but typically will be similar to those of controlled vocabulary indexing, described earlier. The advantages of these methods are likely to lie in the potential for decreased expense and increased thoroughness of indexing, and the ability to associate numeric weights with categories. It is unclear, however, how effective a simple combination of word level semantic features is at representing a document. This is particularly a question for semantic vector approaches, which typically do not attempt to disambiguate ambiguous words.

Vocabulary control is also an important feature of text representations based on logical assertions, conceptual graphs, semantic nets, frames, and similar structures. I discuss these representations in Section 9.7.2.

9.7   Precoordination

Precoordination refers to any method for combining members of an initial set of indexing terms (controlled or uncontrolled) into larger structures used to represent a document. A distinction can be drawn between precoordinate methods that create new isolated terms (*phrasal indexing*), and those that represent documents by structured entities. As with vocabulary control, we will look both at examples of recent approaches, using NLP and knowledge representation techniques, and at those from past IR research.

9.7.1   Phrasal Indexing

An *indexing phrase* is a term that is assigned to a document only when two or more of its component terms (usually words or word stems) are present in the document. The goal of phrasal indexing is to address the problems of polysemy and breadth of meaning that plague many single-word indexing terms. Cleverdon describes it this way ([Cleverdon *et al.*, 1966], pp. 52–53):

> This [phrasal indexing] was to remove the first level of vagueness and ambiguity inherent in words taken singly, by not accepting adjectival forms alone but only in conjunction with the terms they qualified. So terms which in isolation are weak and virtually useless as retrieval handles were given the necessary context; such terms as High, Number, Coefficient, Main, Trailing, Angle, Aspect which in practice do not form classes for which requests are made, appeared in conjunction

with other terms, to produce meaningful class terms – e.g., High subsonic speeds, Mach number, Pitching moment coefficient, Main wing, Trailing edge, Low angle of attack, High aspect ratio.

The components of a phrasal term may be required to have some specified statistical, proximity, syntactic, or semantic relationship in a document for the phrasal term to be considered present in that document. (For instance, see Maarek and Fagan in this volume.) From a document sentence such as:

This paper describes applications of parallel processing to medicine.

we might extract as phrases all pairs of content words in a direct syntactic relationship. This would yield as phrases:

paper describes, describes applications, applications processing, parallel processing, applications medicine

but not:

paper applications, parallel medicine,...

Phrasal representations are appealing because each word in an indexing phrase provides a context that helps disambiguate the other. For instance, *parallel* and *processing* are both highly ambiguous words. The indexing phrase *parallel processing* is much less ambiguous, and a document containing this phrase will in general be a better match for a query about *parallel processing* than will be a document that contains one or both of those words outside of a modification relationship. A disadvantage of phrasal indexing in comparison to term categorization methods is that the implicit disambiguation in phrasal indexing can be taken advantage of only when a query phrase exactly matches a document phrase.

Indexing phrases also tend to have a semantic scope that is narrower than that of words, and perhaps closer to that of typical queries. On the other hand, in comparison with words, an indexing language consisting of indexing phrases will usually have more terms, more redundant (nearly synonymous) terms, higher noise (since synonymous terms are not assigned to the same documents), and lower document frequency for terms.

The use of phrasal indexing has seen considerable attention from IR researchers both in the past and more recently. To date, this technique has not yielded reliable performance improvements, but a good deal has been learned about the properties of phrasal representations. For instance, in one text categorization experiment [Lewis, 1992a], we found that a representation based on simple noun phrases reached its maximum performance when using 20 times as many classifier terms as a word-based representation. Knowledge of such properties of representations can aid in the design of user interfaces and in choosing techniques for query expansion.

9.7.2   Structured Representations

An alternative approach to precoordination is to depart from a feature value representation of documents, and explicitly include relationships among terms as part of the document representation. I present in this section a few examples of such representations. More are discussed elsewhere in this volume, and in other sources [Lancaster, 1972; Chan *et al.*, 1985; *International Journal of Intelligent Systems*, 1989].

As an extension of work on manual controlled vocabulary indexing, a number of structured indexing languages have been tested over the years. The Western Reserve University metallurgical indexing language included structures such as this (adapted from [Aitchison and Cleverdon, 1963], pp. 67 and 161):

> **PRODUCT:**
> **Product:**
> **Major-Component:** "Cb"
> **Minor-Component:** "Cb"
> **Property-Given:** "Arc melted", "Electron beam melted"

An example article indexed under this system had 36 words and multi-word indexing phrases distributed among 23 small partitions grouped into 3 larger partitions. Users could require that words be present with particular roles and occur together within partitions of a particular granularity.

The text fragment *purifying water by precipitating impurities* would be expressed in Farradane's Relational Indexing as (adapted from [Farradane, 1980]):

```
    water /- purifying
      /;              /(
    impurities /- precipitating
```

In Farradane's notation, /- stands for "Action" (i.e., having an effect), /; for an unspecified association, and /(for either a part-whole or a genus-species relationship. This system had a set of 9 binary relations among terms. Yates-Mercer describes a number of strategies for matching queries and documents via Relational Indexing, including allowing semantically related words to match and inferring some relations from others [Yates-Mercer, 1976]. These were apparently never implemented mechanically, however.

The above systems were intended for use in manual indexing. (Farradane's obviously for use with a typewriter!) There has been increasing interest in producing structured representations from text by NLP methods.

Mauldin's FERRET system analyzed sentences such as:

Pioneer 10 was the first spacecraft to venture out of the solar system.

producing representations of this form (adapted from [Mauldin, 1989], p. 52):

```
ptrans
  actor: *pioneer-spacecraft*
  object: *pioneer-spacecraft*
  to: *solar-system*
        type: outer
        ref: def
```

FERRET queries are expressed in the same language, and a document is retrieved if the query matches exactly some substructure of the document representation, with the allowance that slot fillers in the query representation can be semantically more general (as specified by a knowledge base) than slot fillers in the document representation.

Complex structured representations have been considered for some time for legal text retrieval [Hafner, 1978]. Dick [Dick, 1991] proposes a representation based on conceptual graphs. A small fragment of the representation for one document is:

```
[REASONS: #2] → (INCL) → [
    (JD) → [[PROMISE-n: #S1]-
                (¬EQUIV) → [OFFER: #S1]
                (CHRC) → [[PHRASE: ...
        (CAUS) → [[ANXIOUS_FOR: ...
    [HYPO: [PROMISE-n: #S2] → ...
```

The tests reported by Dick were on hand-coded document representations, and only on a few examples. However, the inference methods used are novel, and suggestive of approaches to text retrieval that will be of interest as NLP systems become able to produce more complex representations of text.

How these structured representations stack up on our text representation characteristics depends strongly on how they are used in text retrieval. I discuss this when considering research directions in the next section.

9.8   Opportunities for the Future

I have made the point, as Sparck Jones did in the previous chapter, that there are strong similarities between recent proposals for text representation and those explored in past IR research. These similarities may seem discouraging, since past research on vocabulary control, precoordination, and combinations of the two has not shown them to provide significant effectiveness improvements over word-based natural language indexing ([Lancaster, 1972], pp. 124–129; [Sparck Jones, 1981]; [Keen, 1981]).

However, two differences between recent and past work provide reasons for optimism. The first is the increasing ability to use natural language analysis of document text, rather than human indexing, to produce complex text representations. To the extent that the same sort of representations produced manually in the past can now be produced automatically, they can be applied more economically, consistently, and thoroughly. The total number of indexing structures, of whatever form, that can be assigned to a document manually is strongly limited by patience and expense. If the structures can be produced automatically from the text, this is much less the case.

The other difference is a shift from viewing a text retrieval query as something to be matched (partially or exactly) against a document, to a view where the query is to be inferred from the document. As Croft and Turtle discussed in Chapter 7, a variety of knowledge sources can be used in such an inference framework, and various forms of uncertainty can be managed.

Most systems using vocabulary control in the past have required exact matches between controlled vocabulary items in a user query and those assigned to documents, or at best have allowed matches on hierarchically related categories. Redundancy and noise are, therefore, problems. Most precoordinate systems have required that the query match exactly some substructure of the document representation, again possibly allowing hierarchical matches on controlled vocabulary items. When precoordinated structures must match directly to contribute to retrieval, the effect is similar to having defined a very large set of indexing phrases, with the same disadvantages.

If, however, additional knowledge can be drawn upon to enable matches of non-identical items, many of the disadvantages of controlled vocabulary and precoordinated representations can be eliminated. As an example, the GRANT system [Cohen and Kjeldsen, 1987] retrieves textual descriptions of funding agencies by partial matching of hand-built frame representations of queries and documents. Partial matches are found by spreading activation through a semantic network, with link labels determining how plausible the resulting inference is. Any document can match any query via inferences with greater or lesser degrees of plausibility.

The idea of annotating components of a document's representation with different degrees of belief has long been used in IR in the form of probabilistic indexing and other forms of term weighting [Salton and Buckley, 1988; Fuhr, 1989]. NLP analyses of text and knowledge-based inference provide much richer sources of evidence about the plausibility of a document being on a particular subject than do counts of word occurrences in the document, the most common basis for document-specific term weighting.

Whether text retrieval systems using NLP-constructed text representations and knowledge-based inference will look more like feature-based statistical classifiers, or more like inference systems that manage uncertainty, will depend on the accuracy of NLP techniques and the comprehensiveness of available knowledge bases. For the foreseeable future, statistical classification is likely to remain the dominant framework. Partial text representations at multiple levels will be the best achievable (see Hirst in this volume), and statistical associations will be crucial to bridging the gap between document and query, where incomplete NLP interpretations and knowledge bases fail. The greatest successes are likely to come from methods that integrate NLP and knowledge-based inference with traditional word-oriented text retrieval in a robust statistical framework.

9.9 Conclusion

Any classification task requires producing, by human insight or machine-learning algorithm, a classification function defined on a particular text representation. Statistical properties of the representation, such as high dimensionality, very low or high frequency, redundancy, and noise, as well as linguistic properties, such as ambiguity and scope of meaning, have a strong impact on the ease of producing such a function. Therefore, these properties are important to any representation, traditional or AI-based, used for text classification.

This paper has emphasized text classification systems, but the representation characteristics discussed are relevant to text understanding systems as well, since text categorization is becoming more widely used within understanding systems [Sundheim, 1991]. In addition, the line between text classification and text understanding tasks is less clean than we may have implied. There have been IR systems oriented toward the retrieval of text passages answering specific questions [O'Connor, 1975], and question answering systems that incorporate text retrieval and classification [Jacobs and Rau, 1990].

Text representation will be a particularly interesting problem in systems that combine text understanding with text retrieval. When question answering or data extraction fails, it will be desirable to use any partially successful inferences left from the question answering for improving the representation of texts for retrieval. Methods that can effectively use a variety of partially complete representations are likely to be the most successful.

Acknowledgments

The Computer and Information Science Department at the University of Massachusetts at Amherst, and the Center for Information and Language Studies at the University of Chicago supported this research. Funding was provided by the NSF (grant IRI-8814790 and an NSF Graduate Fellowship), AFOSR (grant AFOSR-90-0110), and Ameritech. Jessica Milstead, Don Swanson, Paul Jacobs, Karen Sparck Jones, Rick Yee, and an anonymous reviewer provided many helpful comments on earlier drafts of this chapter.

Bibliography

[Aitchison and Cleverdon, 1963] Jean Aitchison and Cyril Cleverdon. A report on the test of the index of metallurgical literature of Western Reserve University. Technical report, The College of Aeronautics, Cranfield, Cranfield, England, October 1963.

[Buchanan et al., 1983] Bruce G. Buchanan, David Barstow, Robert Bechtel, James Bennett, William Clancey, Casimir Kulikowski, Tom Mitchell, and Donald A. Waterman. Constructing an expert system. In Frederick Hayes-Roth, Donald A. Waterman, and Douglas B. Lenat, editors, *Building Expert Systems*, chapter 5. Addison-Wesley, Reading, MA, 1983.

[Chan et al., 1985] Lois Mai Chan, Phyllis A. Richmond, and Elaine Svenonius, editors. *Theory of Subject Analysis: A Sourcebook*. Libraries Unlimited, Littleton, CO, 1985.

[Clancey, 1985] William J. Clancey. Heuristic classification. *Artificial Intelligence*, 27:289–350, 1985.

[Cleverdon et al., 1966] Cyril Cleverdon, Jack Mills, and Michael Keen. Factors determining the performance of indexing systems. Vol. 1, Design. Parts 1 and 2. Technical report, Cranfield Institute of Technology; College of Aeronautics, Cranfield, England, 1966.

[Cohen and Kjeldsen, 1987] Paul R. Cohen and Rick Kjeldsen. Information retrieval by constrained spreading activation in semantic networks. *Information Processing and Management*, 23(4):255–268, 1987.

[Croft, 1983] W. B. Croft. Experiments with representation in a document retrieval system. *Information Technology: Research and Development*, 2:1–21, 1983.

[Croft, 1987] W. Bruce Croft. Approaches to intelligent information retrieval. *Information Processing and Management*, 23(4):249–254, 1987.

[Croft and Das, 1990] W. Bruce Croft and Raj Das. Experiments with query acquisition and use in document retrieval sytems. In *Thirteenth Annual International ACM SIGIR Conference on Research and Development in Information Retrieval*, pages 349–365, 1990.

[Dick, 1991] Judith P. Dick. Representation of legal text for conceptual retrieval. In *Third International Conference on Artificial Intelligence and Law*, pages 244–253, 1991.

[Farradane, 1980] J. Farradane. Relational indexing: Part I. *Journal of Information Science*, *1*:267–276, 1980.

[Fuhr, 1989] Norbert Fuhr. Models for retrieval with probabilistic indexing. *Information Processing and Management*, *25*(1):55–72, 1989.

[Hafner, 1978] Carole D. Hafner. *An Information Retrieval System Based on a Computer Model of Legal Knowledge*. PhD thesis, University of Michigan, Ann Arbor, MI, 1978.

[Hayes et al., 1988] Philip J. Hayes, Laura E. Knecht, and Monica J. Cellio. A news story categorization system. In *Second Conference on Applied Natural Language Processing*, pages 9–17, 1988.

[*International Journal of Intelligent Systems*, 1989] *International Journal of Intelligent Systems* *4*(3). Special issue on knowledge-based techniques for information retrieval, Fall 1989.

[Jacobs and Rau, 1990] Paul S. Jacobs and Lisa F. Rau. SCISOR: Extracting information from on-line news. *Communications of the ACM*, *33*(11):88–97, November 1990.

[James, 1985] Mike James. *Classification Algorithms*. John Wiley and Sons, New York, 1985.

[Keen, 1981] E. Michael Keen. Laboratory tests of manual systems. In Karen Sparck Jones, editor, *Information Retrieval Experiment*, chapter 8. Butterworths, London, 1981.

[Kittler, 1986] J. Kittler. Feature selection and extraction. In Tzay Y. Young and King-Sun Fu, editors, *Handbook of Pattern Recognition and Image Processing*, pages 59–83. Academic Press, Orlando, 1986.

[Krovetz and Croft, 1989] Robert Krovetz and W. Bruce Croft. Word sense disambiguation using machine-readable dictionaries. In *Twelfth Annual International ACM SIGIR Conference on Research and Development in Information Retrieval*, pages 127–136, 1989.

[Lancaster, 1972] F. W. Lancaster. *Vocabulary Control for Information Retrieval*. Information Resources Press, Washington, D.C., 1st edition, 1972.

[Lewis, 1992a] David D. Lewis. An evaluation of phrasal and clustered representations on a text categorization task. In *Fifteenth Annual International ACM SIGIR Conference on Research and Development in Information Retrieval*, 1992. In press.

[Lewis, 1992b] David D. Lewis. *Representation and Learning in Information Retrieval*. PhD thesis, Computer Science Dept.; Univ. of Massachusetts; Amherst, MA 01003, 1992. (Available as Technical Report 91–93.)

[Mauldin, 1989] Michael Mauldin. *Information Retrieval by Text Skimming.* PhD thesis, School of Computer Science; Carnegie Mellon University, August 1989. (Also TR CMU-CS-89-193.)

[O'Connor, 1975] John O'Connor. Retrieval of answer-sentences and answer-figures from papers by text searching. *Information Processing and Management*, 11:155–164, 1975.

[Quinlan, 1983] J. Ross Quinlan. Learning efficient classification procedures and their application to chess end games. In Ryszard S. Michalski, Jaime G. Carbonell, and Tom M. Mitchell, editors, *Machine Learning: An Artificial Intelligence Approach*, pages 463–482. Morgan Kaufmann, Los Altos, CA, 1983.

[Rau and Jacobs, 1991] Lisa F. Rau and Paul S. Jacobs. Creating segmented databases from free text for text retrieval. In *Fourteenth Annual International ACM SIGIR Conference on Research and Development in Information Retrieval*, pages 337–346, 1991.

[Salton and Buckley, 1988] Gerard Salton and Chris Buckley. Term-weighting approaches in automatic text retrieval. *Information Processing and Management*, 24(5):513–523, 1988.

[Salton and Buckley, 1990] Gerard Salton and Chris Buckley. Improving retrieval performance by relevance feedback. *Journal of the American Society for Information Science*, 41(4):288–297, 1990.

[Salton, 1986] Gerard Salton. Another look at automatic text-retrieval systems. *Communications of the ACM*, 29(7):648–656, July 1986.

[Sparck Jones, 1971] Karen Sparck Jones. *Automatic Keyword Classification for Information Retrieval.* Archon Books, 1971.

[Sparck Jones, 1981] Karen Sparck Jones. Retrieval system tests, 1958–1978. In Karen Sparck Jones, editor, *Information Retrieval Experiment*, chapter 12. Butterworths, London, 1981.

[Sundheim, 1991] Beth M. Sundheim, editor. *Proceedings of the Third Message Understanding Evaluation and Conference*, San Diego, CA, May 1991. Defense Advanced Research Projects Agency, Morgan Kaufmann.

[Sutcliffe, 1991] Richard F. E. Sutcliffe. Distributed representations in a text based information retrieval system: A new way of using the vector space model. In *Fourteenth Annual International ACM SIGIR Conference on Research and Development in Information Retrieval*, pages 123–132, 1991.

[Svenonius, 1986] Elaine Svenonius. Unanswered questions in the design of controlled vocabularies. *Journal of the American Society for Information Science*, 37(5):331–340, 1986.

[Vickery, 1970] B. C. Vickery. *Techniques of Information Retrieval.* Butterworths, London, 1970.

[Vleduts-Stokolov, 1987] Natasha Vleduts-Stokolov. Concept recognition in an automatic text-processing system for the life sciences. *Journal of the American Society for Information Science, 38*:269–287, 1987.

[Wendlandt and Driscoll, 1991] Edgar B. Wendlandt and James R. Driscoll. Incorporating a semantic analysis into a document retrieval strategy. In *Fourteenth Annual International ACM SIGIR Conference on Research and Development in Information Retrieval*, pages 270–279, 1991.

[Yates-Mercer, 1976] P. A. Yates-Mercer. Relational indexing applied to selective dissemination of information. *Journal of Documentation, 32*:182–197, 1976.

Automatic Text Structuring Experiments[*]

Gerard Salton and Chris Buckley
Department of Computer Science
Cornell University
Ithaca, NY 14853-7501

Abstract

This study describes sophisticated text matching methods designed to insert structural links between semantically related portions of running text, or between text portions in different documents. Such links may provide useful access points to the text and simplify text utilization for many purposes. In particular, text traversal prescriptions may be obtainable that can guide information seekers to particular text excerpts in accordance with expressed user interests.

10.1 The Text Linking Problem

The time is at hand when large collections of natural-language text are becoming freely available in machine-readable form. Automatic processing aids are therefore needed to access and utilize the available data. Fortunately, the technology has evolved rapidly over the past few years: Optical disk equipment can now store hundreds of megabytes of information, and fast, parallel retrieval techniques have been developed that provide rapid access to the stored data for a large diversity of users. Among the text collections available for processing, some are of special interest because the stored data must be accessed selectively rather than sequentially. Such collections include mail and messages of many kinds, manuals of operation, textbooks, dictionaries and encyclopedias, and many other kinds of data. In such cases, it becomes useful to build structured images of the documents that reveal relationships between text pieces, and make it possible to access particular text portions or to skip from one section to other related ones.

[*]This study was supported in part by the National Science Foundation under grant IRI 89-15847.

The hypertext community distinguishes logical text relations from semantic ones, where the term *logical* covers both the normal hierarchical breakdown into chapters, sections, subsections, and so on, as well as the objective relations between main text and auxiliary pieces, such as footnotes, annotations, and bibliographic references. For text accessing purposes, both logical and semantic text relations are needed: the former to recognize the objective relationships that characterize the text, and the latter to enable the user to access simultaneously text excerpts covering semantically related subject matter.

The conventional wisdom is that the logical text relations can be automatically determined—for example, from a text product prepared for automatic typesetting purposes specifying the exact location of all titles, sections, paragraphs, footnotes, and so on. The corresponding formatting codes can be interpreted in an automatic publication process where they control document layout and format. While logical text similarities are relatively easy to deal with in an automated text linking system, it is generally felt that the semantic text relationships between related subject matter must be identified by human, intellectual effort [Conklin, 1987; Furuta *et al.*, 1989].

Two major problems arise when an intellectual construction of text links is contemplated:

1. The person charged with the identification of semantic text links must be expert in the subject matter under discussion. When the subject matter varies widely, as it often does, it will be difficult to find anyone with the required subject know-how.

2. For large text pieces, the number of possible text relations soon becomes unmanageable. In such a case, it is easy to become confused among the large multiplicity of possible relations and links. Even the text authors themselves will meet difficulties in placing useful linking information in their own texts.

This suggests that methods are needed for an automatic placement of semantic text links to relate text segments with similar subject coverage. Such a task raises a number of interesting questions:

1. How to define an appropriate text unit for text linking purposes.

2. How to measure the closeness in subject matter coverage between distinct text units.

3. How to fix the subject similarity threshold, which controls the actual text linking operation for texts whose similarity exceeds the stated threshold.

In the current study, the choice of an ideal semantic text unit will not be treated. Instead, the assumption is that text links are placed between connected text segments, such as text paragraphs, or text sections (a piece of text appearing between adjacent subheads), depending on the application. Subject matter closeness in then measured for text excerpts of paragraph or section length.

10.2 Automatic Text Analysis

The text linking operations must necessarily depend on a prior analysis of the subject matter for the texts under consideration. For large, heterogeneous text databases, the preferred linguistic and knowledge-based approaches to text understanding are not applicable because these methodologies are not well-enough understood, and are in any case useful only in restricted text environments [Salton, 1991]. Instead, the text analysis system must be based primarily on a study of the available text collections themselves. Since very large text collections are now readily processed, a great deal can be learned about the occurrence characteristics of individual text words and expressions. Linguistic approaches based on statistical and/or probabilistic considerations have, in fact, been used previously to identify term phrases [Choueka, 1988], to assign syntactic tags to text elements [DeRose, 1988; Church, 1988], and to design machine translation systems [Brown *et al.*, 1990].

In the standard Smart approach to text analysis, each text or text excerpt is represented by a set of weighted terms, known as a term vector, and the similarities between distinct texts are then computed by measuring coincidences between the corresponding term vectors [Salton, 1975; Salton, 1989]. The following procedures may serve for this purpose [Salton, 1971]:

1. The individual text words are recognized, and certain common function words (such as *and*, *or*, *but*, etc.) are eliminated by consulting a short list of "stop words".

2. The remaining words are reduced to word-stem form by suffix removal and/or truncation. This reduces words such as *analysis*, *analyzer*, *analyzing*, etc., to a common form such as *analy-*.

3. Optionally, term co-occurrence criteria are used to construct term phrases for sets of words that tend to co-occur frequently in the texts under consideration.

4. Term weights are assigned to the remaining terms (word stems and/or phrase stems). In particular, a term weight w_{ik} is then assigned to each term T_k occurring in document (or text) D_i, and a text is represented by a term vector of the form $D_i = (w_{i1}, w_{i2}, ..., w_{it})$, where t terms in all are assumed to be available in the system. A zero weight is used for terms absent from a document, and positive weights characterize the terms actually assigned.

5. The similarity between two different documents, D_i, is computed by using a vector similarity function such as the inner product $sim(D_i, D_j) = \sum_{i=1}^{t} w_{ik} \cdot w_{jk}$.

6. A threshold is defined for the vector similarity, and a text link is placed between two items, D_i and D_j, whenever the global vector similarity (inner product function) is sufficiently large. Alternatively, document D_i is retrieved when query text Q_j is submitted, provided the global similarity threshold between them is reached.

The assignment of useful term weights capable of distinguishing the important terms from the less important ones is crucial to the success of the automatic indexing process. A high performance term weighting system assigns high term weights to terms that occur frequently in particular documents, but rarely on the outside, because such terms are able to distinguish the items in which they occur from the remainder of the collection. A typical term weight of this type, known as a $tf \times idf$ (term frequency times inverse document frequently) weight, may be defined as

$$w_{ik} = \frac{tf_{ik} \cdot log(N/n_k)}{\sqrt{\sum_{k=1}^{t}(tf_{ik})^2 \cdot (log(N/n_k))^2}} \qquad (10.1)$$

where tf_{ik} is the frequency of occurrence of term T_k in D_i $tf_{ik} = 0$ for terms not assigned to D_i, N is the size of the document collection, and n_k represents the number of documents in the collection with term T_k. The summation in the denominator, taken over all terms in a particular vector, is used for length normalization purposes, to insure that all documents have an equal chance of being retrieved. (Without length normalization, the longer documents with more assigned terms and higher term frequencies would generate higher document similarities, and exhibit higher retrieval potential than the shorter items [Salton, 1991; Salton, 1975; Salton, 1989].)

The previously described text analysis system based on global similarity computations between weighted term vectors may suffer from two main shortcomings. The recall performance may be inadequate when many documents exist with similar subject orientation but quite different vocabulary patterns. Such cases undoubtedly exist, but it is difficult to tell how prevalent they are. In practice, some overlapping vocabulary must be expected when different documents cover similar subject matter, and these coincidences should be detectable by the vector matching process. Thus, Swanson found matching vocabulary patterns for documents covering related subject areas, even when the text items were formally disconnected in the sense that the respective bibliographic citation patters were completely disjoint [Swanson, 1991].

In addition to the recall question, a possibly more serious precision problem must also be considered. Many terms are highly ambiguous, and some of these are expected to carry high weights. When such terms occur in different documents, the meanings may differ, and the joint occurrence of such words in different environments may not provide any indication of subject similarity.

A satisfactory proof does not exist for the recall question because, for large document collections, the necessary relevance judgments are not available between all possible query texts and all stored documents. The expectation is that the recall performance is satisfactory, but this remains to be shown formally. To solve the precision problem, we appeal to the "use theory" of meaning proposed by Wittgenstein and others. That theory states that the meaning of words and expressions is determined by the use of the linguistic entities in the language [Wittgenstein, 1953]. Word use can, to some extent, be determined by studying the context in which the words are used. Hence, to determine coincidence in the meanings of the occurrences of particular words and expressions, a context check is required. When the local context in which the common vocabulary occurs is the same, the texts are accepted as related. Otherwise the global similarity computations are disregarded and the texts are assumed to be unrelated.

10.3   Local Context Processing

To identify the local context similarities for different texts, the same vector similarity computations previously used for the determination of the global text similarities are applied again. However, these similarity measurements are now used for smaller text units. Thus, different texts may be accepted as related when the global vocabulary similarities exceed a stated threshold, and when, in addition, one or more text paragraphs, or one or more text sentences, included in the documents exhibit sufficient local text similarities. (Note that the detection of local text similarities, for example, between particular text sentences without corresponding global similarities, is not significant. Sentences such as "Consider the following example" can occur in any context, and the occurrence of two such matching text fragments reveals little about the text content.)

To compute the local text similarities, term vectors must be constructed as before, and applied to the local text segments, such as text paragraphs and text sentences. In principle, the term weights and similarity measures already used to perform the global text measurements may also serve for the local text similarity measurements. In practice, this implies that very short text segments — for example, very short sentences — with only a few matching terms will control the text matching process. It is therefore preferable to use unnormalized term weights without the denominator of expression (1) to perform the local similarity computations [Salton and Buckley, 1991]. When this is done, text similarities between larger fragments (larger sentences or large paragraphs) are treated as more important than similarities between shorter excerpts.

Normally, the detection of local similarities between text fragments is not

Table 10.1: Comparison of Paragraph and Sentence Similarities

Paragraph- paragraph Similarity Ranks	Paragraph Similarity Range	Number of Document Pairs with Significant Sentence Links
1 - 100	0.89 - 0.66	90/100
101 - 200	0.66 - 0.60	82/100
201 - 300	0.60 - 0.58	74/100
301 - 400	0.58 - 0.55	68/100
401 - 500	0.55 - 0.53	67/100

independent of the size of the corresponding global text similarities. The information of Table 10.1 is derived from an analysis of the 1,140 text paragraphs included in a recent textbook [Salton, 1989]. The table shows that very large proportions of the paragraph pairs with the highest global similarities also exhibit significant local sentence similarities (defined as sentence similarities that reach a threshold of 75.0 in the unnormalized text similarity). For example, 90 of the top 100 paragraph pairs with the highest pairwise paragraph similarities also exhibit high sentence similarities. This suggests that the corresponding texts may, in fact, cover similar subject matter.

A refined text accessing (or text linking) process involving both global as well as local text comparison methods may then be carried out in the following way:

1. Use a query statement, or a text excerpt, that describes the needed subject matter, and compare it with all existing texts, or text segments, using global vector similarity measurements.

2. Identify the stored text segments with sufficiently high global query similarities. Optionally repeat the search using a new query formulation obtained by relevance feedback [Salton and Buckley, 1990], or from the text of previously retrieved items.

3. For texts with sufficiently high global similarities with the query, the

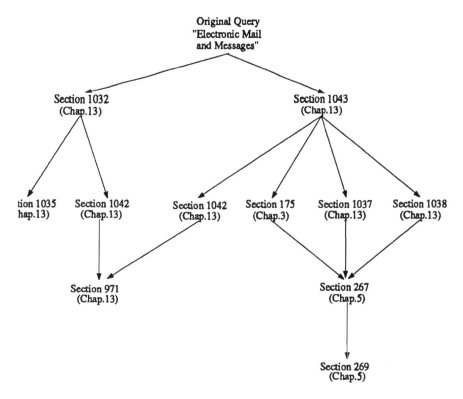

Figure 10.1: Typical linked text structure (paragraph and chapter numbers in [Salton, 1989]—Chapter 13: Paperless Information Systems, Chapter 5: Text Compression, Chapter 3: Automated Office)

local precision filter based on paragraph or sentence similarities can be introduced to reject query-document pairs that do not meet the stated local similarity criterion. Accept as related and retrieve all items with sufficient global as well as local text similarities; alternatively, insert a text link between the corresponding text items.

A sample linked text structure obtained by using the combined vector matching strategy is shown in Figure 10.1. A natural-language query is introduced first and compared with all text sections included in [Salton, 1989]. The two highest matching sections are then used as queries, and additional text sections are identified on the next lower search level. Text sections with sufficient global and local similarities are linked to produce the text traversal prescription shown in Figure 10.1. In the example, the query "electronic mail and messages" identifies sections in three different chapters of the textbook, including the primary chapter 13 where mail and message systems are dis-

Query Article

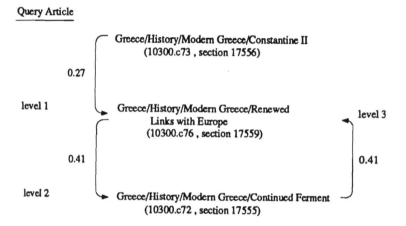

Figure 10.2: Narrow, depth-first search using Section 73 of Document 10300 (10300.c73) as query

cussed, as well as two sections from chapter 5 and one section from chapter 3. Chapter 5 covers text compression and the entropy of message systems, and chapter 3 deals with office automation, and incidentally, with the office mail system.

10.4   Text Traversal Strategies

In constructing linked text structures, and identifying relevant text excerpts in answer to available search requests, a reasonable search strategy must be chosen. In particular, a decision must be reached whether to conduct a single search, or a staged (iterated) search, where several searches are conducted with additional queries derived from previously retrieved text excerpts. In addition, the needed similarity thresholds must be set, and the retrieval size must be specified.

These questions cannot be treated in detail in the present context. Examples are shown, instead, of searches conducted in the 29-volume Funk and Wagnalls encyclopedia [FW, 1979]. The encyclopedia includes about 25,000 articles, broken down into 44,000 text sections, 130,000 text paragraphs, and 410,000 text sentences. The output of Figures 10.2, 10.3, and 10.4 shows the results of the searches conducted with the text of section 73 of article 10300. This section, entitled Greece/History/Modern Greece/Constantine II, covers material related to the reign of Constantine II as king of Greece.

A narrow, depth-first search is illustrated in Figure 10.2. Here, one article only is retrieved at each stage, and that retrieved article is used for a new search as an additional query. The output of Figure 10.2 indicates that two

Query Article

Greece/History/Modern Greece/Constantine II
(10300.c73, section 17556)

1.	Greece/History/Modern Greece/Continued Ferment (10300.c72, section 17555)	0.33
2.	Greece/History/Modern Greece/Renewed Links with Europe (10300.c76, section 17559)	0.27
3.	Prime Minister (18640.c6, section 32559)	0.25
4.	Long Parliament (14211.c6, section 24249)	0.25
5.	Belgium/Government/Executive (2474.33, section 4296)	0.22
6.	Spain/Government/Executive (21417.38, section 37447)	0.22

Figure 10.3: Broad, breadth-first search for query 10300.c73

new text sections are identified by the search, both located in the immediate vicinity of the query section in the encyclopedia (sections 72 and 76 of article 10300 [10300.c72 and 10300.c76]). These new items cover related aspects of the history of modern Greece. The chain comes to an end on the third search step, because a loop is formed when section 10300.c72 retrieves section 10300.c76 that led to its own retrieval. In a depth-first search, the danger exists of shifts in the subject matter because a large number of different queries are utilized in the search effort. For this reason, depth-first searches and depth-first text linking should be used with care in practical retrieval environments.

A breadth-first search for query section 10300.c73 is illustrated in Figure 10.3. Only a single query is then utilized, and all retrieved documents appear on the first retrieval level. The output of Figure 10.3 shows that the search now captures a broader array of documents and subject matter, including some questionable items entitled "Prime Minister" and "Long Parliament". These items should be eliminated by using the previously described local context search.

A mixed depth-breadth search may produce satisfactory search output for many purposes. The results of a depth 3 - breadth 3 search is shown in Figure

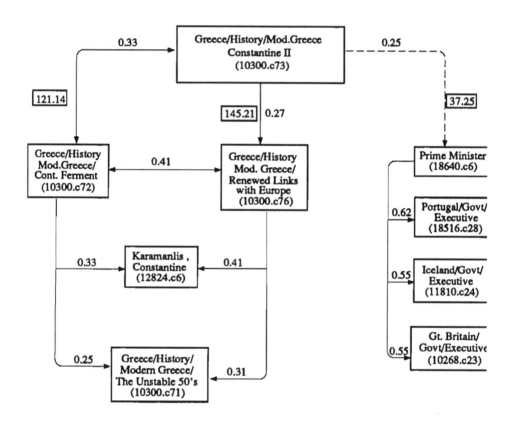

Figure 10.4: Typical linked section structure (Depth 3, Breadth 3) (Boxes
show maximum sentence similarity; dotted line shows a questionable link)

10.4. Here the initial search retrieves 3 items. Each of these items is then used in an additional search to retrieve 3 more items. Two of the three items retrieved at the second stage represent sections that treat modern Greek history, and these items retrieve new sections also concerned with recent Greek history. The third item, entitled "Prime Minister", produces new items concerned with the executive branch of government of various countries.

The results of the local context check are indicated in Figure 10.4 by using boxed numbers that appear alongside the ones that connect pairs of text sections. The box contains in each case the maximum similarity for all pairs of sentences included in the corresponding text pair. It is seen that substantial sentence similarities exist between the query section and the two sections concerned with Greek history (121.14 and 145.21). However, the maximum sentence similarity between the query and section 18640.16 (Prime Minister) is only 37.25. A reasonable sentence similarity threshold that distinguishes relevant from nonrelevant items lies in the vicinity of 75.0. Applying such a threshold rejects the retrieved items shown in the right-hand branch of Figure 10.4 including "Prime Minister" and all other items linked to it.

The available experience indicates that the local context check catches a large proportion of the questionable items that are accepted by the global text comparison system. The combined global-local text comparison system may be expected to produce high precision output as well as reasonable levels of search recall. The operations described in this study are designed to handle large collections of text materials in unrestricted subject areas. The needed linguistic analysis techniques are based entirely on the available texts, and the overhead involved in building large vocabulary schedules and other preconstructed language analysis tools is avoided. The techniques introduced here may become more widely used in future operational text processing systems.

Bibliography

[Brown et al., 1990] P.F. Brown, J. Cocke, S. Della Pietra, V.J. Della Pietra, F. Jelinek, J.D. Lafferty, R.L. Mercer, and P.S. Roussin. A statistical approach to machine translation. *Computational Linguistics*, *16*(2):79–85, 1990.

[Choueka, 1988] Y. Choueka. Looking for needles in a haystack, or locating interesting collocational expressions in large textual databases. In *Proceedings of the RIAO*, pages 609–623, March 1988.

[Church, 1988] K.W. Church. A stochastic parts program and noun phrase parser for unrestricted text. In *Proceedings of the Second Conference on Applied Natural Language Processing*, pages 136–143, Austin, TX, 1988.

[Conklin, 1987] J. Conklin. Hypertext: An introduction and survey. *Computer*, *20*(9):17–41, September 1987.

[DeRose, 1988] S.J. DeRose. Grammatical category disambiguation by statistical optimization. *Computational Linguistics*, *14*(1):31–39, 1988.

[Furuta et al., 1989] R. Furuta, C. Plaisant, and B. Shneiderman. Automatically transforming regularly structured linear documents into hypertext. *Electronic Publishing*, *2*(4):211–229, December 1989.

[FW, 1979] *Funk and Wagnalls New Encyclopedia*. Funk and Wagnalls, New York, 1979. 29 volumes.

[Salton, 1971] G. Salton, editor. *The Smart Information Retrieval System - Experiments in Automatic Document Processing*. Prentice-Hall Inc., Englewood Cliffs, NJ, 1971.

[Salton, 1975] G. Salton. A theory of indexing. In *Regional Conference Series in Applied Mathematics, No. 18*. Society for Industrial and Applied Mathematics, Philadelphia, PA, 1975.

[Salton, 1989] G. Salton. *Automatic Text Processing — The Analysis, Transformation and Retrieval of Information by Computer*. Addison-Wesley, Reading, MA, 1989.

[Salton, 1991] G. Salton. Developments in automatic text retrieval. *Science*, 253:974–980, 1991.

[Salton and Buckley, 1990] G. Salton and C. Buckley. Improving retrieval performance by relevance feedback. *Journal of the American Society for Information Science*, *41*(4):288–297, 1990.

[Salton and Buckley, 1991] G. Salton and C. Buckley. Global text matching for information retrieval. *Science*, *253*:1012–1015, August 1991.

[Swanson, 1991] D.R. Swanson. Complementary structures in disjoint science literatures. In *Proceedings of the Fourteenth International Conference on Research and Development in Information Retrieval*, pages 280–289, 1991.

[Wittgenstein, 1953] L. Wittgenstein. *Philosophical Investigations*. Basil Blackwell and Co., Ltd., Oxford, England, 1953.

Part III

Emerging Applications

Part III: Emerging Applications

We have only begun to explore the range of applications of advanced technologies for handling on-line texts. This group of papers includes two of the more mature applications of "intelligent" text processing techniques, and two promising new sorts of applications.

The Stanfill and Waltz paper describes work that has been implemented and deployed within a massively-parallel architecture called the Connection Machine. What's notable about this work is not only that it shows some of the remarkable functionality of the most successful of a new breed of computers, but that handling volumes of text was behind one of the first real commercial installations of these machines—a text retrieval application for Dow Jones and Co. The Hayes paper reports on other real applications, including text categorization for Reuters. These are illustrative of the current use of advanced methods in handling on-line news.

Maarek's report describes the problem of producing "smart" manuals, or converting documentation into user-helpful systems. Although the content of the first AI-based text systems has been news, manuals and other on-line documentation will be the main force in applications to come, as computer networks and documentation standards flourish. Hearst describes another "direction" entirely—an application where the content of a text must be reduced to answering a simple question: "pro or con?" As easy as this seems, this well-motivated work pushes beyond the current state-of-the-art of current NL and IR work.

This volume ends with the applications because this is where the excitement in text-based systems will be during the years to come. The techniques described earlier will come to solve new problems, and problems will give rise to new techniques, feeding the cycle that has created this whole line of work along with the progress that's reported in this collection.

Statistical Methods, Artificial Intelligence, and Information Retrieval

Craig Stanfill
Thinking Machines Corporation
David L. Waltz
Thinking Machines Corporation, and
Center for Complex Systems, Brandeis University

11.1 Introduction

AI as it has been formulated in the past is, if not yet dead, dying; a new AI is taking its place. The old AI was based on rules and logic. The new AI is based on statistics—but not statistics as it has been formulated in the past. The practice of statistics itself is undergoing a substantial transformation.

The fundamental problem with the old AI is that it is inwardly directed: Given a set of propositions which embody the fundamental truths of the world, logic derives the consequences. The difficulty arises because the world is so complex that, beyond the Unified Field Theory (if one is ever found), it is doubtful that there are any fundamental truths, only approximations to truth. Statistics, by way of contrast, is outwardly directed: Given a set of observations, it estimates the probabilities of various outcomes, using past observations as a basis.

Perhaps the best illustration of the relationship between logic and statistics can be seen in their different handling of incomplete knowledge. In a well-known syllogism, we all accept the proposition that most birds fly. However, some birds (such as ostriches, dead birds, and birds with their feet set in concrete) cannot fly. The regular propositional logic, concerned as it is with certainties, breaks down in the face of such statements. Attempts to formulate alternative logics (e.g., logic with circumscription and non-monotonic logic [McCarthy, 1986; McDermott and Doyle, 1980]) have proved difficult. By way of contrast, the formulation of the problem in probability theory is generally taken care of in Chapter 1 of introductory texts, using the concept of conditional probabilities. Of course, the problem of determining conditional probabilities can become quite difficult, but at least the mathematical basis of statistics is not hostile to the notion of uncertainty.

This is not to say that AI has been ignorant of probabilistic/statistical methods. There was a substantial body of work in the 1960's on statistical pattern classification [Dasarthy, 1990; Cover and Hart, 1967; Anderson and Rosenfeld, 1988]. Much of the work on rule-based expert systems in the 1970's and 1980's used the language of probability theory (Bayesian estimation [Cheeseman et al., 1988], Dempster-Schafer theory [Dempster et al., 1977], and fuzzy logic [Zadeh, 1989]) to rationalize rules incorporating statements of uncertainty. However, the center of gravity of AI has remained in the general area of logic and rules; thus, Dempster-Schafer theory was used as a basis for changing the formulation of rule-based reasoning. For a long time the logical formulation seemed to hold promise, and it remained in the ascendency. However, for all the work that has been put into rule-based systems, there is not a vast difference between what could be done via rules in the early 1970's and what can be done today.

There is now a growing movement away from rule-based approaches and toward more statistically-oriented techniques. The back-propagation learning method, now widely used, can be viewed as a gradient descent algorithm searching for non-linear discriminant functions [Rumelhart et al., 1986]. Recent work done by Poggio and Girosi on radial basis functions also has a statistical orientation [Poggio and Girosi, 1990]. Memory-based reasoning is based on a nearest-neighbor classification rule that is well known in the statistical literature [Stanfill and Waltz, 1986; Waltz, 1990b]. Impressive results have been achieved recently on part-of-speech assignment using statistical methods [Church, 1988]. These methods have strong synergy with massively parallel computer hardware advances [Waltz, 1990a], while it is notoriously difficult for rule-based systems to exploit massive parallelism [Forgy, 1979].

This paper first considers the use of statistics in information retrieval. The next sections discuss recent trends in the field of statistics, and recent trends in information retrieval. The paper concludes with brief descriptions of three sample applications: CMDRS, a text retrieval system based on relevance feedback; a system for automatically assigning keywords to documents, based on a database of already-classified docoments; and PACE, a system for classifying Census Bureau long forms by occupation and industry.

11.2   The Example of Information Retrieval

Information retrieval is a good example of the triumph of statistical methods over rule-based systems. In an information retrieval system, the user tries to describe the information he is seeking; the system tries to use those descriptions to locate the appropriate information.

How would this be done in classical AI? One can imagine something like the following: The database is processed by a natural-language understanding system, which extracts the meaning of the documents. When the user enters a request, the retrieval system uses the same natural-language understanding system to figure out what the user wants, then retrieves the documents that contain that information using an "intelligent" memory with deductive inference. All aspects of the system are implemented as (rule-based) expert systems. Such systems have been constructed for suitably narrow domains of discourse [Sundheim, 1991]. [1]

Information Retrieval has never had the luxury of working within semantically limited domains. In practice, it must cope with wide areas of information, such as "Medicine," "The Law," "Computer Science," etc. A typical IR system takes the following approach: It pre-processes the database, making statistical inferences as to the degree to which various words reflect the content of each document. The user queries the database by specifying certain words that he believes might be used in the documents he is interested in. The system, using the query plus the statistical model produced in pre-processing, estimates the probability that each document is relevant to the user's request, and presents the user with those documents most likely to be of interest. Further interactions between the user and the system allow these probability estimates to be refined, which results in a more targeted set of documents being retrieved [Salton, 1971].

The surprising thing (from the point of view of AI) is that the statistical approach, using no domain-specific knowledge at all, works. And it works for quantities of information (gigabytes) that are unimaginably large by the standards of AI [Stanfill and Thau, 1991].

11.3   Statistics is Changing

The above discussion has remained noncommittal about the meaning of the term *statistics*, and the reader may think that, by including such work as back-propagation and information retrieval under the heading of "statistical methods" the term *statistics* is being broadened beyond its traditional meaning. In this the reader is correct, because statistics is also undergoing some fundamental changes in response to the advent of computers.

Statistical analysis, in its broadest sense, is the search for structure in collections of data, using probability theory as the standard for judging what constitutes "structure." This structure may be interpreted directly, or it may be used to make predictions of future behavior.

Most of classical statistics was developed before the coming of computers, and consists of various methods of parameter estimation. Typically, the analyst posits a parameterized model to explain a set of observations. For example, in linear regressions the analyst posits a model of the following form:

---

[1]This is the aim of the TIPSTER program. TIPSTER is a current DARPA project to extract and fill frames from business and technology news articles, and to detect (i.e., retrieve) facts from databases of filled frames. Research under contract began in 1991; all contractors must handle both English and Japanese.

$$y = \beta_0 + \sum \beta_i x_i$$

The statistical task is to collect a set of measurements on the data which allow the parameters β_i to be estimated, and to determine the accuracy of those estimates.

There are many sorts of statistical models that can be constructed, but most of the commonly used ones have a flavor similar to the above, i.e., of positing a model and then collecting statistics that allow the parameters in the model to be estimated. It is no accident that these methods were developed before digital computers were widely available and that, for modest amounts of data, the required computations can be carried out by hand [Spiegal, 1968].

Recent developments in statistics can be most easily characterized by the ways they differ from the sort of parametric statistics described above:

They are non-parametric. Parametric statistics requires that the analyst posit the form of the model, for example, as the linear sum of analytic expressions. Non-parametric methods relax this restriction; rather than hypothesizing a linear relationship between Z and Y, the analyst may simply posit that some relation exists, and permit the computer to produce a numerical model (e.g., a quadratic spline) for that relationship [Duda and Hart, 1973].

They are non-analytic. Most of traditional statistics produce analytic formulae that proceed directly from measurements to model. For example, in many cases the dimensionality of data being worked on is unreasonably high (e.g., 100+ dimensions). The traditional approach is to reduce the dimensionality of the data by principal component analysis. This method produces an analytic formula, defined in terms of eigenvalues and matrices, that finds (for example) a projection from 100-space to 3-space, preserving as much variation in the data as possible. There is, however, a newer non-analytic approach to this problem, called *projection pursuit*, which frames the problem as a heuristic search for a projection that exposes as much information as possible [Huber, 1985].

They are non-global. In traditional methods, a single model is constructed that explains all the data. More recent techniques are based on discovering and exploiting local structure. For example, one might use a clustering algorithm to divide the database into subsets. If the population being studied is, in fact, a collection of smaller subpopulations that differ one from another, then this method is likely to yield superior results.

11.4   What This Says About Information Retrieval

Although most fielded IR systems are based on Boolean operations, a significant part of Information Retrieval research has long been statistically oriented. For example, many Information Retrieval systems operate by variations on best-match procedures. Such methods are well-known alternatives to parametric statistics, and are being actively explored in the Artificial Intelligence community. However, these methods depend on a global metric, which is directly generated from statistical measurements of the document base. Applying the new statistical thinking, it might be possible to devise new metrics that exploit local structure, and that are formed by an exploratory process rather than by grinding through formulae based on measurements of term-frequencies.

For example, information retrieval has long sought to exploit local structures by the use of clustering algorithms (see the papers by Lewis and Salton and Buckley). However, clustering generally requires that the data first be embedded in a metric space; at this point it runs into the same shortcomings described above, namely, that the method is dependent on a single global metric that does not reflect the local structure of the data. This leads to an interesting (and fundamental) dilemma: One *wants* to exploit local structure. In order to exploit that structure, it must first be found. The most common method of finding that structure is clustering. However, clustering depends on metrics that suffer from the problem that they do not capture local structure.

And what of applications of traditional AI to Information Retrieval? These can take several forms. One approach that has had a certain amount of success is the construction of expert systems for locating very specific types of information in large quantities of data. For example, one might construct a set of rules for reading articles in business publications, looking for articles where one company acquires another, and use this to maintain a database of corporate acquisitions. This sort of system seems to be buildable and could be useful.

However, it seems quite unlikely that such methods will be successful when applied to less constrained problems, and, in any event, there are relatively few applications where the effort needed to build and to maintain the rule set is justified. Hand-built rule-based systems have, in the long run, little to offer Information Retrieval, because they do not work very well (see [Lewis, 1992] and the paper by Lewis in this volume), and because they require vast amounts of (very expensive) human labor [Creecy *et al.*, 1992; Lenat *et al.*, 1986].

11.5   Sample Applications

This section describes three applications that use statistically-oriented methods to successfully accomplish tasks that traditional AI has (or would have)
solved quite differently.

11.5.1   Text Retrieval

The first application is the CMDRS text retrieval system, based on the idea
of relevance feedback [Salton, 1971; Stanfill and Kahle, 1986]. CMDRS (for
Connection Machine Document Retrieval System) has run continuously as
the DowQuest commercial service from Dow Jones [Jones, 1989], searching
about 1 gigabyte of text from over 400 sources (news wires, newspapers,
magazines, business sections of local and regional papers, etc.). CMDRS
could work interactively on much larger databases [Stanfill and Thau, 1991].
In fairly extensive testing, CMDRS achieves a precision-recall product of
about .65 [Wilensky, 1992], far better than traditional Boolean search [Blair
and Maron, 1985], and difficult to compare with any AI programs, which
cannot today deal with text databases of this size and diversity.

The algorithm used by CMDRS has the following steps: (1) collect all
query terms, remove stopwords, rank order them by score (proportional to
the negative log of the probability of each term), and truncate the list to
no more than the 100 highest scoring terms. This gives the highest score
to words and terms that are rare in the database, and ignores very common
words (*the*, *in*, *and*, etc.). *Terms* refers to pairs of words that are both capitalized somewhere in the database. Terms are formed when any such pair of
words occur together with sufficiently greater frequency than one would predict from their independent frequencies. Examples: "White House", "West
Bank", "George Bush".

(2) Compare all remaining query terms with each 30-word section of the
database, and compute scores for each such section. Section scores are the
sum of the scores of all query terms that appear in them. Sections are given
extra credit if query terms appear more than once. This process is carried out
in parallel: Each processor in a massively parallel Connection Machine [TMC,
1989] stores numerous 30-word sections, and all are searched simultaneously
after the query terms are broadcast to all processors. The algorithm uses 30-
word sections for two purposes: (a) allowing searches to locate the best pairs
of even very long documents, and (b) allowing appropriate normalization of
searches in databases where there is a very large discrepancy between the
smallest and largest documents (from under 100 words to over 100K words
per document in DowQuest). (3) "Blurring". Combine the scores of 30-word
sections that are adjacent in texts to form scores for 60-word sections. This
compensates for cases where a very good section has been split into two 30-
word sections that each exhibit only moderately good matches. (4) Find the
best n documents, where the "best document" is the one that contains the

best 60 word "blurred" section. A user can choose to see either the best sections or the heads of the best documents.

The importance of probabilistic operation in CMDRS should be obvious!

11.5.2   Automatic Keyword Assignment

The second example, automatic keyword assignments [Masand *et al.*, 1992], calls CMDRS as a subroutine, using a variant of the Memory-Based Reasoning (MBR) paradigm [Stanfill and Waltz, 1986; Waltz, 1990b]. For this application we use an article we wish to classify to form a query, and search a database of 50,000 articles that have been assigned keywords (by human editors at Dow Jones in our case) from a set of about 300 possibilities. The system finds the best 20 documents, together with their overall scores, and lists of their keywords. Each keyword returned in one or more documents is assigned a score by summing the scores of the documents in which it occurred.

We performed tests for the quality of this method by (1) stripping keywords from a test subset of the database, (2) using the rest of the database to propose keywords for each test article, and (3) giving proposed keyword-article pairs to human experts to evaluate. Keyword-article pairs generated automatically were mixed with human-assigned pairs from the database. Human experts graded each pair as "correct", "borderline", and "incorrect". If "borderline" is lumped with "incorrect", experts judge the original human-assigned keywords to have a precision of .87 and recall of .86. The corresponding scores for the automatically-generated keywords were .80 and .72 in our initial test. We believe that reasoning on the basis of a larger database of articles will improve our performance, as will parameter adjustments and cleverer pruning of low-scored potential keywords. Still, this is very good performance, especially considering that the total effort required to build and test this system was only two person-months (not counting the building of CMDRS).

11.5.3   Classifying Census Returns

The third example, PACE (Parallel Automatic Coding Expert) performs automatic classification of Census Bureau long forms [Creecy *et al.*, 1992] using MBR [Stanfill and Waltz, 1986; Waltz, 1990b]. It does not, however, use CMDRS. Each Census long form has questions that require free-text responses for occupation, company, duties, and industry type. We used a database of 132,000 carefully classified returns as our reasoning base. The 132,000 examples database was originally constructed to test AIOCS, an expert system built by the Census Bureau for the same task solved by PACE [Appel and Scopp, 1987]. PACE uses different MBR variants to perform its two tasks—industry classification and occupation classification. The industry task uses a single nearest-neighbor, selected using the "error metric"—a metric devised during research for PACE, while the occupation task uses a k-nearest neighbor method with k approximately equal to 10. Detailed operation is beyond the scope of this paper, but can be found in [Creecy et al., 1992].

Results were impressive: PACE outperformed AIOCS 63% to 57% on the industry task, and 57% to 37% on the occupation task. (The percentages represent the fraction of the Census returns that can be handled automatically with a confidence score that ensures performance equal to human classifiers.) More significantly, the time to build PACE was only 4 person-months, including testing and several dead ends versus nearly 200 person-months for AIOCS.

We believe that PACE provides a dramatic demonstration of the advantages of statistically-based AI.

11.6   The Future

We are not entirely negative on rule-based systems. They are a useful technology, and the effort involved in studying the logical basis of rules, the implementation of rules, and the construction of sets of rules has been justified. However, as a mechanism for constructing truly intelligent systems, they are a dead end, because such systems are too large to build by hand, and expert systems seem inherently to involve extensive human effort ("knowledge engineering"). We are not at all negative about AI in general. There is a great deal of excitement at the intersection of AI and statistics, where the neat logical formulae of AI and the neat mathematical formulae of statistics must be abandoned. In this zone one finds back-propagation, nearest-neighbor, genetic algorithms, projection pursuit, and clustering, as well as hybrid computational methods. This is the region where Information Retrieval has always been, and is where it should stay.

Bibliography

[Anderson and Rosenfeld, 1988] J. Anderson and E. Rosenfeld, editors. *Neurocomputing: Foundations of Research*. MIT Press, Cambridge, MA, 1988.

[Appel and Scopp, 1987] M.V. Appel and T. Scopp. Automated industry and occupation coding. development of statistical tools. In *Seminar on Development of Statistical Expert Systems (DOSES)*, Luxembourg, December 1987.

[Blair and Maron, 1985] D. C. Blair and M. E. Maron An evaluation of retrieval effectiveness for a full-text document retrieval system. *Communications of the Association for Computing Machinery*, 28(3):289–299, 1985.

[Cheeseman et al., 1988] Peter Cheeseman et al. Bayesian classification. In *Proceedings of the Seventh National Conference on Artificial Intelligence (AAAI-88)*, Saint Paul, MN, 1988.

[Church, 1988] K.W. Church. A stochastic parts program and noun phrase parser for unrestricted text. In *Second Conf. on Applied Natural Language Processing*, pages 136–143, Austin, TX, 1988.

[Cover and Hart, 1967] T. Cover and P. Hart. Nearest neighbor pattern classification. *IEEE Transactions on Information Theory*, *13*:21–27, 1967.

[Creecy et al., 1992] R. Creecy, B. Masand, S. Smith, and D. Waltz. Trading MIPS and memory for knowledge engineering. *Communications of the ACM*, 1992. In press.

[Dasarthy, 1990] B.U. Dasarthy, editor. *Nearest Neighbor (NN) Norms: NN Pattern Classification Techniques*. IEEE Computer Society Press, Washington, DC, 1990.

[Dempster et al., 1977] A.P. Dempster, N.M. Laird, and D.B. Rubin. Maximum likelihood from incomplete data via the em algorithm. *Journal of the Royal Statistical Society, Series B*, *39*(1):1–38, 1977.

[Duda and Hart, 1973] R. Duda and P. Hart. *Pattern Classification and Scene Analysis*. John Wiley and Sons, New York, 1973.

[Forgy, 1979] C. Forgy. *On the efficient implementation of production systems*. PhD thesis, Carnegie Mellon University, Pittsburgh, 1979.

[Huber, 1985] P. Huber. Projection pursuit. *Annals of Statistics*, 13(2):435–475, 1985.

[Jones, 1989] Dow Jones. What's different about Dow!uest? Ease, content and text-retrieval. *Dowline, 2nd Quarter*, 1989.

[Lenat et al., 1986] D. Lenat, M. Prakash, and M. Shepherd. CYC: Using common sense knowledge to overcome brittleness and knowledge acquisition bottlenecks. *AI Magazine*, *6*(4), 1986.

[Lewis, 1992] David D. Lewis. *Representation and Learning in Information Retrieval*. PhD thesis, Computer Science Dept.; University of Massachusetts, Amherst, MA 01003, 1992. (Available as Technical Report 91-93.)

[Masand et al., 1992] B. Masand, G. Linoff, and D. Waltz. Classifying news stories using memory-based reasoning. In *Fifteenth Annual International ACM SIGIR Conference on Research and Development in Information Retrieval*, 1992. In press.

[McCarthy, 1986] John McCarthy. Applications of circumscription to formalizing commonsense knowledge. *Artificial Intelligence*, *26*(3):89–116, 1986.

[McDermott and Doyle, 1980] Drew McDermott and J. Doyle. Nonmonotonic logic I. *Artificial Intelligence*, *13*:41–72, 1980.

[Poggio and Girosi, 1990] T. Poggio and F. Girosi. Regularization algorithms for learning that are equivalent to multilayer networks. *Science*, *247*:978–982, 1990.

[Rumelhart *et al.*, 1986] D. Rumelhart, G. Hinton, and R. Williams. Learning internal representation by error propagation. In D.E. Rumelhard and J. McClelland, editors, *Parallel Distributed Processing: Explorations in the Microstructure of Cognition*, volume 1, pages 318–362. The MIT Press, Cambridge, MA, 1986.

[Salton, 1971] G. Salton, editor. *The Smart Information Retrieval System— Experiments in Automatic Document Processing*. Prentice-Hall Inc., Englewood Cliffs, NJ, 1971.

[Spiegal, 1968] M. Spiegal. *Mathematical Handbook of Formulas and Tables*. Academic Press, New York, 1968.

[Stanfill and Kahle, 1986] C. Stanfill and B. Kahle. Parallel free-text search on the connection machine system. *Communications of the Association for Computing Machinery*, 29(12):1229–1239, 1986.

[Stanfill and Thau, 1991] C. Stanfill and R. Thau. Information retrieval on the connection machine: 1-8192 gigabytes. *Information Processing and Management*, *27*(4):285–310, 1991.

[Stanfill and Waltz, 1986] C. Stanfill and D. Waltz. Toward memory-based reasoning. *Communications of the Association for Computing Machinery*, *29*(12):1213–1228, 1986.

[Sundheim, 1991] Beth Sundheim, editor. *Proceedings of the Third Message Understanding Conference (MUC-3)*. Morgan Kaufmann Publishers, Los Altos, CA, May 1991.

[TMC, 1989] TMC. CM-2 technical summary. Technical report, Thinking Machines Corporation, 1989.

[Waltz, 1990a] D.L. Waltz. Massively parallel AI. In *Proceedings of the Eighth National Conference on Artificial Intelligence (AAAI-90)*, pages 1117–1122, Boston, August 1990.

[Waltz, 1990b] D.L. Waltz. Memory-based reasoning. In M. Arbib and J.A. Robinson, editors, *Natural and Artificial Parallel Computation*, pages 251–276. MIT Press, Cambridge, MA, 1990.

[Wilensky, 1992] U. Wilensky. Paper in progress discussing performance of CMDRS, the system used by Dow Jones for DowQuest. Technical report, Thinking Machines Corporation, 1992.

[Zadeh, 1989] L.A. Zadeh. Knowledge representation in fuzzy logic. *IEEE Transactions on Knowledge and Data Engineering*, *1*(1), 1989.

Intelligent High-Volume Text Processing Using Shallow, Domain-Specific Techniques

Philip J. Hayes
Carnegie Group Inc
5 PPG Place
Pittsburgh, PA 15222

Abstract

Carnegie Group has substantial experience in the implementation and commercial deployment of text-based intelligent systems. Specifically, we have deployed systems that categorize text for routing and retrieval purposes and systems that extract key facts from text for summarization and database filling purposes. In what follows, I review that experience and describe additional intelligent text-based applications that we have explored and view as important and tractable. These additional applications include methods of structuring access to large bodies of technical documentation and methods of combining text and expert systems in intelligent support environments for diagnostic or other advisory systems. I end with some of the challenges still to be solved in creating intelligent text-based applications.

12.1 Carnegie Group Experience in Text Categorization

Carnegie Group has been working in the area of automatic text categorization for several years, using shallow, domain-specific techniques. The techniques are shallow so that they can operate fast enough to process large volumes of text, but allow the incorporation of enough domain knowledge to provide very high accuracy on the kind of text categorization tasks we have pursued. This balance has evolved from the requirements of our commercial customers, who need systems that are accurate enough to meet task goals while being fast and robust enough to be deployed in an operational setting. We see the tradeoff between speed and accuracy mediated by depth of processing as a central design issue in the automatic processing of the extremely large volumes of text that occur in real-world applications. We have adopted a minimalist strategy with respect to depth of processing, only going as deep as necessary to achieve our customers' goals. We have been pleasantly surprised by how much can be accomplished by simple techniques.

The essence (see [Hayes *et al.*, 1990] for a detailed description with examples) of our approach to categorization is to identify themes or concepts in a text by matching phrases related to the concepts. *Phrases* are specified as patterns of words built using arbitrary nestings of disjunction, negation, skip (up to *n* words), and optionality operators. An example might be the phrase "cold rolled bars" or the word *lead*, so long as it is not preceded by *to* or followed within 3 words by the word *manager*. Morphological equivalence sets (noun forms, verb forms), case (upper case, lower case, capitalized), punctuation, and wildcards may also be specified. Individual patterns are weighted by how strongly they indicate the concept, and the sum of the weights of the patterns that match give a strength of occurrence of the concept in the text. Categorization decisions are made by if-then rules, which take into account what concepts are identified in the text, what part of the text they appear in, and what strength they occur at. The patterns, concepts, and categorization rules are all application-specific. Their development for a particular application is a knowledge engineering task. The approach is appropriate for categorization tasks in which the categories can be defined in advance, have definitions that are specific and firm, and are directly related to the content of the text, rather than to the interest of the reader. Thus, corporate acquisitions would be an appropriate category, but events of political significance would not.

A major commercial application of this approach is the CONSTRUE system [Hayes *et al.*, 1988; Hayes and Weinstein, 1991], a news story categorization system developed for Reuters Ltd. and delivered in 1988. CONSTRUE classifies a broad stream of economic and financial news stories into one or more of 674 categories using the above techniques. It also detects the presence of company names in the stories, using close to literal matching techniques and a database of around 17,000 companies. CONSTRUE was delivered to run on Digital VAXStation (TM) 3100s in a manner fully integrated with the customer's computing environment and is designed to operate non-stop, 24 hours a day. Its processing speed on typical Reuters news stories (average length 151 words) averaged 4.36 seconds on the 2.7 Mips 3100. CONSTRUE's accuracy averaged across all 674 categories was 94% recall and 84% precision, [1] measured on a set of 723 stories not previously processed by the system and not previously examined by CONSTRUE developers.

Following is a news story representative of those categorized by CON-

---

[1] *Recall* is the number of stories accurately placed in a category divided by the number that should have been placed in that category; it is a measure of how many of the stories CONSTRUE was looking for it actually found. *Precision*, on the other hand, is the number of stories accurately placed in a category divided by the total number that were placed in the category; it is a measure of how many of the stories that CONSTRUE found were relevant.

STRUE.

DOWA MINING TO PRODUCE GOLD FROM APRIL

TOKYO, March 16 - Dowa [Mining Co Ltd said it will
start commercial production of gold and lead] from its Nu-
rukawa Mine in northern Japan in April. A company spokesman
said the mine's monthly output is expected to consist of
1,300 metric tons of gold ore and 3,700 of black ore. A
company survey shows the gold ore contains up to 13.3 grams
of gold per metric ton, he said. Proven gold ore reserves
amount to 50,000 metric tons while estimated reserves of
gold and black ores total one mln metric tons, he added.

The categories assigned in this case are GOLD-COMMODITY, LEAD-
COMMODITY, JAPAN. Note that CONSTRUE is able, through its rule-
based approach, to apply the LEAD-COMMODITY category correctly despite only one occurrence of the very ambiguous word *lead*.

The first deployment of CONSTRUE to provide value to Reuter sub-
scribers was with Reuter Country Reports in November, 1989. The second
was with Reuter Textline in December 1990. Both of these services use CON-
STRUE to generate index terms for a large textual database of news stories.
The indexes were previously generated by humans, with a delay that frequently extended to several days. CONSTRUE now provides the indexes
within seconds. To meet the specific indexing needs of existing subscriber
groups, both services use rulebases that are modified subsets of the 674 category rulebase delivered with CONSTRUE. Country Reports deals with 200
categories, 196 countries, and 4 general categories. It has been measured on
a sample of 700 stories at 98% recall, 99% precision for the country categories
and 94% recall, 96% precision for the four general categories. Textline deals
with 80 general topics and was measured at 92% recall, 90% precision.

Cost-benefit analysis by Reuters has made it clear that CONSTRUE will
handsomely repay its initial investment. CONSTRUE/TIS has shown that an
automated knowledge-based text categorization system can provide indexing
that is comparable to human indexing in quality on a commercially important
indexing task, but at a much lower cost and much more rapidly. Moreover,
CONSTRUE/TIS goes beyond simple replacement of functionality already
provided by people. It can generate index terms in a fraction of the time
required by human indexers and with greater consistency. It is too soon
to know for sure what impact these service enhancements will have from
a market perspective, but Reuters expects to gain from them a significant
competitive advantage and hence an increased market share.

We have generalized CONSTRUE into a marketable software package
called Text Categorization Shell (TCS) [Hayes *et al.*, 1990]. TCS can be
used to determine the subject matter of entries in textual databases or high
volume streams of text from a potentially large predefined set of categories.
The resulting categorizations can then be used for various purposes: to route

texts to appropriate people, to retrieve texts from a database, and to create indexes into large documents. Creation of a specific text categorization application using TCS involves creation of a rulebase of the same kind of patterns, concepts, and if-then rules used in CONSTRUE, plus some I/O customization to deal with the format of the texts being processed.

TCS has been used by HRB Systems Inc. for a classified US Government application involving the routing of messages to analysts who are each interested in a subset of the incoming messages. An initial version of the HRB system handles five categories. It demonstrates very high accuracy levels on all categories despite misspellings, ungrammatical language, and significant overlap in vocabulary between documents that are and are not of interest. Specifically, HRB has measured recall at 95% and precision at 97% as weighted averages across all five categories on a test set of 700 messages, just under 20% of which fell into one or more of the five categories. This compares very favorably with the categorization/retrieval system that HRB's system is designed to replace. This existing system, based on traditional inverted indexes and Boolean keyword search, has comparable recall, but its precision is less than 10%. A deployment of the HRB system at the same accuracy levels would thus reduce the amount of irrelevant information more than 10 times the relevant information to about 3% of it, with obvious major benefits for analyst productivity.

12.2   Other Approaches to Categorization

Readers familiar with the information retrieval literature or having practical experience of information retrieval systems will have been struck by the high levels of accuracy reported for the various systems discussed in the previous section. There are two basic reasons why the numbers are so high. First, the problem tackled by those systems is categorization against a predetermined set of categories (see Lewis, this volume). This task is a subset of, and is inherently simpler than, the general information retrieval problem of determining relevancy of texts against ad hoc queries. Second, the approach we have used permits more selectivity in the phrases used to determine relevancy, and provides a framework for allowing domain-specific pieces of knowledge to be brought to bear. The second reason means that even on the limited task of categorization against pre-determined categories, the TCS approach is likely to produce higher accuracy than information retrieval techniques. However, this higher accuracy comes at a significant cost in terms of the effort required to build a TCS rulebase. Finally, it is worthwhile to note that even within the limited task of categorization against pre-determined categories, what constitutes a good accuracy level is dependent on the particular task. The categorization task for the Reuters Textline database is inherently harder than the one for Reuters Country Reports database, thus accounting for the difference in accuracy figures reported above for those two applications. It would be entirely possible to define a categorization task where a TCS-based system could not get over 90%. However, we think it likely that a knowledge-based approach like TCS would continue to provide an edge over information retrieval techniques, even in such a case.

The information retrieval methods categorize texts based on the presence or absence of certain words. The simplest information retrieval technique is the Boolean keyword method used by most commercial text retrieval systems. With the Boolean keyword approach, users specify texts they are interested in via Boolean combinations of words, fixed phrases, pairs of words within a certain distance of each other, or other such constructs. This method can be made to run very fast (through the use of inverted file techniques [Salton and McGill, 1983]). Also, because the method does not rely on the detection of any language structures or involve any knowledge of language on the part of the system, it is highly robust, easily maintainable, and straightforward in application development. Furthermore, because the users of such systems effectively specify a new category with every Boolean combination they compose, the approach is, unlike TCS, appropriate when categories cannot be defined in advance or are rapidly changing.

Unfortunately, however, it is hard to capture the conceptual content of text using the Boolean keyword approach to categorization, and hence it is not highly accurate. Average recall and precision figures of little better than 50% are typical for retrieval on ad hoc queries [Salton, 1986]. There are two basic problems. First, a user may not think of the words that were actually used by the author of a relevant text. For instance, a user might specify *takeover* to find texts about one company buying another, but the author of a relevant text might have used only *acquisition*. (See [Furnas *et al.*, 1987] for an indication of the pervasiveness and difficulty of this problem.) The second problem is that the method takes no account of the way words relate to each other or are contextually modified. *Acquisition* can just as easily refer to the purchase of a piece of capital equipment as the takeover of another company.

The first of these problems can be ameliorated by the use of more modern statistically-based information retrieval techniques, such as latent semantic indexing [Dumais *et al.*, 1988], which attempts to determine a pool of words related to each of a set of semantic concepts, and relevance feedback [Salton and McGill, 1983; Stanfill and Kahle, 1986] (see the Stanfill and Waltz paper in this volume) in which weighted collections of words from texts in a category are used as the basis of a search for other texts in the category. However, these advances do not address the problem of the meaning of words being contextually determined.

TCS addresses the problem of finding the right word by using a rulebase in which a knowledge engineer can list a comprehensive set of vocabulary words relevant to a particular pre-determined category. A similar approach could, of course, be taken with information retrieval, and indeed some commercial systems provide facilities for building libraries of terms for use in repeated queries. TCS is more differentiated from information retrieval approaches on the second issue, i.e., the meaning of words being contextually determined. The pattern matching language used by TCS to specify vocabulary is significantly richer than the languages used for expressing queries in typical Boolean systems. In particular, the use of position-specific negated elements in TCS patterns, a feature not found in Boolean systems, gives discriminatory power that we have found very important in gaining high accuracy. The ability to look for the word *gold* so long as it is not followed within three words by the word *reserves* was, for instance, very important for identifying a gold commodity category in the CONSTRUE system. In addition, TCS if-then rules can contain domain-specific knowledge to enhance accuracy. For instance, a rule associated with the same gold commodity category said that if the system saw evidence for both the gold and foreign exchange categories, then it should ignore the foreign exchange evidence and choose gold. The price of using such power is a substantial knowledge engineering effort to produce application-specific rulebases, but the reward is potentially very high accuracy.

12.3   Fact Extraction

A natural next step beyond categorization is fact extraction. This means, for instance, not just determining that a text is about a corporate acquisition, but also determining what company is taking over what other company, price per share, effective date, etc. Once such information is extracted, it can be used to produce concise summaries of the input texts, to fill a structured database with the information extracted, or to perform highly selective document retrieval from a textual database. Clearly, fact extraction requires a deeper level of analysis than categorization. However, we are confident that much (though not all) useful fact extraction can be achieved without a full analysis of the text involved at either the sentence or the text level. This approach contrasts with a system like PROTEUS [Ksiezyk and Grishman, 1986], which attempts to do a complete job of analyzing every sentence in a text and all their interrelations. We give up the potential for total accuracy inherent in full analysis in exchange for major reductions in knowledge engineering and computational load. We believe that such a tradeoff is necessary to field operational systems in the short to medium term.

We have recently developed and deployed a fact extraction system for Reuters Ltd. JASPER (Journalist's Assistant for Preparing Earnings Reports) uses a template-driven approach and partial understanding techniques based on the same pattern-matching techniques as TCS to extract certain key pieces of information from a limited range of text. Specifically, JASPER takes as input a live feed of company press releases from PR Newswire, a commercial wire that distributes company-generated information for a fee. It identifies which of those releases contain information on company earnings and dividends, and for those releases, it extracts a predetermined set of information. It then reformats that information into a candidate Reuters news story and ships it off to a financial journalist for validation or editing. JASPER improves both the speed and accuracy of producing Reuters stories and hence provides a significant competitive advantage in the fast-paced world of financial journalism.

Following is a typical earnings press release received through the PR Newswire service:

/FROM PR NEWSWIRE MINNEAPOLIS 612-871-7200/
TO BUSINESS EDITOR:

GREEN TREE ACCEPTANCE, INC. ANNOUNCES THIRD-QUARTER RESULTS

ST. PAUL, Minn., Oct. 17 /PRNewswire/ -- Green Tree Acceptance, Inc. (NYSE, PSE: GNT) today reported net earnings for the third quarter ended Sept. 30 of $10,395,000, or 70 cents per share, compared with net earnings of $10,320,000, or 70 cents per share, in the same quarter of 1989.

For the nine months, net earnings were $26,671,000, or $1.70 per share, compared with the first nine months of 1989, which had net earnings of $20,800,000, or $1.21 per share.

GREEN TREE ACCEPTANCE, INC. CONSOLIDATED STATEMENT OF EARNINGS
(unaudited)

| | Three Months Ended | | Nine Months Ended | |
	9/30/90	9/30/89	9/30/90	9/30/89
Earnings before income taxes	16,903,000	16,785,000	43,368,000	33,825,000
Net earnings	$10,395,000	$10,320,000	$26,671,000	$20,800,000
Earnings per share:	$.70	$.70	$1.70	$1.21
Weighted average common shares outstanding	11,599,918	11,494,622	11,597,319	11,450,509

-0-   10/17/90

A Reuters reporter would generate the following corresponding Reuters news story from this release. Some abbreviations understood by the target audience of securities traders and analysts are employed, but the correspondence between the facts in the release and those in the story should be clear.

GREEN TREE ACCEPTANCE, INC <GNT.N> Q3 NET
    ST. PAUL, Minn, Oct 17
    Shr 70 cts vs 70 cts
    Net 10.4 mln vs 10.3 mln

```
Avg shrs 11.6 mln vs 11.5 mln
Nine Months
Shr 1.70 dlrs vs 1.21 dlrs
Net 26.7 mln vs 20.8 mln
Avg shrs 11.6 mln vs 11.5 mln
```

JASPER gets excellent results in terms of both accuracy (76% recall, 92% precision, for an average of 84% on a per slot basis) and speed (less than 20 seconds per press release). Details of the experiments used to calculate these results and the precise meaning of the accuracy measures can be found in [Andersen *et al.*, 1992]. That paper also finds that JASPER compares favorably with results obtained in the second Message Understanding Conference. However, the tasks involve different sources and different extraction goals, so direct comparison of raw numbers is not very meaningful.

JASPER employs a layered approach, like SCISOR [Jacobs and Rau, 1990], with an initial categorization phase and a subsequent fact extraction phase using deeper analysis. However, in an effort to maximize processing speed and minimize knowledge engineering effort, the fact extraction phase is significantly shallower than SCISOR and certainly shallower than systems like PROTEUS. The system closest in level of analysis is probably FRUMP [Dejong, 1982]. Specifically, JASPER combines frame-based knowledge representation, object-oriented processing, TCS-like pattern matching, and heuristics, which take advantage of stylistic conventions, including lexical, syntactic, semantic, and pragmatic regularities observed in the text corpus. The pattern matching is driven from category-specific frames whose slots represent a pre-defined set of facts that need to be extracted for each category of text with associated patterns. The heuristics are encoded in procedures associated with each frame slot. These heuristics specify which patterns to match against the text. They use the strings from the text that match or objects derived from those strings to fill their own and possibly other slots.

JASPER's architecture facilitates transfer to other fact extraction applications. The domain-independent core, which controls processing, is separate from the application-specific knowledge base, which makes decisions about extracting information, so only the latter needs to be rewritten for other applications. Still, the knowledge engineering required to build an application is significant. The knowledge engineer must analyze a large corpus of texts, decide on a frame of facts to look for, create patterns of words to be matched against the text, and write procedures to make decisions about how to fill the frame from information found in the text. We estimate that the JASPER application involved approximately eight person-months in knowledge engineering, apart from basic system development.

Our experience with JASPER suggests that our techniques are effective in the following circumstances:

- The information to be extracted can be identified in advance as a set of related facts (e.g., the net income, per share income, revenues, etc., of a corporate earnings report)

- Texts that contain information from one or more of those sets can be readily identified through categorization techniques (e.g., identifying earnings reports out of a stream of press releases containing other information such as product releases and management changes);

- The information tends to occur in an unambiguous, predictable, though possibly wide-ranging, set of linguistic contexts and forms (e.g., there are a limited number of ways in which press releases typically express earnings per share);

- The information can be represented by values of well-defined types (earnings reports are issued by companies, earnings per share is in dollars or some other currency).

- The information to be extracted occurs as foregrounded information in the texts (press releases tend to focus on a single event or announcement).

We believe there are many business problems that could be solved using fact extraction and that meet these constraints.

12.4   Other Potential Application Areas

We have explored three other application areas for automatic text processing, as detailed in the following subheads. We have done implementation work in the first of them, but believe that useful applications can be built in all three of them using straightforward extensions of the techniques developed for TCS. As in TCS, we are not aiming for 100% solutions. Rather, we are aiming for solutions that are fast enough for large volumes of text and offer acceptable accuracy for a specific task. This means they will be shallow in their analysis and hence likely to make some errors, but at a level that we believe can be kept within acceptable bounds for many tasks.

12.4.1   Document Indexing

If we view index entries as categories, and the pages (sections, sentences) of large documents as separate texts, then the creation of an index is a categorization problem. Automatic index creation is valuable when the documentation is voluminous (because it is hard for people to index consistently) or changes frequently (because it is difficult for people to index incrementally and too expensive to re-index from scratch for each change). Maintenance documentation for large systems (airplanes, telephone switches, etc.) is often voluminous (tens or hundreds of thousands of pages) and is updated frequently (substantial revisions as often as every 90 days).

The problem of index production is different from the kind of routing/retrieval problem addressed directly by TCS in that index entries cannot be predetermined before starting to index. All system components mentioned in a maintenance manual, for instance, should have index entries, but determining what components are mentioned is part of the indexing task. We believe that TCS-like techniques can be used both to determine what entries should be made and to create the index entries. Determination of what entries should be made involves inferring what phrases in the text are component descriptions from context. We believe that this could be done by combining general knowledge of the contexts in which parts occur (structural descriptions, replacement procedures, etc.) with pre-existing parts lists and hence should not require substantial knowledge engineering for each new manual. Adding a structural or process model of the system under maintenance may be a way to increase the accuracy of the resulting system, but it will also increase the knowledge engineering effort.

After some initial exploration in this area [Hayes and Pepper, 1989], we have built a prototype system called ARTIST. ARTIST does not address the problem of identifying what index entries should be made and focusses on the creation of the indexes themselves. It is oriented toward technical documentation. It assumes the existence of a model of the system described by the documentation. One example domain we worked with was an aluminum rolling mill. The models we worked with were dependent on the point of view of the prospective users of the index. A model for the electricians working in the mill would consist of a hierarchical breakdown of the electrical components of the mill, whereas the model for hydraulic engineers would include the hydraulic components and the physical components they actuate. Both of these would bear some resemblance to each other, mediated by the physical structure of the mill, but the model for operators of the mill consisted of a classification of operating events that could occur in the mill. The idea is to structure the model in whatever way best corresponds to the technician's way of thinking about the system described by the documentation.

Once the model is established, a knowledge engineer associates descriptive phrases with each node or object in the model. The phrases can be positive or near-miss negative examples of references to the object or event the node describes. The function of ARTIST is first to create TCS patterns and rules from the example phrases. Once this is done, ARTIST uses TCS with those patterns and rules loaded to find references to the model nodes in a body of documentation. ARTIST then creates links between the model and the parts of the documentation in which appropriate references have been found. Finally, these links are used in a run-time system that allows the technician to navigate through the system model and find the desired information by following links from the appropriate point in the model into the documentation. No systems of this kind have yet been deployed, but experimentation has yielded encouraging results on a variety of documentation, including aluminum mill maintenance documentation, aluminum mill operating logs, and heavy equipment service manuals.

12.4.2 Knowledge Acquisition for Expert Systems

As part of the kind of document analysis envisaged above, knowledge will be obtained that could be used in an expert system. For instance, if the analysis of a maintenance manual (specifically the structural descriptions it contains) yields the component hierarchy of the system under maintenance, that knowledge could provide a valuable start on creating a diagnostic expert system for that system. Knowledge acquisition for expert systems has typically focussed on interaction with human experts. Such interaction will continue to be essential, but much valuable and necessary knowledge is already encoded in written form, and we believe that automatic text processing can make a great deal of it available in machine-manipulable form.

12.4.3 Integrated Text/Expert Systems

Even with automated knowledge acquisition from text, the knowledge engineering effort involved in creating expert systems will still remain large and will continue to limit the size of expert systems that can be built. The creation of a diagnostic expert system using currently deployable technology for something of the complexity of an automobile engine pushes the limits of current knowledge engineering capabilities. The knowledge base required is large enough to pose substantial problems in construction, management, and, particularly, validation. An expert diagnostic system covering an airplane or even a full automobile is beyond those limits. This means that expert systems will continue to co-exist with text-based systems for the foreseeable future as aids to human performance. Moreover, recent work has shown that for some diagnostic applications, text-based systems can produce results superior to expert systems [Peper *et al.*, 1989] with far less knowledge engineering effort.

One way to take advantage of these facts is to base a maintenance support system on a hypertext of maintenance documentation plus a set of specialized expert diagnostic subsystems for components/tasks that humans have particular difficulty with. Creation of the appropriate cross-referencing between nodes of the hypertext and between the hypertext and the diagnostic subsystems is an indexing task similar to the document indexing task described above, and hence potentially susceptible to automatic text processing techniques.

12.5 Challenges for Text-Based Intelligent Systems

There are many technical challenges in creating text-based intelligent systems capable of dealing with texts of the volume and diversity found in current databases or message streams. I discuss four of them here.

12.5.1   Rule Development

The rule development effort for CONSTRUE was around four person-years. With the TCS system as it now stands, we believe that it could be reduced to a little less than one person-year, but that still represents a very substantial investment to produce an application. In general, the more knowledge intensive the approach to text processing, the higher will be the knowledge base development effort. This is another pragmatic reason for limiting the depth of processing as much as is consistent with system goals. However, fact extraction is inherently more complex a task than categorization, because unlike categorization it involves recognizing relations between components of sentences. Accordingly, our analysis will become necessarily deeper as we move from categorization to fact extraction, and we must expect the associated knowledge engineering effort to increase correspondingly. The rule development effort for the JASPER fact extraction application was around eight person-months, but JASPER has much smaller scope than CONSTRUE, dealing in depth only with earnings and dividends reports. The rule development effort for a JASPER-like system dealing with a wide range of financial journalism would be huge.

We need ways to simplify and/or automate the rule development process for both categorization and fact extraction. The TOPIC [Lane, 1988; McCune et al., 1985] system has shown that the rule development process for categorization can be simplified in the context of a supportive user interface, albeit at the cost of some expressive power in the rules. For TCS, we are working toward semi-automated methods for generating good patterns to use in the concept recognition phase. We believe that some techniques developed through the statistical corpus-based approach to natural language processing, e.g. [Smadja, 1991], have much to offer in this area, but expect that some degree of human tuning will be necessary to attain very high accuracy. We are also interested in neural net methods for adjusting the weights associated with individual patterns and the strength thresholds for concepts used in the if-then rules.

12.5.2   Processing Speed

CONSTRUE processes texts of average length 151 words in an average of just under 5 seconds, approximately 200 characters per second, or 1,800 words per minute. At this rate, a gigabyte of text would take almost two months of cpu time to categorize. A large textual database like Nexis contains more than 100 gigabytes of text. Even if a suitable rulebase could be developed, it is effectively impossible to find the 20 years or more of cpu time required to categorize a text base of this size using TCS. Processing techniques that perform a deeper analysis are likely to be even worse. However, some experimentation using table-driven parsing techniques in C (TCS is written in Lisp) has yielded a 200-fold speed up in processing. If this could be achieved for TCS as a whole, it would bring the time for processing 100 gigabytes down to around 1 month of cpu time, still large, but not unfeasible for a fixed categorization scheme that could be computed once in advance and used as an aid to retrieval.

12.5.3 Complete Solutions

TCS is a categorization engine. Even with a rulebase, it does not constitute a complete application. People need to have a way and a reason to use the categorizations generated. Reuters used the categories automatically generated by CONSTRUE to replace human-generated categories in a retrieval system that was already set up for use with such categories. The categories could also be used in a similar way to words in full-text Boolean keyword retrieval systems.

It seems likely that other, more innovative, complete systems are possible in the information retrieval or other areas (such as maintenance support). For instance, if rule development could be reduced to judgments on the relevance of texts or phrases to categories the user wanted to define, then it would be possible to envisage a personalized information management tool, using TCS-like techniques. The TOPIC system is the closest approach so far to this goal for categorization systems. Analogous advances for fact extraction would require an ability to correlate the structure of selected texts with a user-supplied summary of them, a daunting task.

12.5.4 Text and Intelligent Systems

Text is and will remain for the foreseeable future the primary method for representing human knowledge. When the knowledge is extensive or complex enough, text is the only method currently practical for representing that knowledge. Experience with developing large-scale knowledge-based systems has shown the limitations of current knowledge representation techniques. A trend is emerging in such systems of combining knowledge expressed formally with knowledge expressed in text and graphics, which is not fully interpretable by the system. The task of such a system is to use its encoded knowledge when possible and appropriate, and otherwise to guide the human user to the right piece of written knowledge. Automatic text processing techniques, based on some level of understanding of the texts involved, will be essential for managing this type of knowledge.

12.6 Conclusion

Text is used everywhere and is available in ever-increasing volumes. It contains enormous amounts of useful information, but its very quantity often renders that information inaccessible. Classic information retrieval techniques are invaluable in locating information in large volumes of text, but they have their limitations. A new generation of intelligent content-based text processing systems promises considerably more power.

I have described an approach to content-based text processing that has already led to commercially deployed intelligent text-based applications for both categorization and fact extraction. Its essence is to make the understanding as partial as possible for the task at hand. This allows us to provide practical processing speed for the large volumes of text involved and to minimize the human knowledge engineering effort required. This, in turn, allows us to meet the requirements of our commercial customers. I believe that there is a large potential market for the kind of systems I have described, and hope to be part of the large industry we foresee arising in the future to satisfy it.

Bibliography

[Andersen et al., 1992] P.M. Andersen, P.J. Hayes, A.K. Huettner, I.B. Nirenburg, and L.M. Schmandt. Automatic extraction of facts from press releases to generate news stories. In *Proceedings of the Third Conference on Applied Natural Language Processing*, Trento, Italy, April 1992. Association for Computational Linguistics.

[Dejong, 1982] G. DeJong. An overview of the FRUMP system. In *Strategies for Natural Language Processing*, chapter 5, pages 149–176. Lawrence Erlbaum Associates, Hillsdale, New Jersey, 1982.

[Dumais et al., 1988] S. T. Dumais, G. W. Furnas, T. K. Landauer, S. Deerwester, and R. Harshman. Using latent semantic analysis to improve access to textual information. In *CHI '88 Conference Proceedings*, pages 281–285, Washington, DC, May 1988. ACM Press.

[Furnas et al., 1987] G. W. Furnas, T. K. Landauer, L. M. Gomez, and S. T. Dumais. The vocabulary problem in human-system communication. *Communications of the ACM*, *30*(11):964–971, November 1987.

[Hayes and Pepper, 1989] P. J. Hayes and J. Pepper. Towards an integrated maintenance advisor. In *Hypertext '89*, Pittsburgh, November 1989.

[Hayes and Weinstein, 1991] P. J. Hayes and S. P. Weinstein. Construe/TIS: A system for content-based indexing of a database of news stories. In *Innovative Applications of Artificial Intelligence 2*, pages 49–64. The AAAI Press/The MIT Press, Cambridge, MA, 1991.

[Hayes et al., 1988] P. J. Hayes, L. E. Knecht, and M. J. Cellio. A news story categorization system. In *Proceedings of the Second Conference on*

Applied Natural Language Processing, pages 9–17, Austin, TX, February 1988. Association for Computational Linguistics.

[Hayes et al., 1990] P. J. Hayes, P. M. Andersen, I. B. Nirenburg, and L. M. Schmandt. TCS: A shell for content-based text categorization. In *Sixth IEEE AI Applications Conference*, Santa Monica, March 1990.

[Jacobs and Rau, 1990] P. S. Jacobs and L. F. Rau. SCISOR: Extracting information from online news. *Communications of the ACM, 33*(11):88–97, November 1990.

[Ksiezyk and Grishman, 1986] T. Ksiezyk and R. Grishman. An equipment model and its role in the interpretation of noun compounds. In *DARPA's 1986 Strategic Computing Natural Language Processing Workshop*, pages 81–95. Information Sciences Institute, Marina del Rey, CA, May 1986.

[Lane, 1988] C. Lane. Topic - A document management/textual retrieval program. *Research Newsletter SWIS 1988-13*, Dataquest, June 1988.

[McCune et al., 1985] B. P. McCune, R. M. Tong, J. S. Dean, and D. G. Shapiro. Rubric: A system for rule-based information retrieval. *IEEE Transactions on Software Engineering*, SE-11(9):939–945, September 1985.

[Peper et al., 1989] G. Peper, D. Williams, C. MacIntyre, and M. Vandall. Comparing a hypertext document to an expert system. Technical report, IBM, Boulder, CO, November 1989.

[Salton and McGill, 1983] G. Salton and M. J. McGill. *Introduction to Modern Information Retrieval*. McGraw-Hill, New York, 1983.

[Salton, 1986] G. Salton. Another look at automatic text retrieval systems. *Communications of the ACM, 29*(7):648–656, July 1986.

[Smadja, 1991] F. Smadja. Retrieving collocations from text: Xtract. *Computational Linguistics, 17*, 1991.

[Stanfill and Kahle, 1986] C. Stanfill and B. Kahle. Parallel free-text search on the connection machine system. *Communications of the ACM, 29*(12):1229–1239, December 1986.

Automatically Constructing Simple Help Systems from Natural Language Documentation

Yoëlle S. Maarek

IBM T.J. Watson Research Center

P.O. Box 704

Yorktown Heights, NY 10598

Abstract

With the increasing size and complexity of software, help systems that can assist the user in locating tools and understanding their functionality become critical. Help systems are intended to *help* and should constrain the user as little as possible. For this reason, natural language help systems that accept free-style natural language queries are more desirable than traditional keyword-based or menu-driven systems. Very few existing software systems come with such a help facility. This is due to the fact that current elaborated help systems require a lot of manual encoding and are therefore expensive to build. It would be preferable to have simpler help systems as long as they can be built automatically. The help system should be able to give information about components of a large toolkit. More precisely, it should accept natural language queries and should provide retrieval facilities to identify software components performing a desired functionality, as well as some kind of hypertext links to allow browsing between conceptually related components.

The key idea of our approach is to take advantage of the natural language documentation that comes with most modern software systems. We use information retrieval techniques specifically adapted to the software domain in order to build help facilities that provide not only retrieval information, but also some basic explanatory information, under the form of summarized descriptions, and related information, under the form of simple hypertext links. We embodied this approach in a tool, GURU that allowed us to generate help facilities for various documented software systems such as AIX, SunOS, INTERVIEWS, EMACS, etc..

13.1   Introduction

Two approaches can be distinguished when constructing help systems: the knowledge-based approach and the text-based approach.

Knowledge-based systems aim at interpreting the queries before providing an answer. This task is domain intensive and requires the use of a knowledge base that stores semantic information about the domain and also often about the English language itself. Examples of knowledge-based help systems are numerous, e.g., UC, the UNIX Consultant [Wilensky *et al.*, 1984], INTERIX [Guez, 1987], NLH/E [Tichy *et al.*, 1989], etc. Most knowledge-based systems do more than simply give pointers to tools or documentation. Some of them are context sensitive and generate answers adapted to the user's expertise. As a tradeoff, the encoding of the knowledge base is often tedious and expensive, especially for large toolkits. Moreover, the knowledge base is so domain dependent that a large part of the help system has to be rebuilt for each new domain of application.

In contrast, text-based help systems draw information from some natural-language documents rather than from a human expert. They do not need any semantic information and do not try to *understand* the queries. Text-based help systems adopt what can be termed a traditional information retrieval (IR) approach. Indeed, information retrieval[1] deals with the storage and accessing of unstructured data, such as textual documents. Most IR systems follow the same general scenario: First, documents are indexed in order to build characterizing profiles. Then, these profiles are stored in repositories so as to be easily accessible, via an inverted file index, for instance. At the retrieval stage, the user expresses a query according to an authorized vocabulary, e.g., controlled or uncontrolled, using Boolean connectors or natural-language syntax, etc. This query directs a search in the repository, and a list of candidates, possibly ranked, is returned to the user. A primitive example of such system is the man -k or apropos command in UNIX, which uses the manual pages as its only information source. This command takes as argument a string, and returns a list of all the manual pages that contain this string in their NAME section. It was then proposed by Frakes and Nejmeh [Frakes and Nejmeh, 1987] to use more elaborated IR techniques on software documentation. Since then, more efforts have been made in this direction. Thus, the AIX 3 documentation on the RS/6000 series comes with a CD-ROM hypertext information base library, INFOEXPLORER [InfoExplorer, 1990], which replaces the man command. Similarly, ANSWERBOOK provides help for SunOS 3.1. Both systems allow querying and searching documentation. Their search mechanisms do not require any manual encoding since they are based on standard IR techniques. In INFOEXPLORER, documentation can be searched via Boolean queries (AND, OR and BUTNOT connectors) in which wildcard characters are allowed for more flexible matches. ANSWERBOOK allows more sophisticated queries. They are

---

[1]See [Salton and McGill, 1983] for a general introduction to information retrieval.

expressed as search phrases, which can be refined via the use of special characters (quotations, parentheses, asterisks), in order to look for literal phrases, unspecified suffixes and terms near each other in text. Unfortunately, none of these systems provides a true free-style natural-language interface and therefore are not optimally user friendly. Both systems allow users to navigate between documents via hypertext links. Typically, under a window interface, users can click on some highlighted topics or section titles and access directly documents relevant to the highlighted item. This is done by following hard-coded links between documents. These underlying hypertext networks require expensive manual encoding and thus present the same drawback as the knowledge-based approach. Providing the hypertext links information is worth the effort for widely used systems such as AIX or SunOS, but not for many smaller applications. One solution would be to enforce a standard format that defines these links while writing documentation, so as to be able to generate them automatically. Unfortunately, enforcing the writing of documentation in software systems is difficult; it is therefore unrealistic to expect users to write in a specific format.

In this paper, we describe an approach for automatically building help systems with retrieval facilities and some kind of hypertext links that do not require any specific formatting. The help system thus generated draws all the information it needs from an existing free-style textual database, such as manual pages. The system does not use any semantics when extracting information, but only IR techniques to analyze them and to return some conceptual information that the user will be able to interpret easily even if the system itself cannot. In other words, it "explains things without understanding them".

13.2   A Basis for Representing Conceptual Information: The Lexical Affinity

Extracting valuable conceptual information from documentation without using semantic knowledge can be done by using richer indexing units than single words. It has been proposed in the past to use multiple-word units [Klingbiel, 1973], [Dillon and Gray, 1983], [Sparck Jones and Tait, 1984], [Fagan, 1989], etc. We adopt this approach and propose to use as basic indexing units, *lexical affinities* (LAs). An LA (also termed *lexical relation*) between two units of language stands for a correlation of their common appearance in the utterances of the language in a similar syntactic construct [de Saussure, 1949]. An LA is more restrictive than a simple co-occurrence since it necessarily relates words that are involved in a modifier-modified relation. The observation of lexical affinities in a text has been shown to convey information on both syntactic and semantic levels, and provides us with a powerful way of taking context into account [Smadja, 1989].

For our purposes, we restrict the definition of LAs by observing them within a finite document rather than within the whole language so as to retrieve *conceptual* affinities[2] rather than purely *lexical* ones. Those LAs thus characterize the document rather than the whole language.

Consider the following sentence, taken from the AIX manual page describing the command **mv**:

''mv displays the permission code of the file to be overwritten'

Some of the potential lexical affinities in this sentence are:

- of type verb-direct-object, e.g. (display code), (file overwrite).

- of type verb-subject, e.g., (mv display).

- of type noun-noun, e.g., (permission code).

Note that the constituents of an LA correspond to the lemma (or base form) and not to the inflected form of the utterance of the words.

Ideally, lexical affinities are extracted from a text by parsing it since two words share a lexical affinity if they are involved in a modifier-modified relation. Unfortunately, automatic syntactic parsing of free-style text is still not effective [Salton and Smith, 1989]. As an alternative, we make use of a co-occurrence compiler. It has been shown that 98% of lexical relations relate words that are separated by at most five words within a single sentence, [Martin *et al.*, 1983]. Therefore, most of the lexical relations involving a word w can be retrieved by examining the neighborhood of each occurrence of w within a span of five words (-5 words and +5 words around w).

Conversely, not all extracted pairs of words are true lexical affinities. In the context of computational linguistics, Smadja in [Smadja, 1991] made use of statistical techniques also based on Martin's results to extract lexical relations, and demonstrated that about 40% of such affinities were valid. After more filtering that involved the use of a bottom-up natural language parser, the rate of true affinities reached 80%. In our context, however, we are not as much concerned with this validity issue as we are interested in conceptual rather than purely lexical affinities. Any extracted pair of words, even if it is not a valid lexical affinity, in the lexical sense, provides useful information about the document. For instance, in the above sentence from the **mv** manual page, the co-occurrence compiler would also extract (code file) which is not a true lexical LA, but still carries information about the sentence. This information should not be rejected if it can be useful when searching the documentation. Thus, the best way to evaluate whether LAs are useful in the IR sense is to compute the recall and precision of our LA-based scheme as compared to a traditional single-word scheme. This is done in Section 13.3. Note that the main difference between LAs and other interrupted phrase indexing such as [Fagan, 1989], is that using co-occurrence

---

[2]We only consider LAs involving *open-class words* as meaning bearing. In general, open-class words include nouns, verbs, adjectives, and adverbs, while closed-class words are pronouns, prepositions, conjunctions, and interjections.

represents only an approximation of a lexical reality, as was shown above, and that the window size of 10 words is not a parameter but a property of the English language.

For each document, LA-based indices that will represent conceptual information are built in three stages. The first stage consists of extracting all the potential LAs and storing them under their canonical form, in which each word is represented by its lemma, and the lemmas forming the LA are in lexicographic order. An example of the potential LAs extracted from the **mv** manual page and ranked by frequency of occurrence is presented in Table 13.1. For the sake of comparison, a list of the open-class words extracted from the same manual page is shown in the first column, also ranked by frequency of appearance. Intuitively, we can see that the LAs outperform single keywords in terms of meaningfulness. The extracted LAs represent potential conceptual affinities. Some correspond to important abstractions of the considered document and some do not.

Table 13.1: LAs and open-class words for **mv**

open-class words	freq	LAs	freq
file	30	file move	9
directory	14	be file	8
mv	11	directory file	7
files	8	file system	5
new	7	file overwrite	5
name	7	file mv	5
move	7	file name	4
newname	6	name path	3
is	6	do file	3
system	5	directory move	3
one	5	different file	3

In a second stage, we isolate the most important ones by observing the statistical distribution of the potential LAs. In order to evaluate the resolving power of an LA, we use a measure, noted ρ, based on the quantity of information of the words involved in the LA within the considered corpus (e.g., the set of all the manual pages), as well as on the probability of appearance of this LA within the considered document [Maarek and Smadja, 1989]. More precisely, we define the resolving power[3] of an LA in a document d as

$$\rho = -P_d \log P_c$$

where P_d is the observed probability of appearance of the LA in the document d, P_c the observed probability of the LA in the corpus, and $-\log P_c$,

---

[3]This notion is related to that of mutual information [Ash, 1965].

is the quantity of information of the LA as defined in information theory. Using the resolving power measure rather than simple frequency allows us to reduce noise due to context words. In order to be able to evaluate the relative performances of different documents, we also perform a standard normalization (using the z-score and cosine normalization). In the rest of this paper, the ρ-values we give as examples will represent the normalized score rather than the raw score.

In Table 13.2, we compare the list of LAs for the **mv** manual page ranked by frequency and by resolving power. As we see, the LA *(file move)* has a resolving power clearly greater than the following ones. Moreover, some non-valuable LAs, such as *(do file)* or *(be file)* (in italics in the table), have disappeared because both the words involved in the LA have a low quantity of information.

Table 13.2: Comparison of frequency and ρ-value for the LAs in **mv**

LAs	freq
file move	9
be file	8
directory file	7
file system	5
file overwrite	5
file mv	5
file name	4
name path	3
do file	3
directory move	3

LAs	ρ_z
file move	8.38
file mv	4.36
directory file	4.03
file overwrite	3.87
directory move	1.98
file system	1.95
mv rename	1.71
move mv	1.58
different file	1.40
name path	1.33

Finally, in a third stage, we select as indices those LAs that represent peaks in the distribution of ρ values. Peaks are identified as ρ values that are at least one standard deviation above the average of ρ values in a given profile.

All the available documentation can thus be indexed. A profile of representative indices is produced for each document and stored in an inverted file index. These profiles represent the basic source of conceptual information for the help system. They are used in order to provide three kinds of information:

1. **Retrieval information**

   This is the most important one. Users can locate and identify a component fulfilling a desired functionality by issuing a query in free-style natural language. The query is analyzed using the same LA-based indexing technique, and a set of LAs is extracted from the query that will direct the repository search. This query's profile is compared to the profiles via the inverted file index. By using an adequate ranking measure, those documents that are the most similar to the query are returned to the users as a ranked list of candidates. We have defined a ranking measure specifically adapted to our LA-scheme by taking into account not only exact matches between LAs from the query and from documents, but also partial matches, where only one of the constituent words matches. An example of retrieval is given in Figure 13.1. The user typed a query in the top left window and issued it, and a list of candidate documents was returned in the top right window.

2. **Explanatory information**
In order to evaluate the relevance of a retrieved candidate, among those returned at the retrieval stage, users can consult the associated original document as well as a summarized conceptual description of the document via its profile. Using an LA-based profile that lists key concepts rather than a traditional single-word profile makes the interpretation of the candidate document easier for the user. An example of such a profile is given in Figure 13.2: The pop-up window lists the index LAs for the document displayed in the bottom window. In this example, the top LA represents the key concept: (copy file) for the command cp. Most of the other LAs also represent important conceptual information. This explanatory information allows a much faster scanning of candidates.

3. **Related information via hypertext links**
Hypertext links can automatically be established between concep-tually related documents by using the LA-based profiles. For each document, a list of related documents is produced by measuring the similarity between profiles. At the retrieval stage, users can start from a candidate that answers a query, and then find related docu-ments that were not returned by the retrieval. They can thus nav-igate among related documents so as to identify some unexpected candidates that would be missed via regular search. An example use of the related information is shown in Figure 13.3. The user wants information about Source Code Control System (SCCS) commands in the AIX corpus, and issued the query "source control" in the top left window. Since the query was not specific enough, some irrelevant candidates, such as cc, are also retrieved (fifth candidate in the top right window). Worse, some relevant SCCS commands such as comb are not retrieved, simply because in the comb manual page, only the acronym SCCS appears and there is no reference to either "source code control", or "source control".

However, by asking for the list of documents that are related to the first relevant candidate **sact**, which is displayed in the bottom window, comb is found as well as other relevant SCCS commands (see

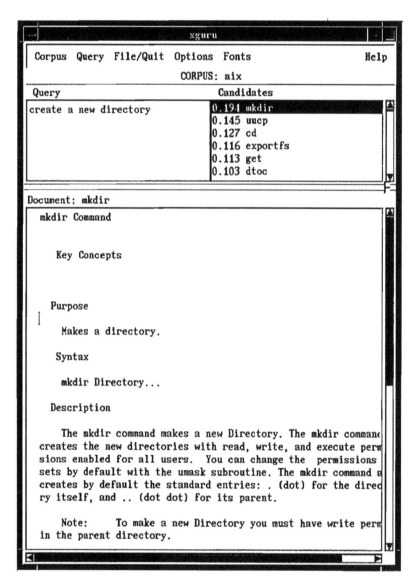

Figure 13.1: Session example with Guru

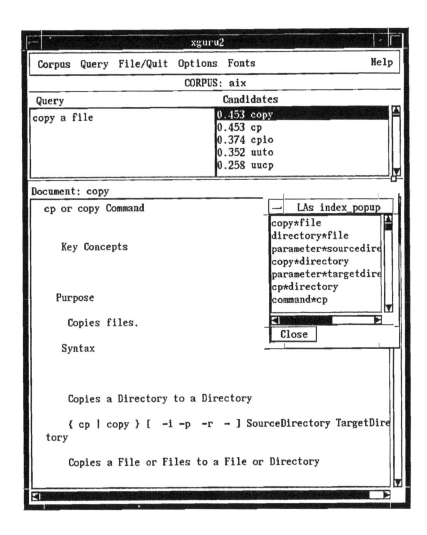

Figure 13.2: Explanatory information for the cp command

pop-up window). These hypertext links are not at the same level of granularity as those existing in manually encoded hypertext systems, i.e., the hot buttons are not at the word level, but at the document level. However, they still provide valuable information and present the advantage of being automatically generated.

These three kinds of help are not as elaborated as the help provided by more intelligent help systems such as the UNIX CONSULTANT, for instance; however, they can still be very valuable. Our experience with GURU showed that users understand easily the underlying mechanism of the help system and are satisfied with the fast response time. Indeed, by using usual retrieval techniques (such as an inverted file index) the help system we generated for the AIX documentation, for instance, answers regular queries of about 10 words long in less than a second on an RS/6000 530. More important, users were satisfied with the answers they got. A more formal evaluation of retrieval effectiveness is presented in the next section.

13.3   Evaluation

In order to evaluate the usefulness of our LA-based scheme compared to more traditional single-word schemes in terms of retrieval effectiveness, we have used the standard IR evaluation procedure based upon recall and precision. Remember here that *recall* is defined as the proportion of *relevant* material; i.e., it measures how well the considered system retrieves *all* the relevant components, and that *precision* is defined as the proportion of retrieved material that is relevant; i.e., it measures how well the system retrieves *only* the relevant components. The evaluation procedure consists of measuring, on a given test collection, precision at several levels of recall, and comparing the values achieved by different systems on the same test collection. In [Maarek, 1991], I have shown that usual IR test collections are not adequate in the software domain and proposed an empirically built test collection for AIX 3 with its relevance judgments.

Another way of obtaining test collections is to require authors of the documentation to provide a standard query for each document [Tague, 1981]. This can be done artificially for the AIX 3 documentation, for instance, by taking as queries the **Purpose** section of each manual page. For instance, from the mv manual page, the query ''moves files'' is automatically produced, the associated relevant candidate being obviously mv. Let us note that this collection is far from being the ideal test collection since it does not allow to measure retrieval effectiveness when the original terminology is not used. Users should be able to retrieve the "mv" manual page by using the words *rename* or *overwrite*, rather than *move*. This is not evaluated with our artificial test collection. However, this test collection presents the advantage of being as large as the collection itself, which is difficult to achieve in manually built test collections. Indeed, standard IR test collections such as MED

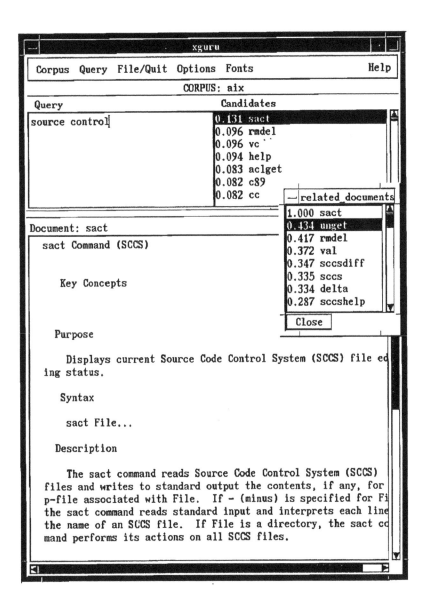

Figure 13.3: High level hypertext information in GURU

or Cisi, only count 30 queries for 1,033 documents, and 35 queries for 1,460 documents, respectively, whereas we have 1,033 queries for 1,033 documents. This allows testing each and every document.

Using this test collection, we have evaluated the precision/recall values for our LA-based scheme, and for a single-word scheme with the same entropy-based numerical and the same morphological analyzer. Note that the only interesting value in the recall/precision plot is the precision achieved for a recall of 100%, since in most cases, there is only one relevant component for each test query. We found that for a recall of 100%, the precision was 80% for our LA-based scheme, and 71% for the single-word scheme. We obtained similar results on the much smaller empirical test collection proposed in [Maarek, 1991].

13.4 Conclusion

In this paper, I describe an approach for automatically generating help systems providing three kinds of information. First, retrieval information is used to locate components that answer natural-language queries. Once a candidate component is selected, explanatory information can be provided in the form of a list of key concepts. Finally, one can obtain pointers to all the components related to a specific component via conceptual hypertext links.

These three kinds of information are obtained by using information retrieval techniques based on a conceptually meaningful indexing unit: the lexical affinity. The LA-based indexing scheme mentioned here was introduced in [Maarek and Smadja, 1989] and developed in [Maarek et al., 1991]. The LA-based scheme allows us to achieve higher retrieval effectiveness than traditional single-word schemes. Moreover, the scheme allows free-style natural-language queries, which makes the dialogue with the help system as user friendly as possible, unlike in other IR-based help tools, such as INFOEX-PLORER or ANSWERBOOK. The main advantage of this approach is that it is entirely automated. Thus, help systems can be built for any software as long as textual documentation exists. The information extracted from text can also be integrated with other kinds of information obtained from code analysis. We are currently working on this issue in the context of object oriented class libraries [Helm and Maarek, 1991].

Bibliography

[Ash, 1965] R. Ash. *Information Theory*. Interscience Publishers (John Wiley and Sons), New York, 1965.

[Dillon and Gray, 1983] M. Dillon and A. S. Gray. FASIT: A fully automatic syntactically based indexing unit. *JASIS*, *34*(2):99–108, 1983.

[Fagan, 1989] J. L. Fagan. The effectiveness of a nonsyntactic approach to automatic phrase indexing for document retrieval. *JASIS*, *40*(2):115–132, 1989.

[Frakes and Nejmeh, 1987] W. B. Frakes and B. A. Nejmeh. Software reuse through information retrieval. In *Proceedings of the 20th Annual HICSS*, pages 530–535, Kona, HI, January 1987.

[Guez, 1987] S. Guez. *INTERIX: A UNIX Intelligent Help System.* PhD thesis, Ecole Central de Paris, Châtenay Malabry, France, June 1987. (In French.)

[Helm and Maarek, 1991] R. Helm and Y. S. Maarek. Integrating information retrieval and domain specific approaches for browsing and retrieval in object oriented class libraries. In *Proceedings of OOPSLA '91*, Phoenix, AZ, October 1991.

[InfoExplorer, 1990] IBM. *IBM AIX Version 3 for RISC System/6000. Commands Reference*, 1st edition, March 1990.

[Klingbiel, 1973] P. H. Klingbiel. Machine-aided indexing of technical literature. *Information Storage and Retrieval*, *9*:79–84, 1973.

[Maarek, 1991] Y. S. Maarek. Software library construction from an IR perspective. *SIGIR Forum*, Fall 1991.

[Maarek *et al.*, 1991] Y. S. Maarek, D. M. Berry, and G. E. Kaiser. An information retrieval approach for automatically constructing software libraries. *Transactions on Software Engineering*, *17*(8), August 1991.

[Maarek and Smadja, 1989] Y. S. Maarek and F. Smadja. Full text indexing based on lexical relations. an application: Software libraries. In N.J. Belkin and C.J. van Rijsbergen, editors, *Proceedings of SIGIR '89*, pages 198–206, Cambridge, MA, June 1989. ACM Press.

[Martin *et al.*, 1983] W. J. R. Martin, B. P. F. Al, and P. J. G. van Sterkenburg. On the processing of a text corpus: From textual data to lexicographic information. In R. R. K. Hartmann, editor, *Lexicographiy: Principles and Practice*, London, 1983. Applied Language Studies Series, Academic Press.

[Salton and McGill, 1983] G. Salton and M. J. McGill. *Introduction to Modern Information Retrieval.* Computer Series. McGraw-Hill, New York, 1983.

[Salton and Smith, 1989] G. Salton and M. Smith. On the application of syntactic methodologies in automatic text analysis. In *Proceedings of SIGIR '89*, pages 137–150, Cambridge, MA, June 1989. ACM Press.

[de Saussure, 1949] F. de Saussure. *Cours de Linguistique Générale*. Librairie Payot, Paris, France, quatrième edition, 1949.

[Smadja, 1989] F. Smadja. Lexical co-occurrence: The missing link. *Journal of the Association for Literary and Linguistic Computing. Oxford University Press*, *4*(3), 1989.

[Smadja, 1991] F. Smadja. From *n*-grams to collocations, an evaluation of XTRACT. In *Proceedings of the 29th Annual Meeting of the ACL*, Berkeley, CA, June 1991. Association for Computational Linguistics.

[Sparck Jones and Tait, 1984] K. Sparck Jones and J.I. Tait. Automatic search variant generation. *Journal of Documentation*, *40*(1):50–66, March 1984.

[Tague, 1981] J. Tague. *The Pragamatics of Information Retrieval Experimentation*, chapter 5, pages 59–102. Butterworths, 1981.

[Tichy et al., 1989] W. F. Tichy, R. L. Adams, and L. Holter. NLH/E: A natural-language help system. In *Proceedings of the 11th ICSE*, pages 364–374, Pittsburgh, PA, May 1989.

[Wilensky et al., 1984] R. Wilensky, Y. Arens, and D. Chin. Talking to UNIX in Dnglish: An overview of UC. *Communications of the ACM*, *27*:574–593, 1984.

Direction-Based Text Interpretation as an Information Access Refinement

Marti A. Hearst
Computer Science Division, 571 Evans Hall
University of California, Berkeley
Berkeley, CA 94720
and
Xerox Palo Alto Research Center

Abstract

A Text-Based Intelligent System should provide more in-depth information about the contents of its corpus than does a standard information retrieval system, while at the same time avoiding the complexity and resource-consuming behavior of detailed text understanders. Instead of focusing on discovering documents that pertain to some *topic* of interest to the user, an approach is introduced based on the criterion of *directionality* (e.g., Is the agent in favor of, neutral, or opposed to the event?). A method is described for coercing sentence meanings into a metaphoric model such that the only semantic interpretation needed in order to determine the directionality of a sentence is done with respect to the model. This interpretation method is designed to be an integrated component of a hybrid information access system.

14.1 Introduction

In the light of the increasing availability of computer-accessible full text, an important goal of a Text-Based Intelligent System is to provide a means for answering questions about documents' contents. Standard information retrieval systems have sophisticated methods for grouping documents according to similarities among their terms and the terms in user queries (see [Salton, 1988] and Croft and Turtle, this volume, for overviews). Often the data for these systems are titles and abstracts, as opposed to full text documents. Using this data, given a document whose topic is known, other documents whose terms are similar to it are considered likely to be about the same topic. However, document similarity is only one of many useful criteria for accessing information, and the availability of full text opens up exploration of others.

One way of structuring a corpus is to sort the documents into categories based on their topical content. Current text systems accomplish this task with varying degrees of sophistication. For example, RUBRIC [McCune *et al.*, 1985] allows the user to define an elaborate conceptual hierarchy, bottoming out on keywords, that classifies documents according to what topics they contain. (Hayes, this volume, describes related systems.) Assuming, then, that the main topic of a document can be determined, how can the document be further distinguished from others describing the same topic?

One way to distinguish a document from its neighbors is to answer specific questions about its contents. A good number of systems have been developed that look for answers to a set of predefined questions about a specific topic domain, notably those demonstrated at the Message Understanding Conferences [Lehnert and Sundheim, 1991]. Most of these systems require large amounts of task-specific domain knowledge and complex inferencing capabilities. The process of building up and representing the necessary knowledge bases is time-consuming, and good coverage is difficult to achieve. For this reason, our question should be revised to: How can a document be distinguished from others describing the same topic without the costs associated with domain-dependent approaches?

What is needed is a classification criterion that applies to a wide range of text, a useful question relatively independent of domain. One such criterion is: Where, according to the text, does a semantic attribute lie along a continuum between extremes? For example, given a corpus of newspaper articles and the topic "Environmental issues pertaining to wildlife refuges," one can inquire as to whether public figures are stated as being opposed to, neutral to, or in favor of a proposed cleanup plan. More generally, articles can be classified according to how they answer the query "Is agent A in favor of event E?" Other examples of queries within this genre are: "Is situation S improving or worsening?" and "Is agent A1 dominating or being dominated by agent A2?" I call this criterion *directionality*, in contrast to the *topicality* criterion mentioned above. Directional queries are domain independent; whether the domain is wildlife refuges, Mideast peace agreements, or urban policy, the question can still be applicable.

A mechanism that can classify an article based on the directionality criterion provides a precise interpretation of a narrow slice of the semantic content of the document. The goal is to avoid the expense of a full semantic analysis by *restricting* the type of information extracted from the text. How is sentence directionality to be determined? Clearly, keyword-based analysis alone is not sufficient. Consider the classification criterion "Is the agent in favor of the event?" applied to the following pair of sentences:

(1a) The congresspersons introduced legislation to *lift* the ban on wastewater dumping.

(1b) The congresspersons introduced legislation to *support* the ban on wastewater dumping.

A difference of one word manages to reverse the attitude of the agents toward the situation, even though *lift* and *support* are not antonyms when out of context. To correctly distinguish these sentences, at least a partial understanding must come into play. However, the semantics need not be comprehensive – the interpretation mechanism can take advantage of the restricted nature of the query in order to minimize the degree of inference needed.

To this end I propose a sentence interpretation model called *direction-based text interpretation* (DTI). In direction-based text interpretation, isolated portions of a text are interpreted within the framework of a general, domain-independent metaphoric model. This model is derived from Talmy's theory of force dynamics [Talmy, 1985] and involves coercing the meanings of sentences that satisfy the directionality criterion into a general conceptual framework and then interpreting the sentences with respect to that framework. When working within this restricted model, lexical items require assignment of a value to only one semantic attribute, thus circumventing the need for the large, complex knowledge bases required by full text understanding systems. Integrating this method with an information retrieval system should yield an incremental improvement in the text classification task.

In other words, DTI involves interpreting text in terms of a simple semantic model, only to the amount of detail necessary to accomplish the target task (to answer the query of interest). A sketch of the overall procedure is: Relevant documents are selected by the system's information retrieval component, which makes use of domain-dependent keywords and phrases (assumed to already be supplied) that identify the target concepts (e.g., the system knows about lexical items involved in expressing a topic such as "wastewater dumping"). This information is used to isolate sentences that are likely to contain the answer to the target query (e.g., a sentence that refers both to "congresspersons" and "wastewater dumping" is a good candidate). Once a candidate sentence is found, it is parsed into a feature-structure form. As the analysis proceeds, pieces of the directional model are instantiated and linked together corresponding to elements of the parse. The resulting structure is interpreted in terms of the directional model, and the query is answered.

In summary, this chapter describes a domain-independent, coarse-level text interpretation method intended to be integrated into an intelligent information access system.

The next section, Section 14.2, explains the conceptual model that underlies direction-based text interpretation, and Section 14.3 describes mechanisms for interpreting sentences within this model. Section 14.4 is a short discussion of related work, followed, in Section 14.5, by an outline of the retrieval paradigm into which direction-based text interpretation might be placed. Section 14.6 concludes the chapter with some questions about the feasibility of the approach.

14.2 The Conceptual Model: Applied Cognitive Linguistics

This section explains the conceptual model that underlies direction-based text interpretation. The *path model*, as I call it, is an extension of Talmy's force dynamic model with some influence from Reddy's description of the conduit metaphor.

14.2.1 The Force Dynamic Model

Studies in cognitive linguistics have shown that in some cases a multitude of linguistic phenomena can be well described in terms of a general conceptual framework. Reddy [Reddy, 1979] describes how the *conduit* metaphor can be seen as underlying many English expressions about communication. In this framework a thought is schematized as an object that is placed by the speaker into a container that is sent along a conduit. The receiver at the other end is the listener, who then removes the objectified thought from the container and thus possesses it. Inferences that can be made about conduits (e.g., they can be blocked up, become full, etc.) are applied to notions of communication. For example, English speakers make statements such as "Your meaning did not come through," "I can't put this thought into words," and "She's sending me some kind of message with that remark." Thus it may be the case that speakers unconsciously structure their talk about communication within the framework of this metaphor.

Another example of a claim that an underlying conceptual framework is revealed by its expression in language is found in Talmy's theory of *force dynamics* [Talmy, 1985]. This theory describes how the interaction of agents with respect to force is lexically and grammatically expressed (focusing on English). Notions within the scope of force dynamics include: exertion of force by an agent, resistance to this force, overcoming this resistance, and so on. Talmy claims that force dynamics is a conceptual organizing system, one of the fundamental categories that structures and organizes meaning, akin to more familiar linguistic categories like number and aspect.

The force dynamic model posits the participation of two opposing entities, named the Agonist and the Antagonist. Each entity expresses an intrinsic force, tending either toward motion or toward rest. The relative strengths of the tendencies of the agents is important since the stronger entity is able to manifest its tendency at the expense of its opposer. The balance of relative strengths determines the interaction's resulting state.

To clarify these ideas, consider the following sentences (taken from [Talmy, 1985]):

(2a) The ball kept rolling because of the wind blowing on it.

(2b) The shed kept standing despite the gale wind blowing against it.

(2c) The ball kept rolling despite the stiff grass.

(2d) The log kept lying on the incline because of the ridge there.

In sentence (2a) the ball is seen as the Agonist and the wind as the Antagonist. The Agonist's tendency is toward rest but it is forced against its tendency by the stronger force of the wind. In sentence (2b) the Agonist (the shed) again has a tendency toward rest but in this case it is able to maintain this tendency against the opposing force of the Antagonist (the wind). In (2c) the Agonist is the ball tending toward motion. In this case the Antagonist's force does not succeed in reversing the Agonist's tendency, but in sentence (2d) the Antagonist (the ridge) overcomes the Agonist's tendency toward motion.

These examples illustrate only the simplest form of interactions. Talmy describes more complex examples in which the force interaction changes dynamically, and situations in which the Antagonist is the stronger of the two entities, but it remains "out of the way" of the Agonist, thus allowing the description of the concept "letting" (e.g., "The plug's staying loose let the water drain from the tank."). Talmy speculates that the traditional understanding of the scope of causation is too narrow, and should be expanded to include notions like letting since this evidence indicates that both letting and causing are expressed through the same conceptual framework.

Talmy further shows that certain force dynamic concepts have grammatical representation. For example, when the Agonist appears as the subject, the role of a stronger Antagonist can be expressed by conjoining a clause headed by *because* (as in (2a)). Similarly the interaction with a weaker Antagonist can be expressed by a clause headed by *although* or a prepositional phrase headed by *despite*. The preposition *against* indicates force dynamical opposition as well as the particles *still* and *on* (e.g. "The ball was still rolling."). Talmy argues that the form *keep* (e.g., "The ball kept rolling.") might be considered an honorary auxiliary in the way that "have to" can act like a modal.

Whether or not the force dynamical system truly underlies the language user's conceptual system, it is a useful device for interpreting expressions of causal interaction. For example, the theory could be helpful for the problem of determining, given a sentence describing two entities engaged in an interaction, which one is relatively stronger.

14.2.2 The Path Model

If an agent favors an entity or event, the agent can be said to desire the existence or "well-being" of that entity. Furthermore, if the agent favors an impedance to the existence or well-being of an entity, then it can be said to be opposed to the entity. A useful heuristic can be inferred from this: If an agent favors an entity's triumph in a force-dynamic interaction, then the agent favors that entity.

In a particular sentential description there may be a string of occurrences that affect the state of the entity. The force dynamic model does not have the expressive power to represent this, so it must be augmented. Instead of focusing on the relative strength of two interacting entities, the model should represent what happens to a single entity through the course of its encounters with other entities. Thus, the entity can be schematized as if it were moving along a path toward some destination or goal. The entity may encounter barriers in its path, indicating that its tendency is being blocked. Agents independent of the entity have the power to introduce barriers, remove barriers, reinforce or weaken barriers, initiate the entity's journey, speed up or slow down the journey, or bring the entity to its destination. An agent's attitude toward an entity can be determined by how it chooses to affect the movement of that entity along its metaphorical path.

Empirical analysis of directional sentences reveals that the inferences that can be generated based on this path metaphor suffice to answer the directional query: "Is the agent in favor of the event?" This leads me to adopt the path model as the conceptual model for direction-based text interpretation.

Both Talmy and Reddy consider the base metaphors that they investigate to be at least part of the underlying meaning of some subset of linguistic utterances. However, in DTI the base metaphor is used as a *lingua franca* into which the meanings of *all* candidate sentences are coerced. This is useful for two reasons: First, once the system has a representation of the sentence based on the path model, it need perform only a restricted set of inferences. Second, since the model being mapped into is small (compared with mapping into a network of "real-world" knowledge), the assignment of semantic attributes to lexical items is simplified considerably.

Preliminary work reveals that the path model, with some minor modifications, can be applied to answer another general query, namely "Does the event E improve the situation S?" This includes subquestions such as "Does the drug cure the disease?" and "Is the financial situation improving?" These queries all have a directional component.

14.3 Determining Directionality via the Path Model

A descriptive theory like force dynamics is a tool for describing how a conceptual framework is expressed in language, rather than prescribing how to interpret sentence meanings. This subsection presents an initial description of how sentences can be interpreted in terms of the path model.

However, before launching into the details of interpretation, we should consider what kinds of results the system is expected to produce. Consider again Sentence (1a). Assume the user is interested in the opinions of policymakers toward issues involving wastewater management, and that a mechanism for recognizing simple noun phrases involving policymakers and wastewater management is in place. The goal on encountering this sentence is to determine that in this case the policymakers are "the congresspersons," the target entity is "wastewater dumping" and the direction is "pro," i.e., the congresspersons favor the wastewater dumping. It is possible also to draw two other directional conclusions from this example, namely: (a) the congresspersons favor legislation and (b) the congresspersons are opposed to the ban on wastewater dumping. Conclusion (a) in this case is not very interesting because it is quite general; it indicates a mechanism that enables the desired result. If the information were more specific, as in "The congresspersons introduced bill number AJ23 ..." then this information might be worth reporting. Conclusion (b) is undesirable because it can be analyzed more thoroughly, presenting the user with a more concise result. Both (a) and (b) can be concluded using the mechanism described here; the end application should indicate whether or not partial results like these are reported.

14.3.1 Path Actions

Although Talmy's description indicates some grammatical patterns that are involved in the expression of the force dynamical model, it relies as well on the meanings of the open-class lexical items. For example, in Sentences (2a-d) the reader must know that *rolling* indicates a tendency toward motion and *standing* indicates a tendency toward rest. Since one of the main reasons for using the path model as the basis of analysis is to make the interpretive process simple, it is desirable to avoid an open-ended semantics-assignment task.

To this end, I define a set of *path actions* that represent the semantic components of the path model, i.e., they represent what kinds of actions can take place within the model. These actions are: *ENABLE, BLOCK, REMOVE-BLOCK, ACCELERATE, DECELERATE*, and *NEUTRAL*. Their semantics are glossed as:

> *ENABLE:* allow or help the entity to move along a path toward its destination
>
> *BLOCK:* impose a barrier in the entity's path toward its destination
>
> *REMOVE-BLOCK:* remove a barrier from the entity's path
>
> *ACCELERATE:* increase or intensify the potency of the entity's current path-movement tendency; speed up
>
> *DECELERATE:* decrease in potency the entity's current path-movement tendency; slow down
>
> *NEUTRAL:* no effect

Other actions, such as *MISDIRECT*, could have been included but those listed have been found to be sufficient for the sentences examined.

As noted above, in the path model it is not unusual for an entity's progress to be affected by a series of actions. Therefore, I define a function that takes as arguments two path actions and returns a path action; Table 14.1 shows the results of all possible function applications. For example, a *REMOVE-BLOCK* action applied to a *BLOCK* yields an *ENABLE*. For simplicity, I will represent this function as a binary (right associative) operator, indicated by ▷.

When answering the target query, the directionality of two separate components – the attitude of the agent and the progress of the entity or event – must be determined. There are expressions that indicate the agent's attitude relatively directly (e.g., *favored*, *denounced*, and *lauded*). The attitude of the agent can be expressed indirectly, however, as seen in (1a), where the legislator's legislation introduction action is taken to indicate that the legislator favors the legislation. If a series of action applications ends in a state that is one of *ENABLE or ACCELERATE*, then the agent is said to favor the entity that the action is applied to. If the action sequence ends up as a *BLOCK* or a *DECELERATE*, then the agent is assumed to oppose the target entity. Otherwise, no opinion is expressed or can be determined.

The lexical items that comprise a sentence constituent determine which actions are associated with the constituent. For example, from sentence (1a), the simple noun phrase "the ban" is assigned the action *BLOCK*, and the verb group "to lift" is assigned the action *REMOVE-BLOCK*. A constituent whose path action is *NEUTRAL* acts as an end point in a chain of action applications. When this occurs, the lexical items that make up the *NEUTRAL* constituent are considered to be the effected entity, and are placed in a predicate that represents the results of the series of path actions. For example, if "wastewater dumping" is *NEUTRAL*, then "to lift the ban on wastewater dumping" induces the following sequence of operator applications:

REMOVE-BLOCK ▷ *BLOCK* ▷ *NEUTRAL* ⇒

REMOVE-BLOCK ▷ *BLOCK* ⇒

ENABLE ⇒

favor(A, "wastewater dumping")

(The term *A* represents the agent whose attitude is under scrutiny. The example fragment "to lift the ban on wastewater dumping" does not specify an agent, so *A* is left unbound.)

If sentence (1b) is processed instead, "to support" is assigned the *ACCELERATE* action and the sequence would be:

ACCELERATE ▷ *BLOCK* ▷ *NEUTRAL* ⇒

ACCELERATE ▷ *BLOCK* ⇒

BLOCK ⇒

oppose(A, "wastewater dumping")

Table 14.1: Results of Applying One Path-Action to Another

▷	NEUTRAL	BLOCK	REM-BLOCK	ENABLE	ACCEL.	DECEL.
BLOCK	BLOCK	ENABLE	ENABLE	BLOCK	BLOCK	ENABLE
REM-BLOCK	REM-BLOCK	ENABLE	--	--	--	ENABLE
ENABLE	ENABLE	BLOCK	REM-BLOCK	ENABLE	ACCEL.	DECEL.
ACCEL.	ACCEL.	BLOCK	REM-BLOCK	ACCEL.	ACCEL.	DECEL.
DECEL.	DECEL.	ENABLE	ENABLE	BLOCK	DECEL.	ACCEL.

action in row is applied to action in column
NEUTRAL cannot appear as the first argument

The *BLOCK* is "sped up" or "strengthened," rather than removed.

The path actions interact in some interesting ways, as shown in Table 14.1. Notice that the "negative" types, *BLOCK* and *DECELERATE*, tend to flip the polarity of the action they are applied to, while the "positive" types, *ENABLE* and *ACCELERATE*, leave the polarity unchanged. Comparing the phrases "increased the restrictions" and "reduced the restrictions," we see that the lexical item "increased" indicates the *ACCELERATE* action, "reduced" the *DECELERATE* action, and "the restrictions" indicates a *BLOCK*. Analyzing "increased the restrictions" produces:

$$ACCELERATE \triangleright BLOCK \Rightarrow BLOCK$$

whereas "reduced the restrictions" produces:

$$DECELERATE \triangleright BLOCK \Rightarrow ENABLE$$

The heuristic that motivates these transformations is: In the political arena, if an agent is seen as favoring the reduction in potency of a barrier, then in actuality that agent wants the barrier removed entirely but is supporting the reduction as a compromise. Thus to favor a *DECELERATE* on a *BLOCK* is to desire an *ENABLE*. Similarly, *limits*, *restrictions*, and *ceilings* are often proposed as compromise alternatives to outright stoppages, and in this model they are cast as *BLOCK*s. If the system produced detailed semantic interpretations, it would have to know how to reason about partially restricted movement. Although this is a reasonable strategy, it is much simpler to coerce the notion of a limit into that of a barrier.

It would be possible to do away with the *ACCELERATE* and *DECELERATE* actions since their semantics mirror those of *ENABLE* and *BLOCK*, respectively. They are included both to allow for the possibility of graded distinctions (although this exposition does not exploit this potentiality) and to make the coercion process more intuitive.

14.3.2   The Role of Syntax

For the examples of the previous subsection, the syntax of the sentence determines (a) what the path action-bearing constituents are and (b) the order in which the path actions are to be applied to one another. Although the lexicon entry for a lexical item with a directional component must indicate its corresponding path action, (b) can usually be determined from the syntactic category of the constituent that the lexical item ends up being a part of. For example, the direct object of a transitive verb is usually the target of the verb's path action. If the lexical item invokes a non-standard behavior or behaves differently in different syntactic situations, this tendency is indicated in its lexicon entry.

As the sentence is parsed, feature-structure representations [Shieber, 1986] are built. The constituent that immediately contains a lexical item with a path action is assigned the following features:

> **Path-action.** This can take on one or more of the values *NEU-TRAL, BLOCK, REMOVE-BLOCK, ENABLE, ACCELERATE, DE-CELERATE.* This feature indicates the directional contribution the encompassed lexical item makes to the interpretation of the sentence, and can vary depending on the syntactic category of the lexical item. For example, *lift* as a transitive verb can be a *REMOVE-BLOCK* type whereas as an intransitive verb it is *NEUTRAL*.

> **Target-entity.** This indicates which constituent to apply the action to. It may be another action-bearing constituent, as is "the ban" in the phrase "to lift the ban on wastewater dumping" or it may be a constituent that is left unanalyzed, as "wastewater dumping" would be. A null value for this feature signals the end of an action application sequence.

> **Next-constituent.** Usually this is unified to the value of the target-entity. However, there are cases when a constituent has more than one relevant argument, as in "The president shielded the elephants from attacks" where both "the elephants" and "from attacks" are complements of *shielded*. In this case, the value of the target-entity is retained until the end of the action application sequence, and the current path-action is applied to the constituent that unifies with the next-constituent feature.

> **Viewpoint-agent.** This is the entity, usually animate (metonymic agents such as "the White House," "Beijing," etc., are permissible here) and usually the subject of the main clause, whose opinion is being investigated. This feature is optional.

> **Secondary-agent.** This attribute indicates a secondary agent that plays a role in the indication of the sentence's directionality. For example, in "The governor persuaded farmers to implement irrigation measures" it may be desirable to retain the information about who is doing the implementation, although often this is unstated. This feature is optional.

For some lexical items, the path-action assumed depends on the action found in the target-entity. For example, the verb *shield* acts as a *REMOVE-BLOCK* path-action in "The president shielded the elephants from attacks by poachers" because its next-constituent feature points to a constituent containing a *BLOCK* action. However, if the sentence were simply "The president shielded the elephants," the verb would act as an *ENABLE* action since both its target-entity and its next-constituent point to a constituent with a *NEUTRAL* action. Most lexical items that can take on the *REMOVE-BLOCK* action take on a different action when no *BLOCK*-type target-entity follows.

Most (open-class) lexical items will fall into one of a small set of categories, for example, *finite-transitive-remove-block-verb* or *block-noun*, so once an initial set is defined, classification of new words should be relatively simple. Closed-class items, such as prepositions, can require special attention.

An important syntactic consideration that arises when determining the agent's attitude involves clausal attachment. Consider the following sentences:

(3a) The congresspersons introduced the bill that appeased the protestors.

(3b) The congresspersons voted against the bill that appeased the protestors.

(3c) The congresspersons introduced the bill (in order) to appease the protestors.

(3d) The congresspersons voted against the bill (in order) to appease the protestors.

(3e) The congresspersons voted against the bill to ban wastewater dumping.

In Sentences (3a) and (3b) the restrictive clause modifies "the bill." Therefore, since the agent enables the bill in (3a), the agent favors the bill and also what the bill does. Similarly, in (3b) since the agent opposes the bill, the agent opposes what the bill does. Now consider (3c-d). In these sentences the infinitival clause acts as a purpose clause attached to the main verb, instead of a modifier for the object of the verb; this can have an affect on the interpretation. In these sentences the opinion of the congresspersons with respect to the protestors is independent of whether the congresspersons *ENABLE*d or *BLOCK*ed the bill. In both cases the goal is to appease the protestors. Thus when a purpose clause is identified, its contents should be preceded with an implicit *ENABLE* action.

Notice that in both (3a) and (3c) the main clause produces an *ENABLE* action and the attitude toward the complement is the same whether it is an object modifier or a purpose clause. However, when the main clause produces a *BLOCK* action, as in (3b) and (3d), the attitude to the contents of the complement can be affected. It is not always easy to distinguish the two cases, as shown by a comparison between (3d) and (3e), a variation of (1a). Although the sentences are syntactically quite similar, the first can be seen as having a purpose clause[1] and the second an object modifier. Unfortunately, determining the proper attachment requires more detailed interpretation than this model assumes. This issue will be discussed further in Section 14.5.

14.3.3   A Full Example

The following sentence is more complicated:

(4a) President Bush halted hardware sales

(4b) to increase pressure on Beijing

(4c) after its crackdown on the pro-democracy movement.

The first conclusion is that President Bush is opposed to hardware sales because $BLOCK \; \triangleright \; NEUTRAL \; \Rightarrow \; BLOCK \; \Rightarrow$ oppose("Bush", "hardware sales") is easily induced from (4a). The next step is to recognize that (4b) is a purpose clause, thus indicating that again "President Bush" is the agent and that the sequence of path actions begins with an implicit $ENABLE$. The verb introduces an $ACCELERATE$ action and its object is a $BLOCK$ yielding $ENABLE \; \triangleright \; ACCELERATE \; \triangleright \; BLOCK \; \Rightarrow \; ENABLE \; \triangleright \; BLOCK \; \Rightarrow \; BLOCK \; \Rightarrow$ oppose("Bush", "Beijing"). Thus President Bush opposes Beijing, or to interpret the metonymy, opposes some action of the government situated in Beijing. It would be useful to recognize the link between parts (4a) and (4b); namely that the hardware sales that Bush halted were sales to Beijing, but this is beyond the capability of the method as currently formulated.

Notice that in (4b) the noun *pressure* is followed by the preposition *on* which reinforces the indication that *Beijing* is the object of the $BLOCK$ action. Prepositions in noun phrases are often strong directionality indicators. The prepositions *on* and *against* are associated with the $BLOCK$ action, *from* with $REMOVE\text{-}BLOCK$, and *for* with $ENABLE$. The verb *protest* is interesting in this respect. Both "protest against X" and "protest about X" indicate a negative attitude, as does "protest X" with no preposition at all. However, "protest for" flips the polarity. This is another example of a syntactic consideration that can affect a lexical item's directionality.

The adjunct (4c) imposes some difficulties, the foremost being the determination of the referent of the pronoun. In general pronoun resolution requires a more sophisticated interpretation element than is assumed for this method (however, see Section 14.5). Assuming that this difficulty can be overcome, the matter of determining the agent's attitude toward the contents of the adjunct remains. While (4b) describes the desired results (increasing pressure) of the action of (4a) (halting sales), (4c) describes the justification or motivation for (4a) and (4b). In fact, (4c) can be paraphrased as "because Beijing cracked down on the pro-democracy movement."

---

[1] Actually, sentence (3d) is ambiguous if "in order" is omitted, and if context is lacking.

Recall in Sentences (3c-d), that the agent of the main clause favors the contents of the purpose clause. However, the agent of the paraphrased (4c) is one that has been opposed to in (4b). To handle this kind of situation, we need a heuristic that states that if in some sentence S agent A is found to oppose an entity E that happens also to be an agent, if E's actions are described in a purpose clause of S, then A opposes the actions described in this purpose clause. In order to accommodate this heuristic, the *BLOCK* action is prepended to the interpretation of (4c).

Although (4c) is a noun phrase, its analysis proceeds similarly to the verb phrases seen so far. In noun phrase interpretation, a modifier can affect the interpretation of its head noun. For example, in "further slaughter of elephants," *further* is associated with *ACCELERATE*, *slaughter* with *BLOCK*, and *elephant* with NEUTRAL, giving $ACCELERATE \triangleright BLOCK \triangleright NEUTRAL \Rightarrow ACCELERATE \triangleright BLOCK \Rightarrow BLOCK \Rightarrow$ oppose(A, "elephants"). In the case of (4c) it is straightforward to associate *BLOCK* with *crackdown*, but a judgment must be made as to whether to break "pro-democracy" into two pieces. Trying it the first way we get (after prepending a *BLOCK* for the pronoun, see above):

$$BLOCK \triangleright BLOCK \triangleright ENABLE \triangleright NEUTRAL \Rightarrow$$
$$BLOCK \triangleright BLOCK \triangleright ENABLE \Rightarrow$$
$$BLOCK \triangleright BLOCK \Rightarrow$$
$$ENABLE \Rightarrow$$
favor("Bush", "democracy movement")

If we hadn't broken "pro-democracy" in two, we would have ended up with favor("Bush", "pro-democracy movement").[2]

Discussion. The description in this subsection is deliberately high-level since the implementation and grammar (written in Common Lisp, based on a unification-based parser described in [Batali, 1991]) is an experimental prototype and covers only a few sentences. Furthermore, this exposition has omitted discussion of several important issues: how to handle negation, assignment of path actions to lexical items that occur in compounds, noun phrase disambiguation, interpretations of conjunctions, and so on. I leave all of this to future work.

14.3.4   The Role of General Metaphor in Path Action Assignment

How are lexical items assigned path actions? The approach outlined here is motivated by

---

[2]In other situations, *movement* would be assigned an *ENABLE* path-action, but terms occupying a position at the end of the inference chain are generally left unanalyzed, in the interests of having something interesting to report. In other words, favor("Bush", E) is not very informative.

[Lakoff and Johnson, 1980], who observe that the use of "general metaphor" is structurally consistent and surprisingly widespread in "everyday" utterances. An example of a general English metaphor is one in which negative, undesirable things are described in terms of "downness" whereas desirable things are expressed in terms of "upness." This is evident in phrases such as "stocks took a dip," "the quality is declining," "it's going downhill," and so on. The central meaning of metaphors such as these can be considered domain independent, as evidenced by the fact that they are used in many diverse contexts. These observations about general metaphor are useful for deciding what path action to assign to a particular lexical item.

Words that are usually thought of as synonyms do not necessarily work the same way within these metaphoric structures. *Lift* is used to indicate the removal of some obstacle, whereas *raise* indicates an increase of a quantity. The phrase "raise the ban" is confusing to most readers and can even seem to mean the opposite of what "lift the ban" means. An appeal to general metaphor also helps explain the difference between Sentences (1a) and (1b). Lakoff and Johnson identify what they call the Arguments Are Buildings metaphor. It is common to speak of an argument's foundations, whether or not a statement supports the argument or position, arguments that fall or collapse, constructing good arguments, and so on. This observation helps explain why *support* is classified as an *ACCELERATE* action.

The mechanism described here for assigning the value for the direction-type attribute is inspired by the idea of the pervasiveness of metaphoric extension. However, it does not strictly follow the structures that have been observed. Some metaphoric models are too specialized for the path metaphor, and some words participate in more than one metaphor and a choice among them, relevant to the path model, must be made.

14.4   Related Work

Related work in information retrieval and text categorization systems is discussed elsewhere in this volume. Therefore, this section focuses only on work related to the restricted interpretation model.

Like direction-based text interpretation, work in text skimming, such as [DeJong, 1979; Lebowitz, 1983], involves extracting information from only certain parts of a text. These approaches differ from the method described here in that they rely heavily on domain-specific world knowledge. Furthermore, since they use little syntactic information they would have trouble making the directionality distinctions in, say, Sentences (3b) and (3d). Jacobs [1990] describes an approach called *relation-driven text skimming* that is similar in some ways to DTI. In both approaches, the relevant topics must be specified in advance and then only limited semantic interpretation is done and only on a subset of the sentences, chosen by a coarse first pass. The main difference is that relation-driven skimming looks for the kind of information best indicated by predicate-argument relations (e.g., who is the target and who is the suitor of a corporate takeover). In order to determine these kinds of relations it makes more use of syntactic information than the other skimming methods, but the relation determination in many cases only requires a partial parse. This is advantageous since the parser need be less complicated than that needed by DTI, mainly because the kind of relation extracted is less subtly expressed.

The Plot Units strategy for text summarization [Lehnert, 1982] makes use of a distinction between positive and negative events. However, this distinction is made at the conceptual level (e.g., the fact that one's car won't start is a negative event) rather than at the level of a component in the interpretation of the meaning of a sentence. The polarity of these affect states are used to characterize a sequence of events in terms of a narrative primitive. For example, the sequence of a negative events motivating an action that terminates the cause of the negative event is a common sequence termed "resolution of a problem by intentional means." There may be a similar underlying motivation between this work and DTI, but the actual mechanisms are quite disparate.

Several researchers (e.g.,[Carbonell, 1982] [Martin, 1990]) have integrated general, or conventional, metaphor into the process of full text understanding. The goals of these systems are different from that of DTI in that they use an understanding of the workings of metaphor in order to determine the author's intended meaning, instead of trying to coerce the meaning of a sentence into one all-purpose metaphor.

14.5   A Hybrid Text-Based Intelligent System

Direction-based text interpretation is meant to be a component of a hybrid TBIS system, although it is not currently implemented as such. In this section, I attempt to flesh out the architecture that such a system might have.

First, the desired topical information (e.g., "environmental issues" or "wastewater dumping") is specified to an information retrieval system such as that described in Croft and Turtle (this volume). The parameters of the system are set such that sentence-level documents are returned (along with a few sentences of surrounding context) as candidates for directional analysis.

Next, a robust partial parser like that of McDonald (this volume) processes the candidate sentences. The grammar is modified to use a feature-structure representation, and the lexicon is augmented with the appropriate path action information. The conceptual analyzer is replaced by a module that interprets the resulting sentence structures in terms of the path model, as described in Section 14.3.

Since McDonald's parser is designed to be robust but partial, it may not produce some of the constituent attachment and pronoun resolution infor-

mation that DTI is sensitive to. To remedy this problem while still avoiding
the need for complex knowledge bases, we might try integrating results from
statistical methods of text processing (see Stanfill and Waltz, this volume).
For example, Hindle and Rooth [1991] describe an approach for determing
prepositional phrase attachments based on statistical tendencies in a large
corpus. Dagan and Itai [1990] have done similar work on pronoun resolution.
While this kind of approach to text analysis is still preliminary, it is also quite
promising, and it seems likely that in the future, hybrid text interpretation
systems will incorporate statistical results extensively.

The results of the analysis are returned to the user as predicate/document
pairs, where the predicate has the form *direction(agent, event)*, e.g., fa-
vor("congresspersons", "wastewater dumping"). In addition to determining
the answers to directional queries, the analysis component can act as a filter
on the output of an information retrieval component in that if it cannot find
directional content in the candidate sentence, then this information (and perhaps results from other kinds of analyses) should lower the relevance ranking
of the document that contains it.

14.6   Conclusions

Ideally a Text-Based Intelligent System would perform full interpretation of
its document corpus and allow the results to be accessed according to a user's
information need. However, since the state of the art is quite far from this
goal, much of the work in this volume suggests intermediate steps toward the
ideal. These intermediate steps include: partial parsing (McDonald), partial
representation (Hirst and Ryan, Lewis), combination of weak interpretation
methods (Wilks it et al.), and statistical approximations to full understanding
(Stanfill and Waltz, Maarek). This chapter is no exception: It proposes a
question-answering paradigm that yields only a partial interpretation of a
sentence's meaning.

More specifically, I have described a method for answering a general class
of queries without engaging the complexity required by natural language
processing techniques that attempt to generate "all plausible" inferences.
This kind of approach is profitable only if the effort involved in building
and executing the method does not outweigh the depth and quality of the
results. If the effort does get too large, one could argue that a general text
understanding system would be more appropriate, since it could produce
more detailed interpretations for the same amount of effort. In analyzing
the tradeoffs of an approach like direction-based text interpretation, several
questions need to be answered:

How often does the text contain the answer to the query in a form dis-
cernible to the method? In what situations must solutions to problems of
anaphora, attachment, and lexical ambiguity be resolved? How valid is the
assumption that the target queries are general and useful enough to jus-

tify the effort required to answer them? And what kinds of direction-based queries, aside from the agent-attitude one explored here, can be answered using the proposed method?

Any restricted interpretation model must address these issues. The outcome of the tradeoffs can only be determined through empirical studies. If this approach and others like it can tip the balance in their favor, restricted semantic analysis will prove a useful component in the construction of efficient, intelligent text interpretation systems.

Acknowledgments

The majority of this research was completed during an internship at Xerox Palo Alto Research Center. The following people provided much useful discussion in the preparation of this chapter: Per-Kristian Halvorsen, John Batali, Susan Newman, Deborah Tater, Cathy Marshall, and Doug Cutting; additionally, Robert Wilensky, Narciso Jaramillo, and Yoëlle Maarek provided helpful comments on various drafts. Finally, I would like to thank Paul Jacobs for advice on this draft and for continuous, generous encouragement.

Bibliography

[Batali, 1991] John Batali. *Automatic Acquisition and Use of Some of the Knowledge in Physics Texts*. PhD thesis, Massachusetts Institute of Technology, Artificial Intelligence Laboratory, 1991.

[Carbonell, 1982] Jaime G. Carbonell. Metaphor: An inescapable phenomenon in natural-language comprehension. In Wendy G. Lehnert and Martin H. Ringle, editors, *Strategies for Natural Language Processing*, chapter 15, pages 415–434. Lawrence Erlbaum Associates, Hillsdale, NJ, 1982.

[Dagan and Itai, 1990] Ido Dagan and Alon Itai. A statistical filter for resolving pronoun references. In *Proceedings of the 7th Israeli Symposium on Artificial Intelligence and Computer Vision*, 1990.

[DeJong, 1979] Gerald DeJong. *Skimming Stories in Real Time*. PhD thesis, Yale University, New Haven, CT, 1979.

[Hindle and Rooth, 1991] Donald Hindle and Mats Rooth. Structural ambiguity and lexical relations. In *Proceedings of the 29th Annual Meeting of the Association for Computational Linguistics*, 1991.

[Jacobs, 1990] Paul S. Jacobs. To parse or not to parse: Relation-driven text skimming. In *Proceedings of the 13th International Conference on Computational Linguistics*, volume 2, pages 194–198, 1990.

[Lakoff and Johnson, 1980] George Lakoff and Mark Johnson. *Metaphors We Live By*. University of Chicago Press, Chicago, IL, 1980.

[Lebowitz, 1983] Michael Lebowitz. Memory-based parsing. *Artificial Intelligence*, *21*:363–404, 1983.

[Lehnert, 1982] Wendy Lehnert. Plot units: A narrative summarization strategy. In Wendy G. Lehnert and Martin H. Ringle, editors, *Strategies for Natural Language Processing*, pages 375–414. Lawrence Erlbaum Associates, Hillsdale, NJ, 1982.

[Lehnert and Sundheim, 1991] Wendy Lehnert and Beth Sundheim. A performance evaluation of text-analysis technologies. *AI Magazine, 12*(3):81–94, 1991.

[Martin, 1990] James Martin. *A Computational Model of Metaphor Interpretation*. Academic Press, San Diego, CA, 1990.

[McCune et al., 1985] B. McCune, R. Tong, J.S. Dean, and D. Shapiro. RUBRIC: A system for rule-based information retrieval. *IEEE Transactions on Software Engineering, 11*(9), 1985.

[Reddy, 1979] Michael Reddy. The conduit metaphor—A case of frame conflict in our language about language. In A. Ortony, editor, *Metaphor and Thought*, pages 284–324. University Press, Cambridge, England, 1979.

[Salton, 1988] Gerard Salton. *Automatic Text Processing: The Transformation, Analysis, and Retrieval of Information by Computer*. Addison-Wesley, Reading, MA, 1988.

[Shieber, 1986] Stuart M. Shieber. *An Introduction to Unification-Based Approaches to Grammar*. CSLI Lecture Notes, Number 4. Center for the Study of Language and Information, Stanford University, 1986.

[Talmy, 1985] Len Talmy. Force dynamics in language and thought. In *Parasession on Causatives and Agentivity*, University of Chicago, 1985. Chicago Linguistic Society (21st Regional Meeting).

Index